THE RUSSIAN MIND:

From Peter the Great
Through the Enlightenment

The
Russian Mind

*From Peter the Great
Through the
Enlightenment*

STUART RAMSAY TOMPKINS

NORMAN : UNIVERSITY OF OKLAHOMA PRESS

By Stuart Ramsay Tompkins

The Russian Mind (Norman, 1953)
Alaska: Promyshlennik and Sourdough
(Norman, 1945)
Russia Through the Ages (New York, 1940)

To Dr. *and* Mrs. H. T. Harris,
*whose continued interest
has been a constant inspiration*

Preface

It is now more than a generation ago that psychologists first mooted the existence of the group mind. Whether we accept or reject the idea of a collective mind, there can be no doubt that in most societies there persist certain commonly accepted views and attitudes of mind which are inherited from the past and which are only gradually modified. Without laboring the point, the writer has long held that much of our difficulty in our relations with the Russians is due to our lack of understanding of certain basic habits of mind which seem to distinguish Russian society from that of the West. He is not vain enough to hope that he will be able to describe these accurately or to give an adequate explanation of them. The difficulty of distinguishing native traits from customs and habits that have been borrowed is enormous. All that the writer has endeavored to do is to trace the main trends that have marked the period during which Russia has been exposed to the impact of foreign influence, to observe how these alien influences were either assimilated or rejected, and to arrive at some general ideas about which of these trends are fundamental and which may be regarded as ephemeral. One world may be a grand ideal for the human race, but it is elementary wisdom to recognize basic differences of outlook and approach. These differences may be obliterated by the softening influences of time, or peoples holding opposed views on fundamental things may finally agree to live and let live. At the present time, we find two systems of thought and politics in the sharpest conflict. To adjust ourselves to this condition, we first need to understand it. It is the purpose of this book to give some understanding of Russian ideas during modern times. Not everything in the Soviet system is drawn from the teachings of Karl

Marx; some things are inherited. I hope to contribute something toward enabling the reader to grasp that part which is derived from the past.

The writer wishes to acknowledge the financial assistance received from the Humanities Division, Rockefeller Foundation, which made it possible to assemble the materials for this work. He also would like to pay tribute for generous assistance and counsel from Mr. Johann G. Ohsol of New York City and from Professor V. Riasanovsky of the State University of Iowa. The former gave unsparingly of his time and labor in helping to assemble a bibliography. Both of them read through the manuscript with great care—a formidable task at best—in this case greatly increased by the effort to detect errors and slips that had escaped notice.

The present work carries the story down only to 1855. That year marks a clean break in Russian history and Russian thought. To deal with the momentous development that followed the end of the Crimean War requires a separate treatment, which it is the author's purpose to give in another volume.

STUART RAMSAY TOMPKINS

Norman, Oklahoma
January 22, 1953

Contents

Illustrations

THE RUSSIAN MIND:

From Peter the Great
Through the Enlightenment

I

Russia in the Time of Peter

❧❧❧❧❧❧❧❧❧❧❧❧❧❧❧❧❧❧❧❧❧❧❧

O N the night of December 30–31, 1721, a festive party had gathered in the cell of the monk Ioakim in the monastery of Daniel in the city of Pereyaslavl. The festal season was being duly celebrated with vodka, for which the good Ioakim had dispatched the sacristan to the neighboring grog-shop. There had been heavy potations, and tongues were loosed and voices raised. Finally, the drink began to take effect. One after another the guests had been overcome and had picked out comfortable corners; someone put out the light; one by one all had dropped off to sleep; all, that is, with the exception of Father Ioakim. Drink had merely put him at peace with the world and filled him with a great love of his fellows and of his country.

Suddenly the chorus of snores was broken by the booming voice of Ioakim: "To our noble, benevolent sovereign and autocrat, Peter Alexeyevich, long life."

"Long life!" came a muffled echo from the sleepy Iraklim.

"Long life to our Holy, Governing Synod."

"Long life," parroted Iraklim.

"Now His . . ." began Ioakim.

"Wait, stop," broke in Iraklim. "Why should we not wish long life to the Tsaritsa, Ekaterina Alekseyevna?"

"What do you mean, our Tsaritsa? Our Tsaritsa is the old one —the Tsar's lawful spouse."

The bibulous unanimity of proceedings had been shattered. The jarring note was the reference to the wife, Eudokia, whom Peter had sent away to a nunnery in favor of his new one, Catherine. The conversation had taken a dangerous turn.

"You lie," came from a disembodied voice.

3

"Haven't you made enough noise? Pipe down and go to sleep," a drowsy voice chimed in.

All lay down with one exception. Father Iosaf, who had listened in silence to what went on, waited until the snoring recommenced and then stole away in the gloom. He made his way to the Abbot Harlaam with his story. Three days later the Holy Synod received from the Abbot his denunciation, and the persons denounced were summoned for questioning.

The accused tried at first to deny everything. But the witnesses to whom he looked for corroboration were proved to have been asleep. And the sly Iraklim, whose ebullience had started the pledges of fealty to the Imperial family, had not missed his sally about the Tsaritsa Eudokia. He was backed up by three companions not so far gone (as they said) in their cups that they had not caught the words. So Ioakim broke down: "Yes, I said it, but I was drunk. That evening we had sent out for liquor and were celebrating; I should never have said it if sober."

Accordingly, the Archbishop Theodosius, the examining officer (who was also judge), deprived him of his monk's status and returned him to the world as Yakov Venediktov, the name given him at birth.

The Archbishop reported to the Holy Synod in the person of the Prokuror Peter Andreyevich Tolstoi. The unfrocked monk was turned over to them. One would have thought that the matter was closed. The good Prokuror, however, did not think so. Some secret conspiracy might lurk behind this. The martyrdom of the heir apparent, Prince Alexei, and his alleged conspiracy against his father were fresh in the people's minds. So the former monk was turned over to the secret chancellery to be tortured.

Taken out to the rack, Father Ioakim looked at the crossbeam from which he was to be suspended and then down at the horizontal beam to which his feet would be lashed. The horizontal beam would also be used as a lever to stretch his miserable body to its fullest extent as a prelude to the *knut*. In terror at the prospect, he cried out to his tormentors:

I really said what I did because in the gospel of Matthew it is written: "He who shall divorce his wife without cause and marry another, committeth adultery." And these words I used

The Rack: method of torture used for forcing confessions. *From Abbé Chappe d'Auteroche,* Voyage en Sibérie *(Paris, 1768)*

of the great empress; the thought came into my head when Iraklim began to talk to me about long life to his imperial majesty. I never uttered these words in the presence of any man before this, nor heard them uttered. Whether I said anything more than this, I do not remember, for I was quite drunk. Nevertheless, justice was not to be denied; the hangman proceeded. Up went the rope over the crossbeam. The unfrocked monk was swung up; the horizontal beam between his legs was depressed; as his body yielded to the stretch he groaned; then the *knut* was laid on—once, twice, three times. . . . The count reached fifteen. The ropes were slackened, and he was lowered. His limp body sank to the ground. He was picked up by attendants and hurried away to prison. At first inert and speechless, he lay staring at the ceiling of his cell for two days. On the third, attendants appeared in his cell and once more he was dragged to the rack. Again his poor body, still scarred and raw from the previous ordeal, was hoisted and stretched; again the *knut* hissed and cracked on his shrinking back. This time, the number was twenty-five. Again he was cut down and taken away to freshen up for a third ordeal; and once more the agony was repeated. Nothing new was wrung from the wretched man; there was no more to say. He had told all.

As he lay in his cell in a stupor of exhaustion, he heard the sentence of the court pronounced, based on his original confession, "that you, Yakov Venediktov, for the treasonable words spoken in drunkenness shall by decree of the Senate be banished to a monastery"[1]—a wry admission of the state of religion in Russia that to be shut up in a monastery was equivalent to prison.

This was the method used in Russia in the year of grace 1722 to ferret out crimes against the state—denunciation by a friend, report to the secret chancellery (the equivalent of the modern M.V.D.), torture pushed to the extreme limit to extract a confession and implicate accomplices, and then the useless hulk of a body all but buried for the rest of life.

The above selection throws some light on Russia at the dawn of the eighteenth century. To enforce the authority of the state,

[1] M. I. Semevskii, *Slovo i Dyelo*, 77–80. An adaptation of the Russian original.

5

there had come into existence and developed into a supreme instrument of coercion the secret chancellery of the monarch with its dreaded procedure of denunciation, *slovo i dyelo*. At a time when England was working out the principles of religious toleration and of parliamentary government and when France was already in the midst of the intellectual revolution of the Enlightenment, the Russian state was ruled by a boundless despotism which demanded the complete submission of the individual to its authority; there was still little understanding of human dignity. While the boyar still held over his peasants the most despotic rights, he, too, was subject to extreme coercion of the state; he must serve it without question; and in case of incurring the displeasure of the monarch, he was, like the humblest serf, subject to torture, to public flogging, and to an arbitrary justice at the hands of the executive power. He still, when addressing the throne, used the terms of abject slavery. Indeed, there was little to distinguish his lot from pure bondage.

From the age of adolescence to senility he was at the disposal of the state for service in any capacity to which the state might call him. During the incessant wars of the seventeenth century, he was on repeated campaigns with the military levies or serving on the frontier guards. Only at rare intervals did he visit his family. The estate set aside for him by the state was administered by other hands than his to provide for his children. His sole hope of leisure was when incapacitated for further service; for then he could return to his ancestral acres to enjoy perhaps a few years of idleness until death claimed his enfeebled frame. In turn, he and his agents exercised an equal tyranny over his peasants, whose lot was even more oppressive than his own. When we contemplate the overriding considerations of military security by which the Muscovite state was motivated, the all-embracing character of this servitude will not seem abnormal. "Almost the whole of the territory of Muscovite state," says Klyuchevsky, "was laid out like a great armed camp presenting a front on three sides, the west, the south, and the east."[2]

Why was the autocracy of Russia so different from the absolutism that arose in western Europe in early modern times? The

[2] V. O. Klyuchevskii, *Istoriya Soslovii v Rossii*, 149.

absolute monarch of western Europe rested his power originally on a vague pact with the towns who made common cause with him to curb the common enemy—the feudality. In a sense, he held this power only on sufferance from the *bourgeoisie*. Moreover, in the Western world, even though the kings might become all-powerful at home, none was ever able to assert a lasting supremacy over the Continent. In addition to rival kings, each monarch had to reckon with an independent church; he must always keep an eye on a potentially dangerous baronage; the rising towns clamored for recognition of their rights and privileges; and in time, with the growth of representative systems, these had to be recognized.

How different in the East! The autocracy that emerged in early modern Russia was subject to no such limitations. The church, which had so zealously seconded the efforts of the Muscovite princes to attain dominance, was deprived of its independence and ultimately despoiled. Reduced to complete subservience, it was inclined to stress the rendering unto Caesar of the things that are Caesar's rather than the rendering unto God of the things that are God's; religion thus became a buttress of the existing order. After the absorption of the appanages, the old appanage princes and boyars were brought to Moscow and fused with the native aristocracy. When the latter with their new allies became truculent, the Grand Prince, or Tsar as he now styled himself (as a mark of his new claims to absolutism), called into existence a new "serving class" with whose aid he struck down the old boyars. After the annexation of Novgorod, the towns were too feeble and dependent on the Prince to dispute his claims.

As the new despotism tightened its hold in modern times, there was no field of life excluded from its activity. Argus-eyed officials watched over the citizens and reported any signs of unrest. Official was encouraged to spy on official, citizen on citizen. No secret was so carefully hidden that it could not be ferreted out. The tsar arbitrarily committed to prison or sent into exile, subjected to physical chastisement or even mutilation those, even of highest station in life, who were suspected of being unreliable. There were neither moral restraints nor legal embarrassments in the exercise of absolute power; and to back up all its powers of coercion and intimidation it could call on the church to anathematize rebels and enemies.

How were the people brought to accept so thoroughgoing a despotism? The long and unremitting warfare with the Tartars, their greatest scourge, took on the character of a crusade. As the Tartar menace weakened and new enemies appeared in the West, this religious bigotry turned in that direction; for the Roman church was only slightly less hated than Islam. This religious fanaticism was changed into a sense of world mission by recourse to a unique legend. After the fall of Constantinople an obscure priest hailed Moscow as the third Rome, which, now that the second had fallen to the unbeliever, was destined to carry on the imperial tasks of the first. The idea appealed to the princes. To buttress this claim scribes were sent to search the ancient records for links between Moscow and its predecessor, imperial Rome. It was thus possible to give a new and totally distorted interpretation of Russian history to supplant the older chroniclers—more reliable, but less flattering to the vanity of the princely line of Rurik. On this falsified history, Muscovite patriotism was long nourished.[3]

Thus Russia, on beginning to emerge from her isolation, confronted the states of western Europe not merely as a rival, but as an aspirant for the supreme position of potential successor to the Holy Roman Empire. It is not without significance that Peter the Great assumed the title "Imperator." Logically, in the foreign field such an exclusive claim clashed with the new system of international law—then growing up—based on recognition of the equality of all states. But at home, the new Imperator, like the old Tsar, admitted no limits to its power. With no rallying point for any opposition, it was possible to close the system and exclude all opposition. There were no towns to provide, like the medieval communes, asylums for runaway peasants or to nourish the hope of freedom; there were no universities, no press to foster independence of thought; there was almost no education worthy of the name and, above all, no contact with the outer world to invite

[3] This is the *Synopsis*, first published in 1674, which remained the standard text in Russian history until 1762, when Lomonosov published his.

comparison with their own mode of life or to give birth to thoughts of such disquieting things as freedom. As the seventeenth-century Olearius remarked: ". . . to keep them from seeing the liberty which other nations about them enjoy, the Muscovites are, upon pain of death, prohibited to go out of the country. . . ." Finally, an all-embracing system of service imposed directly on landowners, on a hereditary fighting class, and indirectly on merchants, on townsmen and peasant alike, obligations from which there was no escape.

In time, under this combined pressure these things became accepted as part of the natural order, since Russians knew no other. What the Russian historian Karamzin calls "the vile artifices of slavery" became their protection against those stronger than themselves. In the time of Ivan the Terrible, as he says, they "gloried in what they were reproached with by foreigners; a blind and boundless devotion to the monarch's will, even when in his violent fits of caprice, he trampled upon every law of justice and humanity."

Of course, at times life became intolerable. The peasants ran away to the steppes to become Cossacks. Their lords escaped abroad and denounced their former rulers. But such defections from time to time could not shake the solid structure of autocracy. Far more dangerous were the spontaneous and violent explosions that occurred when a peasantry rendered desperate by their misery rose, massacred their lords, and set fire to manor houses. These periodic convulsions shook the established order to its foundations. Moscow passed through a number of these, but the rebels were helpless against a powerful government, when once it had recovered from its fright and mustered its forces. The revolts collapsed; savage reprisals began; and the people sank back into torpor and despair. So long as the gates were closed to foreign influences there was no way of breaking the iron chain.

It must not be supposed that Russia was devoid of all intellectual life or that foreign influences could not penetrate to her. After all, Christianity had come in from the Black Sea along with Byzantine civilization. She had had a rich church literature, though with a few notable exceptions secular works were lacking. Kiev had traded with Constantinople until access to the Black Sea was closed by nomadic hordes. She had commercial relations with the Danube Valley overland and by the northern rivers to the Baltic and western Europe. But the Tartar yoke had cut her off from the family of peoples to which she naturally belonged. Venetian and Genoese merchants indeed had crossed the steppes to the new Russian capital—Moscow. Intermittent diplomatic relations were established with the Empire from the end of the fifteenth century. Italian architects at the time of the Renaissance found their way to Moscow to aid the building programs of the grand princes. With the opening of the White Sea route by the English in the late sixteenth century, regular commercial intercourse was established with Europe. Western ideas from the Protestant lands began to supplement and eventually supplant those that had trickled in hitherto from Roman Catholic Europe through Poland and the Ukraine. Not only was the West knocking at the doors of Russia, but the grand princes were turning westward for the technology needed to overtake the West.

Ideas from the bustling centers of Europe continued to clamor for admittance. The same Dutch and English bottoms that brought the much-coveted goods of those commercial rivals also brought the seeds of the dangerous Lutheran and Calvinist heresies. These same sailors were themselves examples of political freedom. Even rationalist concepts began to penetrate the Russian frontiers. After the defeat of Poland the very triumph of Muscovite arms which added the left-bank Ukraine opened a new ingress to Western ideas. The much greater freedom to which the Cossacks were accustomed, the contacts with the Latin world through long association with Poland, the very challenge of the Latin faith which could be met only by counterpropaganda, the models for which were drawn from the Roman Catholic schools of the West—all these factors were a disturbing element to Muscovite torpor. Unless Orthodoxy was to succumb in an unequal struggle, some form of higher education to compete with the West must be introduced. There was eventually established at Moscow the Greek-Latin-Slavonic Academy where the rival cultures openly clashed. The ferment of imported ideas was working everywhere in the church and reached its apogee in the struggle over liturgical reform in the time of Nikon. The issues around which it raged seem today bizarre and trivial, but it was the sole framework of ideas with which the Muscovite world was familiar and which was nearest its heart. Compared with Germany or France or England, Russia was centuries behind and could only think in terms familiar to the Middle Ages, which those countries had left far behind.

The supreme events of Russian history in the seventeenth century—the bitter wars with Poland for possession of the Ukraine, the rivalry with Sweden, and at home the acute religious crisis through which the church passed—all these were only the accompaniment which came from contacts with the outer world, to the awakening of the Russian mind. Some of its chief mouthpieces were Krizanich, the Croat cleric and philosopher; Ordyn-Nashchokin, the minister of the Tsar Alexei; and Matveyev, who was married to a Scottish woman, and who also served Alexei and Nikon, the reforming patriarch. All these knew western Europe, had come in contact with some of its greatest minds, and had acquired a love of books, of which they made impressive collections. These men were the heralds of the coming age of the Enlightenment.

But they were far ahead of their own time. The general tone of polite society is described by Olearius who visited Moscow in 1643: "Their [the Muscovites'] boast is that they are descended from the ancient *Greeks*, but, to do them no injustice, there is no more comparison between the brutality of these *Barbarians* and the civility of the *Greeks*, to whom all other parts of the World are obliged for all their literature and civilization, than there is between day and night. They never learn any Art or Science, nor apply themselves to any kind of Study: on the contrary they are so ignorant, as to think, a man cannot make any Almanack unless he be a Sorcerer, nor foretell the Revolution of the Moon and the Eclipses, unless he have some communion with Devils."

Olearius also recounts how he sought to divert some of them with a simple trick in optics and the results: "I showed them upon a Wall of an obscure [i.e., darkened] Chamber, through a little hole I had made in the shutter of the window, by means of a piece of glass, polished and cut for Opticks, all was done in the street, and men walking upon their heads. This wrought such an effect on them, that they could never after be perswad'd than that I held a correspondence with the Devil." This took place at the time when scientific societies were being started in various countries of western Europe, when Bacon's advocacy of the experimental method was beginning to take effect, and when science was beginning to lay its foundations securely on reason and openness of mind.

It is with Peter that the impact of these new forces began to be felt. His plans demanded the acquisition of Baltic ports, which could only be obtained by wresting them from Sweden. This meant war. And to wage war with a first-class power required the introduction of the arts of war as practiced in the West which could only be accomplished by bringing from the West the craftsmen to modernize the Russian armies and the industries with which war is fed. For the first time the barriers were down, and Russia was inundated with a flood of alien influences.

For a hundred years wave followed wave as Russia sought to assimilate the science and technique of the West and with these its culture. Yet there came the time when native elements began once more to stand out above the flood. While the old order had been swept away beyond recall, much of the old reappeared in a new form. The new Russia was not to be a replica of Europe, because the nascent nationalism of the nineteenth century reasserted native characteristics and emphasized its dissimilarity to Europe. Despite the facile use of analogies drawn from France and England, the structure of Russian society stubbornly refused to be fitted into the western pattern. It carried into the modern era features inherited from its Muscovite past.

Classes

IC+IC+IC+IC+IC+IC+IC+IC+IC+IC+IC+IC+IC+IC+IC+IC+IC+IC+IC+

ANY of the great modern controversies in Russia have
turned on the relations of the social classes to one
another. In spite of this, it is difficult at times to define exactly what constitutes a class or what persons
are included in a class. Meanings shifted from age to age and class
boundaries constantly were being blurred. Klyuchevsky in his
History of the Classes focuses on the legislation of the Empress
Catherine in 1785 and seeks to elucidate their history in the light
of this legislation. From earliest times society had been somewhat
loosely stratified into groups with differing rights and privileges,
but the concept of a stratum of persons superimposed on another
and extending over the whole extent of a vast state was then in-
applicable. Political groupings were local, and relations tended,
therefore, to be personal and individual.

The older Kievan social groupings underwent a great change
during the appanage period (1169–1462), when the state was splin-
tered into a multitude of principalities. When the process of gathering up the Russian lands began once more and the older principalities were merged in the new Muscovite state, there was an
increasing tendency to reduce groups to one common category
and to define their relations to the central government. It is in this
Muscovite period that we get the germ of the later class divisions.
This division is for the most part on the basis of their obligations
to the state, though these obligations do not seem to have been
defined by any decrees. At this time, subjects were classified into
serving people, *tyaglo*-paying persons, and nonpaying persons.
These classes were further subdivided into smaller groups. Klyuchevsky emphasizes that the basis of division was their obligation

to the state and in no sense privileges, which were a late development. This classification was completely disrupted by the reforms
of Peter, and for considerable time there was great confusion as
the principle of privilege began to take precedence over obligation.[1]

Since we are dealing at present with the eighteenth century,
we are primarily concerned with these divisions as they then existed. They still carried vestigial characteristics and differences
that hark back to a slightly earlier time. The main classes mentioned were the nobility, the clergy, the merchants, the *myeshchane*
(tradespeople or craftsmen), and the peasants.

The nobility may be regarded as an aristocracy, though hardly
an aristocracy in the western sense. Actually they fall into several
groups. At the top were the grandees, descended from the princes
of early principalities or their own vassals, who lost their local
identity when they became attached to the Muscovite state. Others
of almost equal rank had come from abroad into the service of
the Muscovite tsars and been granted high rank and precedence.
Together these two formed the core of the aristocracy, and their
families were entitled to be called "highborn."

During the course of the fifteenth and sixteenth centuries a new
class had come into existence. This was a group of persons whose
ties with the monarch were very intimate. They were bound to him
by the closest relation of fealty and obedience. In return for their
services for which the state could not afford to pay them, they
were assigned grants of land to exploit. As the landlords were
absent for long stretches of time, it was imperative that the man-
agement and cultivation of their estates should go on uninterrupt-
edly during their absence in order to maintain the lord and his
family. The peasants living on this land accordingly were bound
to the soil.

These changes did not take place without violence. On the
dying out of the older dynasty in 1598, the country went through
a series of convulsions in which foes, domestic and foreign, threatened the destruction of the state. But a national revival saved Rus-

[1] Klyuchevskii, *Istoriya Soslovii v Rossii*, 100, where a classification of the
classes in Moscovite times is given.

sia. A new dynasty was installed, and the order inaugurated by the old dynasty became permanent.

During the seventeenth century the old aristocracy—to whom the name *boyare* (boyars) was sometimes given—and the new—now coming to be called *dvoryane* (court men)—lived side by side. Actually, together they formed the serving people; but the older families sometimes held their land in fee simple—*votchina*—while the newer nobility held theirs on conditional tenure. There were many gradations of rank — Moscow nobles, provincial nobles (*dvoryane gorodovye*), boyars' sons, *stol'niki, stryapchi, okol'-nichi,* and others. Many ranks, like our office of chamberlain, denoted some menial office at court; others had a military connotation; a few—*d'yaki* and *pod'yachie*—were scribes in the chanceries. Rank in the service and family precedence were almost inextricably intertwined. Birth might give one a claim to certain rank, but only when the appropriate post in the service was occupied, while persons of ability might rise to rank without birth. But, generally, precedence was preserved and books were used to keep the record straight.

There can be little doubt that noble birth gave the holder of any position in the service the prestige and authority needed to overawe his subordinates. But with the introduction of European arms and military technique, less and less reliance was placed on rank, and in 1682 the whole system of *myestnichestvo* or family precedence was abolished and the record books burned.

Peter took the next logical step of giving complete recognition to this principle by introducing the Table of Ranks. By this, service was open to all persons of education. Service rank was arranged in three parallel divisions—civil service, military service, and naval service. The attainment of the ninth rank from the top conferred nobility for life, while the fifth automatically conferred on the holder (and his heirs) hereditary nobility. The older titles disappeared. Some new ones, those of prince, baron, and count (the latter two from western Europe), were rewards for special service. The older families still enjoyed certain privileges, such as access to the court, but these were largely social only. All nobles received their land as a *votchina*, and the system of conditional tenure (*pomyest'e*) was abolished.

The new nobles formed a class referred to as *shlyakhetstvo,* a term borrowed from the Polish, the use of which was soon discontinued. It would be a mistake, however, to think of the *shlyakhta* as especially privileged in the western sense. The hand of the administration lay heavy on them. They were enrolled in the state service at the earliest possible age, were drafted into various schools or sent abroad to acquire special training, and from the date of their return were at the state's disposal for the rest of their natural lives (or at least until incapacitated by old age) for state services, visiting their homes only at long intervals. Moreover, they were, like the rest of the tsar's subjects, exposed to demeaning treatment in various ways. When they submitted a request to the monarch, they did so as lowly slaves approaching a master and were forced to make the "kowtow" at least figuratively in support of their petitions.[2] This obnoxious verbiage of slavery was only abolished by Catherine. Moreover, until this time, nobles had been subject to public chastisement as a form of punishment, if not to mutilation.[3] Compared with the aristocracy of western Europe, their lot could be regarded as a form of slavery. Peter introduced primogeniture in Russia for all classes. It was particularly hated by the nobility and was abolished in 1730. But like the French nobility, the nobles were forbidden to engage in industry or commerce. Some few "serving people" were not noble. Such were the Cossacks, the *Stryeltsy.*

The classes of society that corresponded to the burghers of the medieval towns were of slight importance in Russian society. Their distinguishing feature (also shared by some of the peasants) had been the payment of *tyaglo* (tax). In early times townsmen were gathered into communes as were many of the peasants, but the townsmen differed from them in that they did not till the land, but depended for their livelihood on a craft or business. In the seventeenth century, following the general trend, these persons

2 The Russian word for petition—*chelobit*—means to "beat the ground with the forehead."

3 It is notorious that while Elizabeth abolished the death penalty, savage mutilation continued to be inflicted on members of the noble class. Two women—Lopukhina and Bestuzheva—who had offended the Empress were stripped and publicly whipped; they afterwards had their tongues cut out before being exiled.

were freed from dependence on the local authority and came more and more under departments of the central government. Under this new arrangement, they assumed "service" duties, such as the collection of customs and the operation of state industries. During the seventeenth century they were collectively referred to as *tya-glye lyudi posadskie,* falling into two divisions—roughly, merchants and craftsmen.[4] They were drawn together into one unified body by Peter, though still subject to *tyaglo.* During the course of the eighteenth century when Russian travelers went abroad, they noted the division of society in France and elsewhere into the estates. Class divisions in Russia were fluctuating and uncertain, and Peter's reforms themselves further increased this confusion. Gradually western terms began to appear in the literature and people began to speak of townsmen as merchants (*kuptsy*) and petty bourgeois (*myeshchane*).

By the middle of the eighteenth century these terms together had begun to be applied to the class engaged in what we should call business. In Russian life they never assumed the importance that they did in western Europe. For instance, when deputies from the towns were chosen in 1767 for the Commission for Drafting a New Code of Laws, the towns were represented for the most part by nobles.[5] Catherine's own knowledge of Russian classes must have been of the most casual kind. In her *Nakaz* she devotes a special chapter to the "middle sort of people."[6] She seems to have thought of only four classes of subjects—clergy, nobles, townsmen, and peasants. A special commission named to determine the various divisions of subjects divided them into three categories—the nobility, the middle class or *myeshchane,* and the peasants. The middle class or *myeshchane* is a sort of catchall for everybody not included either in the higher class—the nobility—or in the lower class—the peasants. Herein are included the white clergy (parish priests), scholars, artists, merchants, artisans, clerks (*raznochintsy*), and emancipated serfs.[7]

---

[4] Klyuchevskii, *Istoriya Soslovii v Rossii,* 101.
[5] V. I. Semevskii, *Politicheskie i Obshchestvennye Idei Dekabristov,* 55 ff.
[6] Ekaterina II, *Sochineniya* (Works) *Imperatritsy Ekateriny II,* ii, 89.
[7] V. I. Semevskii, *Krest'yanskii Vopros v Rossii v XVIII i pervoi Polovinye XIX Vyeka,* I, 128.

In 1785 a special charter was granted to cities bringing all classes of their inhabitants, irrespective of their origin or rank, under one category—nobles, merchants, craftsmen, traders from other cities, foreigners, and members of the clergy were swept into the catchall. The merchants were organized into guilds with exemption from military service and corporal punishment. Certain citizens who had achieved distinction were to be given the title "distinguished citizen" with the right of applying for entrance to the nobility in the third generation.[8]

By the new legislation it was provided that the city was to be governed by a city *duma* of all citizens, though there was also, and perhaps of more weight, a body known as an Assembly of the Urban Society, i.e., of the wealthiest citizens. The city was to be autonomous, though this was easier to proclaim than to enforce, since the governor and the police were always encroaching on the authority of the cities. Nevertheless this was an important landmark in the history of the towns.[9]

Next in importance were the clergy. As in the West, they formed two major divisions: the black and the white. The black corresponded to the regular clergy of the West; the white to the secular, with this one exception—that in the Orthodox church all the upper hierarchy belonged to the black (regular), which in practice meant that the white clergy consisted of the parish priests and some of the lower ranks of the hierarchy. The parish priests were allowed to marry once, while the monastic orders were celibate as in the West.

There had been a time when the church had been able to challenge the state in its wealth and power. As in the West, the Eastern church had through the ages fallen heir to vast holdings of land and other wealth. At first the land had been tilled by the occupants of the monasteries. Later some of it passed to landowners who served the church. After the establishment of the office of patriarch in 1598, a patriarchal court was set up, which during

---

[8] Grigorii Shelekhov, the actual promoter of the Russian-American Company, received this distinction for his work of exploration and the development of the fur trade on the northwest coast of America. See Ivan Golovine, *La Russie sous Nicolas I*, 276.

[9] Karl Staehlin, *Geschichte Russlands*, III, 551–52.

the seventeenth century rivaled that of the tsar; it had its boyars and vassals.[10] Land held by the monasteries and the dioceses might be worked under the direction of ecclesiastical officers by peasants. With the introduction of serfdom, these peasants fell into serfdom, their lot differing little from that of the domanial serfs.

Perhaps the greatest influence exercised by the church was through the ecclesiastical courts, to which were referred a vast number of cases, especially those arising in connection with marriage, divorce, and testaments.

Eventually in the seventeenth century matters came to a head over the proposed reforms of Nikon; and in the aftermath of the crisis produced by these reforms, the tsar, through the calling of an ecumenical council, deposed Nikon and thus asserted his control over the church. This drastic step was followed up by Peter, who allowed the office of patriarch to lapse and in 1721 set up a special *collegium*, the Holy Synod, a body of clerics under the presidency of a layman to administer the Orthodox church.

In the meantime the relations between church and state continued to be tense. Peter professed solicitude for the church and its traditions, but there remained two major issues between them—the enormous landed wealth of the church and its age-old indifference or active hostility to learning. The latter was in part a Byzantine tradition deriving from the attitude of the church toward pagan learning in the days when the literature and philosophy of the ancients had been Christianity's most formidable rival. While the Russian church had adhered to this attitude, the rest of Europe had not, but had come to regard learning as the handmaid of religion. In any event the world had moved far beyond this position, and science and education had come to be the price which nations paid for survival. Peter had early become a convert to this view and hence looked with disapproval on the concentration of idle wealth in the hands of the church. While he refrained from laying violent hands on it, he did impose on the church heavy

[10] During the course of the eighteenth century, the clerical class was gradually restricted to persons who followed the religious calling by the removal of all laymen. This was done by a series of legislative acts. M. F. Vladimirskii-Budanov, *Gosudarstvo i Narodnoe Obrazovaine v Rossii XVIII Vyeka*, 117.

financial demands in the field of education.[11] By 1762 the church had lost public sympathy to such an extent that it was safe to proceed with the expropriation of its property, and under Peter III and Catherine the government confiscated a great part of the church lands.

The clerical class, by the loss of its land and of its retainers and the cultivators, was thus now reduced to (a) the parish priests and the secular hierarchy and (b) the black clergy (the regular clergy). The clergy no longer constituted a distinct social and political group with great wealth and an independent political position, but had come to be merged with that indeterminate grouping sometimes referred to as "persons of the middle rank" in society.

The great majority of the population of Russia was made up of peasants, grouped in a score of different categories, but one in that they constituted a vast submerged mass who supported the economic and political structure of Russian society. Peter had enormously simplified the classification by imposing on practically all of them the "soul's tax" as well as military service. No detailed list of the different classes of peasants will be given, but an attempt will be made to note the most important.

By the third revision (1762–63), about 53 per cent—or 3,805,073 —of all the male peasants in Great Russia and Siberia were classified in the eighteenth century as "landlords' peasants." In addition to the payment of the soul's tax and the rendering of military service which they owed the state, they were liable to exactions imposed by the landlord—the payment of rent for their land, as well as the performance of labor at the demand of the lord, normally for three days a week, although more work might be exacted. These regular obligations might be supplemented by others—the rendering of dues in kind and putting their draft animals at the lord's disposal. There was no guarantee of their right to land; their land might be taken away or they themselves might be transferred at the whim of the master from one estate to the other. They were completely at the mercy of their master, who might inflict severe bodily punishment on them. They were subject to restriction in

[11] For the church's role in the new education under Peter, see Chap. III below.

entering into marital relations, especially with servants of other masters. They could not file complaints against their lord; but where a landlord became notorious for mistreatment of his peasants, a peasant could be made a ward of his relatives or, if that did not suffice, of the governor of the province.

A second category of male peasants, who occupied a somewhat analogous position to these mentioned above, were the "possessional" peasants. They were peasants taken from the land (where they had been originally domiciled) to work in mills, factories, and mines, to which they became permanently bound. Although their lot was hard, since many of them were located in isolated places of inclement climate, they had some protection against the caprice of their owner, for they could register complaints. There was also no restriction on entering into wedlock.[12]

The next most numerous class of peasants were those on the ecclesiastical estates, who comprised in 1762 not less than one million males and formed 13.8 per cent of the peasant population of Great Russia and Siberia. Their position was somewhat analogous to that of the landlords' peasants, though with some difference. On these estates where exactions were in the form of labor, there was a limit to the work they could be called on to discharge, and many were used for the highly skilled operations in which some of the monasteries specialized. Where the obligations were in money they were frequently moderate. The church authorities had the same right as the layman to inflict severe physical chastisement on the serfs. Wedlock out of the estate involved a payment; and families of the peasant might be broken up, though peasants could not be sold.

These peasants paid the "soul's tax" and were called on for military service to the state. Their position was somewhat better than the landlords' peasants. They had the right to own immovable property and also were permitted to lodge complaints against their masters.

While Catherine on her accession halted the sequestration of church property which had begun under Peter III, she soon made

[12] Although during the first half of the eighteenth century merchants could not own estates or peasants, they could operate mills and possess peasants for the explicit purpose of working in the mills.

up her mind that the only solution of the question was to deprive the church of these lands and their peasants. A College of Economy was created in 1764, and to this body was turned over the administration of the great mass of ecclesiastical estates and their peasants, who came to be referred to as "economic" peasants. About 1,000,-000 peasants were affected.[13]

A considerable body of peasants—about 400,000 of the male sex in 1762—belonged to estates of the crown. Known as "court" peasants, they paid a reasonable rental and sometimes performed obligations in labor. Their lot was somewhat better than the landlords' peasants; they could secure subsistence when crops failed, and they could not be sold either with or without land. Some of the imperial estates with their peasants had become under Peter the personal property of members of the imperial family, and the peasants in this group were somewhat less privileged than they had formerly been. There were about 62,000 in this category. Under Catherine the inferiority of their position was due to the fact that they were the victims of the caprice of their owners. They were subject to the "department [vyedomstvo] of the court peasants."

Probably the most important class of peasants, omitting those belonging to landlords, was that of the crown. This group—about 1,815,000 of the male sex—formed about 25 per cent of all the peasants. If we add to this number the ecclesiastical peasants, who for all practical purposes became state peasants, we get 2,806,812 or 40 per cent of the male peasant population. They are to be distinguished from the court peasants in this: the former belonged to the estates privately owned by the sovereign, while the latter were settled on public lands held by the monarch as the proprietor of the public domain. While circumstances during the seventeenth century were working together to create this somewhat homogeneous class, it was the decrees of Peter from 1719 to 1724 that finally defined their status. The decree of January 22, 1719, undertook to apply to a whole category of peasants the same obligations

[13] In the decree of November 29, 1762, providing for sequestration of church lands, these peasants were called "landlords' peasants." V. I. Semevskii, *Krest'yanskii Vopros v Rossii v Tsarstvovanie Imperatritsy Ekateriny II*, I, Intro. 10. The introduction to each volume should be consulted for a general statement of the peasant question.

of military service and the payment of the poll tax demanded of those living on the land of the landlords. It was emphasized that their relations to the crown were analogous to the relations of the peasants of private owners to their landlords. Hence the state peasants were called on to discharge dues similar to those which the landlords could demand of their peasants. There were some diversities in the status of these peasants living in different parts of the country. In general, they were better off than the peasants of the landlords, but were still circumscribed in their rights; they were collectively responsible for their dues; they were subject to control by the local governmental authorities; they could not leave their land. One inestimable advantage they did enjoy: they were free from the abuse of arbitrary power, such as the gentry was often guilty of exercising.[14]

The relation of the classes to one another and to the state has been of exceptional importance to the Russians. Up to the eighteenth century citizens were graded according to their obligations to the state; but from the time of Peter, class became a matter of privilege. It is difficult to determine the cause for this situation. There can be no doubt that the system of education devised by Peter fostered the change, since it fixed the kind of education for each class and the functions each would perform.

Though all persons were admitted to the state service and accordingly to the nobility, in practice this privilege meant nothing, since few besides the nobility (and possibly the clergy) were so trained. But it is probable that the weakness of the successors of Peter and their dependence on the nobility for their support played into the hands of the gentry, who were able to wring important concessions from them, including emancipation from service. Even in the early part of the eighteenth century, we find the nobility insisting fanatically on their privileged position in the state. Ta-

[14] N. M. Druzhinin, *Gosudarstvennye krest'yane i reforma P. D. Kiseleva*, 23–34. The figures for the state peasants are found on page 44. With regard to the *odnodvortsy*, the government was guilty of a breach of faith. These people were the descendants of a land militia created to guard the southern Russian frontier against the Tartars; they had been given grants of land in return for their services. With the creation of a regular army, the need for this militia disappeared; instead of receiving their land "in fee simple" as the nobles did, they continued to be regarded as tenants of the crown and were finally reduced to the status of state peasants.

tishchev, the distinguished historian of the early eighteenth century, is constantly bewailing the inadequate legislation on the question of class distinctions:

> Because of the absence of a law to fix the rights and privileges of the higher classes, everyone is considered of noble birth. All owners of villages, clerks, sons of priests, townsmen, and peasants having patrimonial estates bought or acquired—all of them adopt some coat of arms according to their own invention and are honored because they are rich. This is one thing we find nowhere else.[15]

Tatishchev further emphasized the importance of discriminating all classes in the interests of the state:

> In view of the fact that we respect only privileges and pomp, everyone is concerned only with getting rights by whatever means possible, and, as seen, as men become rich, they find it easy to buy honors, ranks, and privileges. In trying ostentatiously to gain an advantage over one another, they do not understand that they ruin not only themselves but also the state.[16]

In a later passage he further develops this idea and insists on the clearer definition of class relations:

> This distinction of ranks is temporary, but it is different with a permanent and hereditary distinction, such as the nobility, burghers, and the common sort, but sometimes a fourth is counted—the clergy. Among us in the *Ulozhenie* the nobility is distinguished from the others to some extent, but without indicating the basis on which it rests and thus is inadequate and far from clear. Hence with us everyone who merely has a desire secures by devious means the rank of noble.[17]

Commenting on this statement, K. Bestuzhev-Ryumin in his characterization of Tatishchev says: ". . . And it should in no wise astound us that a careful study of Russia in the eighteenth century

[15] Georgii Plekhanov, *Istoriya Russkoi obshchestvennoi mysli*. This passage was taken from the English translation published by the Board of Education of the City of New York and the Department of Social Science, Columbia University, in 1938, page 102.

[16] *Ibid*. This view bears a striking resemblance to the definition of justice advanced in the fourth book of Plato's *Republic*.

[17] V. N. Tatishchev, *Istoriya rossiiskaya s samykh drevnykh vremen*, cited in K. Bestuzhev-Ryumin, *Biografii i Kharakterisktiki*, 157 ff.

shows that it was exactly at this time, through government measures and the efforts of the *intelligentsia*, that there was called into existence among us class distinctions, which were not clearly recognized in ancient Russia, but existed only in the form of division into *sluzhilie i tyaglie lyudi*, i.e., were based on how and with what a man serves the state and were proportionate to the demands of the state. Acquaintance with conditions in Europe, where class distinctions were strongly rooted, could not fail to be reflected among us in the effort of the nobility (who in the eighteenth century had received the distinguished title of *Shlyakhetstvo*); the 'assembling of the dispersed remnants' applied not only to the urban population; but the nobility also is being formed from 'different ranks and services of the serving people' and is trying to attain to class consciousness. Among the *'nakazy'* [instructions] of the deputies and the discussion of them in the famous commission of Catherine, there is clearly evident this effort, to meet which is directed the government's effort to form a 'third class of persons,' i.e., to create a *tiers etat;* the clergy, owing to circumstances, is being organized into a closed class. From this point of view the remark of Tatishchev becomes intelligible."[18]

The clash of interest between privileged and unprivileged classes was somewhat inchoate in the eighteenth century, and it was not until the nineteenth that it emerged as a major problem. Perhaps the chief factor was that there could be no reason for dissatisfaction as long as all classes felt the hand of the state indifferently heavy upon them. No clash could arise until one class was accorded preferential treatment, which in 1762 took the form of the emancipation of the nobles from obligatory service. Nevertheless, even at an early stage in the development of class differences, certain tensions existed between classes. One of these (perhaps the most significant) was the ill will between the gentry and the townsmen, probably occasioned by the growing wealth of the latter. For instance, in one of his satires, the Russian poet Kantemir (died 1744) has this to say of the "third estate":

[18] Bestuzhev-Ryumin, *op. cit.* The reference to "the assembling of the dispersed remnants" is to an expression used by Peter with regard to the townsmen (*posadskie lyudi*) whom he was trying to form into a class answerable to the central authorities.

The bourgeois—everything is money to him.
He never goes from home without a coach,
And he is followed by a long train of retainers.
In his great house, the floors and walls are gilded.
He heaps up gold for the luxury of an empty name.
His memory delights to recall the deeds of his false ancestors.
The toad swells till he bursts.[19]

It is well known that the gentry for long contested very bitterly the right of the merchants to own land and serfs, and in spite of the Table of Ranks there were few cases where a merchant was admitted to the noble class.[20] Moreover, when the conspiracy was on foot that was to culminate in the Decembrist revolt of 1825, the poet Ryleev proposed to bring in some merchants. He was strongly opposed by Baron Steingel, who urged that such a move was impossible since merchants were nothing but ignoramuses.[21]

In 1843 Baron von Haxthausen, an authority on rural institutions, was invited by the Emperor Nicholas I to make a study of

[19] D. D. Blagoi, *Istoriya Russkoi literatury XVIII vyeka*, 86. The translation is the author's.

[20] Klyuchevskii, *Istoriya soslovii v Rossii*, 189–90. Klyuchevksii admits that in unusual cases they might rise in the seventeenth century to the position of *dyak* or *dumnyi dvoryanin* and be rewarded with a *pomyest'e* for services, but there is no case on record of rising to that of boyar. It is noteworthy that even the *dumnyi dvoryanin* was not strictly regarded as a noble. In the eighteenth century the Table of Ranks enabled persons of all classes to rise in the state service. We have the case of Baranov, chief factor of the Russian-American Company, a merchant of Kargopol, advanced to the rank of Collegiate Counsellor; see S. R. Tompkins, *Alaska, Promyshlennik and Sourdough*, 115.

But we have the celebrated case of the questions published by D. I. Von Vizin in *Byli i Nebylitsy* and the reply given anonymously by the Empress.

The question addressed by Von Vizin to his unknown interlocutor was: "If the nobles are rewarded for services, but the field of service is open to every citizen, why is it that merchants never obtain nobility, but it is always mill-owners or tax farmers?"

The reply was: "Some who are richer than others have an opportunity to perform some service whatever it is, for which they achieve distinction."— D. I. Von Vizin, *Izbrannye Sochineniya i Pis'ma*, 136.

[21] See *Russia* (1917–R.S.F.S.R.) *Tsentral'noe Arkhivnoe Upravlenie: Vosstanie Dekabristov; Materialy*, I, 179.

the condition of Russian agriculture. He was deeply impressed by the total absence in Russia of the material for the formation of a middle class:

> It appears as if mysterious causes existed in the character of the Slavonic people, unfavorable to the formation of a citizen class. . . . For more than half a century the Government has exerted itself to form a citizen class . . . in Russia. Catherine issued regulations for the towns, and several laws concerning their conditions were enacted in the German spirit and after the German model. It must be acknowledged that these laws were on the whole a failure, and have by no means had the effect expected. The German corporate spirit, on which the law was founded, was quite foreign to the Russian national character . . . was opposed to the national habits, the social customs, and ideas of the Russian people; and I do not believe it will ever strike firm root in the soil.[22]

His final verdict:

> . . . for the formation of an honorable and numerous class of citizens, there is at present no hope. The peoples who represent it, artisans, shopkeepers and small traders, are utterly demoralized.[23]

If we ponder these facts, what strikes us is that the old Russian state was founded on the principle that all persons in some way, direct or indirect, contributed service to the state. There was no relaxation of this universal rule under Peter, who drove all classes ruthlessly to the tasks in hand. But the substitution of the system of merit for family rank and precedence required that advance in the Table of Ranks should be sought through the display of superior attainments. However, in his haste for immediate results,

[22] Baron von Haxthausen, *The Russian Empire: Its peoples, institutions and resources*, I, 51.

[23] *Ibid.*, I, 54–55. See also the remarks of a Russian writer, Semevskii, *Politicheskie i Obshchestvennye Idei Dekabristov*, 99: "The *myeshchanin*—a respected and honorable class in all other countries—is here insignificant, poor, loaded with obligations and without means to eke out a livelihood. In other countries, they live in the cities; but here, cities exist only on the map. The craft guilds oppress freedom of craftsmanship in them, and so the *myeshchane* are migratory-like gypsies, engaged in tinkering, peddling, etc. The decline of trade affects them the more in proportion to their poverty, for they are dependent on the merchants as small traders or workers in the factories."

Peter selected for his great experiment the readiest instruments at hand, foreigners brought into his service, at the same time meeting his long-term objective by providing schools for the nobles and clergy. The other classes were to shift for themselves. With the best intentions of opening service to all classes, he more and more came to rely on foreigners and the gentry (and his successors still more), so that service became a monopoly of the nobles. Patents of nobility became claims to preferment and privilege still further stressed by the emancipation from service of the aristocracy in 1763. Catherine's belated efforts in 1785 to raise the status of the townsmen missed fire. A thriving business life was completely lacking in the towns. The total neglect of the interests of the middle class by the government and the failure to associate any large numbers in the state service through education must have contributed to their stagnation. As the aristocratic Decembrists despised the merchants "because they were ignoramuses," so the next generation just as unthinkingly despised the *myeshchane* for their meanness and their vulgarity, without concerning themselves over the causes of their depressed condition, preferring to regard them as outcasts rather than as fellow citizens.

III

Education Under Peter
and His Successors

IN the seventeenth century, Russian schools and heresy were all but synonymous. "Be ye not proud, but abide in humility" runs an epitaph of that age.

If ye are asked, "Do you know philosophy?" ye shall reply, "I have not practiced Greek subtleties nor read eloquent astronomers, nor conversed with wise philosophers. I read the books of divine law, if haply my sinful soul may be cleansed of its sins."[1]

Did one attain holiness by turning his back on the world and its wisdom? The apostle had said, "Hath not God made foolish the wisdom of this world?"[2] The Christian world had taken this teaching to heart and had all but consigned to oblivion the stores of the past in its concern for eternal salvation. But time had brought changes in this attitude. Faith might lead to eternal happiness, but the key to unlock this world's problems and to enjoy its delights had to be sought in the accumulated treasures of man.

In the West a common language and a common culture allowed the stream, once this source had been tapped, to overspread the

---

[1] P. P. Pekarskii, *Nauka i Literatura Rossii pri Petrye Velikom*, I, 2. Toward the end of the seventeenth century Avvakum was wont to cite Gregory of Nyssa: "Do not seek rhetoric and philosophy or eloquence but live according to the true and wholesome word, for a rhetorician and a philosopher cannot be a Christian." N. K. Gudzy, *History of Early Russian Literature*, 396.

[2] I Cor. 1:21.

29

whole West. The East, however, which did not share this common language and common culture resisted, and its resistance was stiffened by the dissimilarity of confession. The Russian looked westward and heard also the discordant clamor of Roman Catholic and Protestant, of Lutheran and Calvinist, of Anabaptist and Quaker. When the clash of armies followed the war of words, he shrank back within his own world, more than ever convinced that to admit reason into religion would open the sluices to a flood that would sweep away both religion and morals.

During the period of the Roman Catholic Reformation the Jesuits had made their schools the chief means for propagating the faith; in Poland they sought thereby not only to extinguish the Lutheran and Calvinist heresies, but also to win over the Orthodox Russians to the Roman faith. In both these tasks they succeeded brilliantly. But among the Cossacks of the Ukraine their efforts encountered stiff opposition. To counter Roman Catholic propaganda, the clergy who clung to the Orthodox church in Lithuania banded into brotherhoods and founded a number of schools. This campaign for education culminated in the founding by Peter Mogila of the Kiev Academy early in the seventeenth century. When Kiev and the left bank of the Dnieper passed into Russian hands, it was from here that the new learning began to spread to the inert masses of Russia proper.

While the Orthodox church proper was comparatively unaffected by the Reformation and the Counter Reformation, it had its own religious convulsions. Thus, in the seventeenth century the schism in the Orthodox church warned the church that tranquillity was not to be found in resistance to new ideas. "I sought out the roots of this spiritual sickness," said the Metropolitan of Gaza, Paisios Ligerides, referring to the trouble with the dissidents of the Solovetskii Monastery, "and at last I traced it to two sources: a lack of schools for the people and the absence of libraries." Yet the most grudging concessions were made to this need. At first the teachers who were available were trained solely in the Latin tongue and were looked on as tainted with Latin heresy.

Recourse was had to Constantinople to furnish teachers to impart to young churchmen the knowledge necessary for transcribing and interpreting the sacred books and the liturgy. But these

"Greek" schools with their Byzantine traditions were also a disturbing element, since some of their teaching challenged Muscovite prejudices.

Eventually in 1685 under the Tsarevna Sophia, protagonists of East and West each set up their own seminary in Moscow. This impossible situation could not last. The deadlock was finally settled by Peter when he merged both Moscow schools into the Greek-Latin-Slavonic Academy. It was manned, it is true, by the Greeks Iohannikii and Sophronii Likhudis, sent by the Patriarch of Constantinople; but it also dispensed at least some of the free learning of the West. "The Moscow Academy," says Soloviev, "was a citadel which the Orthodox church sought to construct to protect itself in the inevitable clash with the heretical West: it was not a school at all but a fearful inquisition." But the hated Latin teaching continued to creep in. Finally Peter, who preferred "to tear things down and build them afresh to making any attempt to repair them," swept away all the halfhearted conservative measures. The Likhudi brothers were dispatched home, and the Academy was reorganized under the dominance of the westernizing party and with teachers drawn from the dangerous academy of Kiev.

We have spoken up to now of what might be called higher education. But one class, the parish clergy, was the repository of what elementary knowledge was needed for one's eternal salvation, and literacy of a sort could be regarded as the necessary tool of their craft. Yet from the fifteenth century on, complaints on this score multiplied. Gennadius had appealed at that time to the Metropolitan of Moscow to start schools:

> My counsel is above all to teach the alphabet in school, the words under the tilda and the psalter; when they learn this, then they can read all books. But the ignorant peasants teach their children only to spoil them. First they teach them the vespers, and for this they bring the master a grivna's worth of kasha. The same rule is applied to the matins, and for the hours a special sum. They also bring a gift in addition to the sum agreed on. And he goes forth [such a pupil] from the master and knows nothing. He merely stumbles through the book.

Is it to be wondered that illiterate candidates were admitted to the priesthood merely because their voices were adequate for singing?

31

At the Church Council of the Stoglav (1551), when a complaint was made that many of the clergy were illiterate, the explanation given was that "We learn from our fathers or our masters, for there is no other means for us to be taught. We learn as much as our fathers or our masters know."[3] On the basis of this complaint, the Council resolved that schools should be opened in the homes of the wealthiest town clergy, in which the young should be taught reading, writing, church singing, and reading from the lectern. But there is no evidence that even this modest provision for instruction was actually made. The degree of literacy attained by the clergy continued to be the very minimum that would qualify them for their clerical posts. Until the seventeenth century they continued to receive their instruction from their fathers.

Peter gave a sharp turn to education, as he did to many things. His views were naturally colored by the political system which he had inherited and the purpose which he had in hand. In the Muscovite state the service to the state was the paramount duty, and Peter regarded education merely as a preparation for service or even as service itself. He had no other tradition by which he could be guided. He set forth his views in a conversation with the Metropolitan Adrian: "Persons well-learned are needed from the schools for all purposes. They can go into the service of the church or into the civil service; they can serve in the army; they know how to build and have the doctor's art of healing."[4]

His break with the old system was the greatly expanded concept of service to achieve the immense tasks he had in hand. All other considerations had to go by the board—even religious ones. For Peter took little thought of the danger of heresy, a fear of which had inspired the seventeenth-century schools. He affronted churchmen by the easy familiarity with which he associated with Protestants during his sojourn abroad. Lutherans and Calvinists were invited without questions being asked. Indeed he was as ready to invite Roman Catholics as any.[5] The sole yardstick by which he

---

[3] The writer here has followed P. N. Milyukov, *Ocherki po istorii Russkoi kultury*, II, 233–37. It is on his authority that the above quotations are given.

[4] N. G. Ustryalov, *Istoriya Petra Velikago*, III, 511–12.

[5] One of Peter's most trusted officers was Patrick Gordon, a Scottish Roman Catholic.

measured men was their qualifications for a special job, not their religious affiliations.

Peter had sent persons to western Europe to study as early as 1692, but only after his return from abroad in 1698 did the exceptional become the normal. The revolt of the *stryeltsy* during his absence disclosed how untrustworthy was this motley rabble of warriors. New evidence was not needed to prove the inadequacy of their equipment and tactics. The professional soldiers from the German quarter of Moscow, who helped him whip his "play regiments" at Preobrazhenskoe into shape for the Azov campaign, had already convinced him of the primitive nature of Russian armaments. Peter dreamed of creating a Russian navy to challenge Sweden. A war with that power was now all but a certainty. Her armies had already made the Swedish name dreaded. The chief reliance in such a clash was placed in the new Russian navy and army, and Peter might well have balanced what he could gain from the elimination of this unreliable warrior caste against the loss of his chief military force, but he does not seem to have hesitated. The ringleaders of the revolt were promptly brought to trial, the guilty punished. The whole corps was disbanded and exiled to distant frontiers. This gap had to be filled. With characteristic energy, Peter gathered together from among the gentry and others the most eligible men. In some haste he dispatched scores of young Russians to Italy, to France, to the Netherlands, to Germany and the German universities to prepare themselves not only for posts in the army, but also for positions in the nascent navy and in the chancelleries.

However necessary, these heroic measures were attended with hardships. On arriving at their destination, the students were frequently left without proper supervision and were shamefully neglected by the home government. Often without funds, they were reduced to the direst extremity—they ran into debt if that were possible; when this possibility was exhausted, they were forced to enter menial employment. Those who had ample funds often acquired only a taste for French wines and other luxuries and fell into habits of idleness and vice. They brawled in the streets; their uncouth manners frequently involved them in quarrels with the people. The authorities, for diplomatic considerations, hesitated to adopt firm measures with them. The purpose for which they went abroad was in many cases defeated. Of those who profited by their sojourn many on return to their native land sought merely to resume their old Muscovite ways. They contributed little to the assimilation of western ideas. There was thus a waste of human material. Yet, despite the failure of the plan as a whole, many did bring back a familiarity with western ways and a real taste for western culture.

But, after all, sending students abroad was little more than a stopgap. A basis had to be laid for something more permanent. Peter was dissatisfied not only with the old Muscovite education, but also with that imported from Kiev, which was largely under western and Roman Catholic influence and was little more than a modification of the seven liberal arts of the Middle Ages. He had to have something more practical to meet the specific needs of his day.

The calling of the *white* clergy was hereditary, and the education of their children was therefore imperative. As has been pointed out, some effort had already been made to correct the unhappy condition of clerical education. On the initiative of some of the bishops, schools had been opened in several of the dioceses on the model of the Kiev and Moscow academies, for example, at Chernigov, Tobolsk, Yaroslavl, Rostov, and Velikii Novgorod. The school at Chernigov had been originally a Jesuit school started at Novgorod Seversk. Moved to Chernigov after the annexation of the Ukraine, it continued to offer instruction in Latin, Polish, and Russian, as well as logic. The school at Tobolsk had been founded under Ukrainian influence and was staffed with Ukrainians; hence, it carried the "free studies" over even into Great Russia.

But Peter was not content to leave matters to local initiative. As early as 1701 an edict had been issued directing that elementary schools should be opened in each diocese. In 1714 it was found that few bishops had complied with this order; as a result, the decree of 1701 was followed by one to the effect that where regular diocesan schools could not be organized, monasteries in the dioceses must provide quarters and instruction. If this were not possible, then episcopal buildings must be used. To these schools the name "cypher" was given.

In 1721 came the famous *Dukhovnyi Reglament,* making universal throughout the empire the compulsory establishment of diocesan clerical schools; it was followed by a decree of the Holy Synod on May 31, 1722, and was slightly modified by an *imennoi ukaz* of the emperor, dated January 31, 1724. As foci of the system, two central seminaries were to be established at St. Petersburg and Moscow. This order, however, was carried out only in Moscow (the new seminary was started in the Spasskii Monastery), since there was already a seminary in the capital in the Alexander Nevskii Monastery.

These diocesan schools were intended to be elementary. They were referred to as "Russian" schools, apparently by virtue of the fact that Russian was the only language taught. They approximated the so-called "cypher" (secular) schools, those established in accordance with the decree of 1714. There was no uniform organization or curriculum, although the schools as a rule copied one another in both respects. They were conducted at diocesan expense, the teachers being paid and the scholars clothed, fed, and provided with books at the expense either of the monastery in which they were located or of the diocese.

It was recognized that these schools were to have an elementary character only at the start. As teachers became available at Kiev, the teaching of the classical languages was introduced. Perhaps most notable of these schools was the one opened in 1706 at Velikii Novgorod on the initiative of the Metropolitan Job. For his purpose he brought back the Likhudi brothers (who had left the Greek-Latin-Slavonic Academy in Moscow). Latin, Greek, and Slavonic were taught. From here there spread throughout the district of Novgorod a whole network of elementary schools, all supplied from this center. Indeed it furnished many of the teachers for the schools of the other dioceses. At one time, one thousand students were in attendance at the school of Novgorod and its filial institutions. Gradually all these schools introduced the teaching of Latin and other advanced studies, and thus they evolved into professional schools for the clergy. The transformation of the diocesan schools into secondary schools was complete by the reign of Anne (1730–41). It therefore became necessary to establish elementary schools in the small towns throughout the diocese to prepare students for the diocesan schools. This change was finally rounded out by the decree of the Holy Synod of January 24, 1737, when, in addition, a system of rigid control and supervision by the state was set up. At the summit of the system stood the seminaries in the capitals and in Tobolsk or in the great monasteries —Sergiev-Troitskii, Kruitskii, Vladimirskii, Pereyaslavl-Zalesskii.[6]

The training of the clergy, like the training of the gentry, for the armed services and the civil service, as well as that of the *d'yaki* and *pod'yachie* for clerkships, remained professional.[7] As in the case of the gentry, if no other means were available, parents were required to see that their children received an elementary education at home. The *Dukhovnyi Reglament* of 1721 also called on parents of the clerical class to present their sons at the age of seven to the authorities. By this time their children were expected to have a knowledge of reading and writing.[8] At the age of twelve they were ready for their professional education; the first stage, covering the years twelve to eighteen, grounded them in arithmetic, geometry, and languages—the articles of faith—all as prerequisites for their higher training. This latter phase occupied the last two years. The principle underlying clerical education, as well as that of the gentry, was that the young man before entering on his chosen field should study the special tasks he would later be called on to perform.[9]

Nowhere, perhaps, were the systems begun by Peter so great a failure as in the case of the clergy. Factors working against the system of clerical education were the indifference of the clergy towards learning, aggravated by the natural reaction that took place after Peter's death, and the negligence of the bishops. These clerical schools were frequently embarrassed by lack of financial means, even the revenue in kind required of the parishes for their support often going unpaid. Underlying all these factors was the dislike and distrust of anything in the way of enlightenment imported from Kiev. On the whole the level of learning among the

6 This account is taken from Vladimirskii-Budanov, *Gosudarstvo i Narodnoe Obrazovanie v Rossii XVIII Vyeka.*

7 *Ibid.,* 118, 121.

8 *Ibid.,* 161.

9 *Ibid.,* 272.

clergy remained pitifully low.[10] The efforts of Peter to liberalize ecclesiastical education seem to have been frustrated.[11]

The views of an intelligent native observer on the grave deficiencies in clerical education are interesting. Ivan Pososhkov, a writer of peasant origin who had engaged in various commercial and industrial enterprises, has left a number of valuable treatises on Russian economy and society. Though entirely self-educated, he was sufficiently a child of the eighteenth century (he died in 1725) to believe in the need for education. He was especially appalled at the ignorance of the clergy, which, as a devout member of the Orthodox church, he deplored. He would even have imported Lutheran theologians to instruct the clergy in matters which apparently their own church could not provide. He also believed that schools should be set up in all cities for the instruction of the children of the clergy.[12] On the other hand, he would not have his son learn either Latin or Polish for fear these subjects would wean him from the true faith.[13]

But it was the serving gentry to whom Peter looked for faithful instruments in carrying out his vast projects of reform, and for them a whole series of professional schools were founded. The first of these was the school of mathematics formed in Moscow in 1701, followed by a school of navigation at St. Petersburg to provide officers for Russia's new navy, as well as officers for a future merchant marine; a school on the *gymnasium* level was opened in Pokrova, Moscow. In 1712 a school of engineering was established in Moscow (later moved to St. Petersburg); the same year a beginning was made with a hospital and a school of surgery; in 1715 the Naval Academy was founded and in 1721 a school of artillery. Two schools of mining were opened, one at Olonets and one at Ekaterinburg in the Urals. To enforce upon the nobility the requirement of providing for at least the elementary education of

[10] A. S. Arkhangel'skii, *Imperatritsa Ekaterina II v istorii Russkoi literatury i obrazovaniya*, 23.

[11] P. N. F. Dubrovin, "Nashi mistik-sektanty," *Russkaya Starina*, September, 1894, p. 203. Dubrovin emphasizes that, in contrast with the country clergy, members of many of the monastic orders were well educated and followed some of the intellectual trends prevailing in western Europe.

[12] Aleksandr G. Brückner, *Possoschkow Ideen und Zustände in Russland zur Zeit Peters des Grossen*, 125.

[13] Bestuzhev-Ryumin, *Biografii i Kharakteristiki*, 80–83.

their sons, it was decreed that a certificate of marriage would be refused such sons unless the application was accompanied by evidence that the applicant had completed at least a course in an elementary school.[14]

Peter, with his insistent urge to bring Russia abreast of Europe, extended the principle of service beyond the gentry. Children of *d'yaki* and *pod'yachie* (the professional clerks that manned the chanceries) were required to secure an elementary education and to enter special schools maintained by the government for them. Although merchants were not liable for service in the ordinary way, some merchants were recruited and sent to several of the Baltic seaboard towns to study foreign trade. Even members of the *myeshchane* class were occasionally sent abroad to study foreign craftsmanship.

The innovations Peter introduced into education call for some estimate regarding their merits and enduring results. As we have seen, all that he did was directed solely toward preparing people for his service. Indeed preparation was regarded as service itself. This narrowly utilitarian view permeated the schools and prevented them from achieving much that would have been sound and lasting. For instance, students were constantly being drafted into the services without being given time to finish their work. Moreover, recruits were frequently transferred from one school to another, so that the continuity of their work was destroyed. Sons were required to follow the calling of their fathers, and this determined what education they would normally receive. No allowance was made for individual preferences.[15] Thus, although Peter opened the various branches of the service to all classes, his policies defeated the leveling-down process. One class was forbidden to enter the schools of another.[16] Moreover, circumstances were such that it was the nobles to whom the state looked more and more for the personnel it needed for government service, and

[14] This rule was subsequently relaxed in favor of those proceeding to a military school. Most of this account is drawn from Vladimirskii-Budanov, *Gosudarstvo i Narodnoe Obrazovanie v Rossii XVIII-go Vyeka*, 275 ff.

[15] Vladimirskii-Budanov, *Gosudarstvo i Narodnoe Obrazovanie*, 205.

[16] The *podatnyi* class, the *dukhovnyi* (clerical) class, the nobility, and soldiers were all forbidden to enter the schools for *d'yaki* and *pod'yachie*. *Ibid.*, 121.

other classes were neglected.[17] Summing up these results, the historian Pekarskii says:

Contemplating these proposals, it is not difficult to see that they express above all the need for educated people for filling different posts in the state service, and that a great lack of such was even then evident. Thus education was emphasized because only with its help could they hope to provide more well-informed persons than were then available. One is forced to recognize that this subordination of education to secondary aims, however important the latter were, was bound to react unfavorably on the further spread of knowledge in Russia, since in this direction, fickle caprice and superficiality, a frivolous and irresponsible attitude toward knowledge, and, finally, indifference to its results, if it did not have immediate effect on the matter in hand (which is readily understood)—all these may be phenomena resulting from such a view of education.[18]

We have talked of a general system of schools, but we must not suppose it was anything approaching a modern public school system. The truth is that the schools were public in only a very loose construction of that term. The diocesan schools were supported by diocesan funds, at least a part of which was paid in kind from the lands of the church in the diocese. Even after 1737 when they were turned into seminaries and it was required that elementary schools should be established throughout the diocese to prepare students for them, it was the church lands (both diocesan and monastic lands) that bore the burden of the expense.

When the garrison schools were set up in 1732, statutory enactment was merely being given to what was already in existence. The older garrison schools had been supported from regimental funds; with the *ukaz* of 1732, they received official recognition, and it was agreed that in case of need their revenues would be supplemented by state subsidies. In the Ukraine, the schools of the *odnodvortsy*, a land militia, followed the same rule. In both cases the state undertook to restrict the number of students.

In the matter of attendance the figures indicate how extremely

17 *Ibid.*, 190–92.
18 Quoted in Vladimirskii-Budanov, 143.

meager was the provision for the population as a whole. In his carefully documented study of the Petrine and post-Petrine system, *Gosudarstvo i Narodnoe Obrazovanie v Rossii XVIII-go Vyeka*, Vladimirskii-Budanov cities statistics from reports received during the period 1725–60 by the Holy Synod on school attendance in the diocesan schools. The numbers run ordinarily from 20 to 70 per school. Certain schools, such as Pskov and Novgorod, seem to have been exceptional. Pskov, which was opened in 1725, started with 58 students; from 1738 to 1739 the number jumped to 149. It became a seminary in 1746, but its attendance had already risen to 200; during these years only once did attendance fall below 100 (in 1745 there were 76 students). In 1761 it had 226 students. Novgorod seminary (a sort of teachers' training college for its diocese), together with the elementary schools scattered throughout the diocese, had a total enrolment of 1,000. We have no means of knowing the exact number of students attending the earlier diocesan schools or the later seminaries.

The number attending the professional schools of the gentry must have been considerably larger, at least under Peter, owing to the exigencies of war. After 1731 the Army Cadet Corps gradually took over the training of all army officers and even of noncommissioned officers of less than noble rank. Here the numbers ran into hundreds, and by 1760 the corps had an annual budget of 88,000 rubles. It was one of the few institutions wholly supported by the state. The Naval Academy, which had come into existence under Peter, was abolished, or rather reorganized, in 1752 into the Naval Schlachta Cadet Corps, providing for 360 cadets at its peak with an annual budget of 46,541 rubles. Since the gentry were reluctant to enter the navy, its enrolment declined. Its budget, drawn from a levy on the great noble families, proved to be inadequate and must have been supplemented by a state grant.

Peter introduced a new concept into state service. As we have already seen, he broke completely with the past by making merit instead of birth the sole claim to advancement in all branches of the state service. This was, perhaps, the logical outcome of the abandonment of the principle of *myestnichestvo* during the reign of Fedor Alexeyevich. But he was far from contenting himself with rounding out a reform already underway. He went far beyond this by opening service to persons of other than noble origin. These new recruits were, in many cases, foreigners with special qualifications, invited to join the Russian service. These included such illustrious names as Leibniz and Wolff, the German philosophers who were frequently consulted by Peter, though they never actually settled in Russia. But the number of less renowned aliens who actually came to Russia was legion, of whom Patrick Gordon, François Lefort, and James Bruce are only a few outstanding examples. The favors shown to outsiders were to bring Peter the reproach of his courtiers for preferring the society of upstarts and foreigners to that of his own boyars, and ultimately was to bring in its train a fierce criticism of foreign and other undesirable influences. While the education of all was not such as would render them equally eligible to enter the state service, it is interesting that, at least theoretically, none was barred by humble birth or foreign extraction from aspiring to the highest position in the state.[19]

The establishment of professional schools to train the gentry for service marked Peter's chief break with tradition. In one sense these schools were an improvisation formed under the terrific pressure of war needs. Men were needed to man the guns, to build field fortifications, and to navigate the ships of the new Russian navy. From his journey abroad in 1697–98, the monarch had seen the immeasurable technical superiority of western Europe. As one writer remarks, in old Russia all that a man directing another needed was "authority"; for long this had come from distinguished birth. Peter decided that the government service must be staffed with persons who had acquired outstanding knowledge in their chosen field. Professional training was to be the first prerequisite to advancement.

This leveling-down process made all subjects equal in his sight except as they attained distinction by service. However, it was

[19] As an example, Alexander Baranov, the first chief factor of the Russian-American Company, though a merchant and therefore of humble rank, was rewarded with nobility for his services. In Peter's own day, echoes of this discontent were heard in the work of Philipp Johann von Stralenberg's *Nord-und-östlicher Theil von Europa und Asien*. Stralenberg was a Swedish prisoner of war captured at Poltava who spent years in Siberia. For an account of this discontent with Peter's indifference to birth, see Ivan Golikov, *Dyeyaniya Petra Velikago*, I, Introd.

not the equality of free men, but of slaves. Nor had the claims of a higher education, as a means by which the individual could attain culture, any place in Peter's scheme. He was concerned primarily with the spread of civilization among his people, not as we think of it, but with attaining the European standard in technical and scientific things in order to enable Russia to hold her own with, or even surpass, Europe. He could not grasp the remote consequences of what he did.[20]

Peter's apparent intention to abolish class distinctions was the logical development of the abolition of *myestnichestvo*. In conformity with this aim, the lower schools—those for general education—were in general opened to all; but in the course of time professional schools became more and more narrowly class institutions, on the assumption that the sons would automatically follow the calling of the fathers. Thus the ecclesiastical seminaries that came into existence in the seventeen thirties were restricted to the clergy; the schools for the *d'yaki* and *pod'yachie* were restricted to the sons of *d'yaki* and *pod'yachie*, and the mathematical schools, the schools of engineering, the school of navigation, the school of artillery, and the schools of mining tended to assume a similar relation to the gentry, though here some callings required the same knowledge of all ranks; e.g., the man who served the gun had to know something about ballistics, as well as the man who directed its firing;[21] the man who sank the mine shaft had to know something of the craft of the man who laid out the mine. So, when the government tried to attract into the "colleges" the sons of gentry, there was some overlapping of their education with that provided for the sons of *d' yaki* and *pod'yachie*. Yet the trend of the times

[20] "The glimmer of a recognition that the government ought to concern itself with popular education apart from its application to state service—the glimmer noted by us in the history of the seventeenth century—had been extinguished. The extreme development of the police character of the state which marked the new era, when the state constituted itself the sole source and end of all human activity, was quite unfavorable to the development and consolidation of the above principle. The state was not called on to serve the interests of man's personality but every individual with the aggregate of his moral forces was the submissive servant of the state. . . . The state is concerned with instruction but not with enlightenment." Vladimirskii-Budanov, *Gosudarstvo i Narodnoe Obrazovanie v Rossii XVIII Vyeka*, 155.

[21] Explained in Chap. III below.

was against this. Even in Peter's day there were frequent protests against the mixing of classes; when the nobles were subsequently permitted to learn their three "r's" at home,[22] there was no need for mixing the classes, and the professional schools which trained for service came more and more to be restricted to one class.

The trouble with what Peter did in more than one field was the impossibility of giving permanence to his acts. Indeed, many people, even during his lifetime, regarded the changes he made as only provisional measures which would be swept away at his death. Yet the old Muscovite times did not come back. The political changes, despite their unpopularity and their many inherent contradictions, remained. In education, however, all depended on the driving force of a powerful personality, and when Peter's compulsion was withdrawn, his schools tended to fall into neglect. For one thing the state, always hard pressed for funds, siphoned moneys off into channels that were nearer the heart of the sovereign. Thus much done by Peter had to be done again by Catherine II.

Peter's efforts on behalf of higher learning were destined to have results only in the remote future. Learned societies had come into vogue in the seventeenth century; in France, Louis XIV had, in 1666, called into existence the *Academie des Sciences;* Charles II in England had established the Royal Society in 1662. Savants whom Peter met on his travels—among them Leibniz—made suggestions for a similar institution for Russia. The Tsar began scouring Europe for suitable scholars to form such a learned body, but preparations were not completed until 1724. The first decree establishing the Academy of Sciences came in that year. It was not, however, until after the monarch's death that the definitive decree naming its personnel was issued, on February 26, 1726. But the members who made up that august body had already gathered. The academy was to have two functions—research and teaching; and in the latter capacity it was to fill the role of a university. It was soon discovered that although the academy had a distinguished faculty, it had insufficient students, and that it was necessary for the faculty to go around listening to one another's lectures.[23]

[22] There were in 1732 some 4,000 in attendance at garrison schools.
[23] The government actually brought over eight students from Germany to start the *gymnasium*. Pavel Milyukov, *Ocherki russkoi kul'tury*, II, 288–90.

As a result of this situation it was decided to start a *gymnasium* to prepare students. The first class consisted of 120, the second of 58, the third of 26, and the fourth of 24. To keep up the attendance, the children of soldiers, artisans, and even peasants were enrolled. Since many of these would not graduate, but would leave before the completion of their course to enter on their life's calling, it was decided in 1730 to encourage them to remain by paying them a stipend. The original 20 was increased to 30, later to 40, and in 1760 to 60. Even then it was necessary to draw on some of the older institutions, like the Greek-Latin-Slavonic Academy, for students to fill up the complement. Even with these forced measures the number entering the university was pitifully small. The payment of the stipend gave the government a claim on the services of students, and they were frequently drawn away for state needs. The Academy as a teaching institution completely broke down.

The history of the Academy of Sciences for the first years of its existence makes dismal reading. It was staffed at first exclusively by foreigners. The rise of foreign favorites to power under the Empress Anne in the period immediately after its establishment involved everything foreign (especially German) in general odium, and the Academy was one of the sufferers. This antiforeign feeling laid the basis for a long-standing feud which arose as soon as any considerable body of Russians was added to its membership. There were also personal jealousies, such as that of Lomonosov for the historian Müller and that of Tredyakovskii for Lomonosov. Like all Russian institutions the Academy quickly acquired a bureaucratic character. Its administrative posts gave the holders considerable prestige, which officials such as Schumacher and Blumentrost used to humiliate and frustrate their learned associates who were doing the actual work of research.[24] There was constant friction between the Chancery (the administrative office) and the Conference, whose members were scholars. This unhappy state of affairs did not come to an end until the complete reorganization of the Academy by Catherine II.

[24] Schumacher, without consulting the members of the Academy, authorized the preparation and publication of the *Atlas Rossiiskoi Imperii*, which ignored the results of the second Bering expedition. It was thus neither up to date nor accurate and brought the Academy into disrepute. Schumacher was eventually discredited and retired.

Despite its sorry history some of its individual members made lasting contributions to knowledge. The historian Müller laid the foundation of modern Russian historiography. The Academy, along with the Admiralty College, planned the second Bering expedition and deserves some credit for its achievements. The naturalists Steller and Gmelin did yeoman service among the fauna and flora of Siberia and America and in assembling information about natural resources. Other achievements were the organization and dispatch of various astronomical and geographical expeditions to different parts of the empire.[25] The most distinguished native Russian to adorn the Academy's roster in the eighteenth century was Michael V. Lomonosov, the son of a peasant, who attained renown even in his own day as a sort of universal genius, whom some rank with Leonardo da Vinci. His most enduring claim to fame was his work in the field of physical chemistry, in which he showed himself nearly a century ahead of his time.[26]

An adverse contemporary estimate of the Academy comes from the pen of V. N. Tatishchev. Writing in 1739, he records a most interesting conversation he had with Peter:

In 1724 when I was setting out for Sweden, it chanced that I was at the Summer Palace with His Majesty; His Majesty's personal physician, Blumentrost, as president of the Academy of Sciences, told me to be on the lookout in Sweden for scholars and instructors in the Academy then being founded, to which I replied with a smile: "You are trying to construct a powerful Archimedean machine, but you have nowhere on which to rest it." His Majesty was good enough to ask what I had said, and I remarked to him that he was looking for teachers, but without elementary schools there was no one to teach, and this Academy created at great expense would be useless.

To this His Majesty replied:

Suppose I am able to reap great harvests, but there is no mill; nor is there sufficient water in the neighborhood to construct a watermill; but there is enough water some distance off, but no chance of constructing canals since a long life cannot be counted

[25] See V. F. Gnucheva, *Geograficheskii Department Akademii Nauk XVIII Vyeka, passim.*
[26] See Boris Nikolaevich Menshutkin, *M. V. Lomonosov.*

on. So I build the mill and merely give instructions for the canals to be begun; this will force my successors to bring water to the mill that has been built.

Commenting on Peter's response, Tatishchev says:

The mill is the Academy; the canals are the mathematical schools founded by Peter. But this desire and plan of His Majesty went quite awry for as it turned out, though distinguished scholars soon came together to make up the Academy, yet in the dioceses with the exception of Novgorod [where Feofan Prokopovich was bishop] and Byelgorod not only were schools not built, but even some of those that had been begun fell into ruins.

And Tatishchev further adds:

To everyone it is clear that it [the Academy] was founded only that its members might come together each week that each might present what he thought useful, each in his own field for which he had a reputation in society. This he put forward with great pains and supported it with close reasoning, in order that he might polish it up for publication for the benefit of those who cared to read it. This we can see from the number of books put out by the Academy.[27]

In the period immediately following the death of Peter the expected reaction did not materialize. His reforms lasted, though in a partially atrophied condition. For one thing, the perpetual financial embarrassment of the state seems to have compelled curtailment of his program. On December 31, 1736, there was passed a decree putting on the shoulders of the family of the gentry the obligation of giving their children an elementary education. If, at the age of twelve, the boy's educational attainments were regarded as favorable by the authorities in St. Petersburg or Moscow, he would be allowed to return home to prepare himself for entrance to the *Junker* College or the cadet corps. Boys who failed to pass the tests might be assigned to state schools where their deficiencies would be made good; in extreme cases the deficient ones might be sent to sea.

At the age of sixteen Russian boys were then supposed to be

[27] Bestuzhev-Ryumin, *Biografii i Kharakteristiki*, 130.

"One of the duties of the tutor in the country" (*Von Vizin had in his* Nedorosl' *mercilessly lampooned the so-called education imparted, under the decree of the Empress Anne in 1737, by tutors to the sons of the nobility living in the country. Called a "muddy stream" by Catherine, it nevertheless persisted into the nineteenth century.*)

ready to enter the special schools for military service; and on being turned over to the *Junker* College, they were assigned to the Naval Academy, the Military Academy, the engineering school, the artillery school, or the cadet corps. The system seems to have been subject to gross abuses, for in 1752 after an adverse report on the education of the *nedorosli*,[28] it was reorganized. The *Junkers*, as they were known, were given the lowest rank in the Table of Ranks and assigned to the various ministries (in case they did not enter the fighting services).

It was during this period that the practice arose of making the term of service of the son run concurrently with his education, even when given at home. This is well illustrated by Pushkin:

Through the influence of our near relative, Prince B., who was a major in the Guards, I had been enrolled as a sergeant in the Semenevskii regiment even before my birth. I was to be considered on leave until the completion of my studies. The education of young people in those days was not what it is today.

[28] *Neodorosl* is the title of the play by Von Vizin, which pictures the inadequate education of these callow youths.

At the age of five I was turned over to an ostler, Savel'yich, promoted to tutor as a reward for exemplary conduct. At the age of twelve I had learned under his supervision to read and write Russian, in addition to becoming a good judge of racing dogs. . . . At this time my father engaged for me the services of a Frenchman, Monsieur Beaupré, ordered from Moscow together with a year's supply of wine and olive oil. Beaupré had been a wigmaker at home and had served in the Prussian army, coming later to Russia *pour être ouchitel*, with no understanding of that term. He was a good-natured little fellow but unstable and extremely flirtatious; his *amours* frequently exposed him to beatings that kept him black and blue for days. He was also *an enemy of the bottle*, [a Russian figure of speech, i.e., he often took a drop too much]. But as wine was served only in wine glasses and at dinner at which time it was usual to serve the teacher, Beaupré quickly became accustomed to the Russian *liqueur*, and even began to prefer it to the wines of his own country as incomparably more suited to his stomach. . . . We quickly took a fancy to one another, and though he was engaged to teach me French, German, and other subjects, he shortly chose to learn Russian from me; and each day we then went our own way. But fate soon parted us. These are the circumstances.

Our laundress, a fat, pockmarked girl named Palashka, and our one-eyed dairymaid, Akul'ka, one day put their heads together and made a joint confession to my mother, admitting a moral lapse and blaming Monsieur for betraying their unsuspecting innocence. Mother complained to my father. He at once set out to find the rascally Frenchie. They told him that Monsieur was giving me lessons. My father burst into my room. Beaupré was on the bed sleeping the sleep of innocence. I was busy myself. I might add that a map had been ordered for me from Moscow. It hung on the wall unused and had long fascinated me with its great size and fine paper. I had decided to make a snake from it and, profiting by Monsieur Beaupré's slumber, had set to work. My father came in just as I was pinning a tail on the Cape of Good Hope. Seeing me occupied with geography, my father gave me an affectionate tweak on the ear, then rushed over to Monsieur Beaupré, shook him violently and began to heap reproaches on him. Beaupré in confusion tried to stand up, but could not as he was so very drunk. My father seized him by the collar and, raising him in no gentle manner from the bed, bundled him unceremoniously out of the room. To the glee of Savel'yich he was sent away. So my education came to an end. I had just turned sixteen.[29]

This system anticipated the eventual emancipation of the gentry from service and their return to rural life. It also opened the way for foreign instructors; indeed without them it could hardly have worked, few Russians being capable of acting as tutors. In this way the homes of the nobility were flooded with French and German tutors and governesses, who brought the ideas and tastes of the most advanced countries of Europe into these remote corners of the world.

Tatishchev looked at the new education from the standpoint of utility. Judging it according to the standard of Peter's aims, he found grave defects. He was thoroughly in sympathy with the latter's scheme to establish diocesan schools for the elementary education of the nobles and others and found little to complain of. He did not, however, like the system of home education which developed after Peter's time, which he found to be in the hands of wholly incompetent instructors and subject to grave abuses.[30]

By the year 1760 a complete change had been brought about in the whole tone of education. It was no longer exclusively ecclesiastical and had been to some extent brought into line with the secular trend of western Europe. But it hardly favored learning in the true sense of the word. It was directed entirely toward the rendering of service to the state. It was thus utilitarian and professional, and any contribution it made toward true learning was rather a by-product than its chief purpose. Although it opened service to all classes, it ended by sharply differentiating the training and service of each class. These trends were continued after Peter's death and by his successors with one difference. Peter had probably not intended to advance the interests of the nobility above

[29] Alexander Pushkin, *The Captain's Daughter.*
[30] See Chap. V below where this subject is discussed in greater detail.

other classes, but events had played into the hands of the gentry. More and more they secured continually greater privileges, until in 1762 they acquired complete emancipation from the obligations of service to the state. Their education thus at last was free from the dominance of pure utilitarianism.

Reform did not quite stop with Peter's death. Among significant advances was the foundation in 1731 of the Army Cadet Corps. The compulsory subjects in this curriculum were arithmetic, military exercises, and the Law of God, but in addition there were a number of purely cultural subjects—painting, engraving, sculpture, carving, and dramatics. Two years later garrison schools were founded for the children of enlisted men at Kronstadt, St. Petersburg, Riga, Reval, Narva, Vyborg, Keksholm, Moscow, Kazan, Smolensk, Astrakhan, Voronezh, and Byelgorod. In 1744 these schools were fused with the other schools, the "cypher" (begun in 1714) in the episcopal towns. The general public was indifferent to education; the *posadskie lyudi* (townspeople) and small tradesmen and craftsmen preferred to keep their children at home to teach them a business; the clergy chose to send their sons to the episcopal schools which were ecclesiastical. When the government permitted the withdrawal of these elements from the schools, the secular schools lost out and many were forced to close. Hence the merger with the garrison schools was inevitable.

If the government's solicitude in providing a minimum of literacy for the population overlooked one class, it was the lower middle class. These persons were not, strictly speaking, "serving people," their state obligations being restricted to the payment of *tyaglo*. Peter had, nonetheless, tried to include them in his program of Enlightenment and had sent some members of this class abroad to study business methods.[31] But after 1720 nothing was done by way of education for the urban population.[32] More and more the elementary schools to which all classes had been admitted were restricted to the clergy; after 1737, the gentry generally got its elementary education at home. Each of these two classes had its

[31] M. M. Bogoslovskii, *Petr I*, V, 304. Under the heading, "despatch of persons abroad," the writer cites a number of cases of this kind where tradesmen were sent either to the Baltic states or to western Europe to learn a trade.

[32] Vladimirskii-Budanov, *Gosudarstvo i Narodnoe Obrazovanie v Rossii XVIII Vyeka*, 192, 256.

own institutions in which it could pursue its further education, but the parents (generally of the *myeshchane*), wishing the children to learn the family trade, availed themselves of every pretext to withdraw them. Of course, after the death of Peter, education became more narrowly professional and, as a corollary, more narrowly class. The contempt in which the townsmen were generally held played its part, but it is strange that, as anxious as the government was to stimulate trade and indusutry, a greater share in this scheme of education was not assigned to the townsmen and greater efforts were not put forth to raise their level of education and culture. Had such been done, the history of Russia might have been vastly different.[33]

For the same reasons the university established at St. Petersburg in connection with the Academy continued to experience difficulty in attracting students; the alumni of the *gymnasium* were constantly being drawn away into professional schools; in 1767 when the commission for recodifying the laws was summoned, the state was forced to withdraw from the institution those students who had some knowledge of jurisprudence. These constant inroads ruined the university. It was finally decided to found other institutions of higher learning in localities where conditions would be more favorable. Thus there came into existence the University of Moscow, established in 1755, and the University of Kazan, founded in 1758. The latter, with a *gymnasium* attached, attained more than a local reputation for the thirty years of its existence. It met the needs of poor students, particularly the sons of soldiers.

In 1759 there came into existence at St. Petersburg the Pages Corps, designed to give the sons of gentry some preparation for state service. It also tended to draw students away from the University of St. Petersburg. Indeed, during each of the two academic years, 1782 and 1783, that institution had no more than two students.[34]

---

[33] Bogoslovskii gives a curious instance where a *podyachii* (underclerk in a chancery) had occasion to accept on behalf of his chief the manuscript of a translation made at Peter's own direction. The translator (of non-noble rank) was received in the kitchen and greeted with the words: "In Moscow they whip tradespeople."

[34] Arkhangel'skii, *Imperatritsa Ekaterina II v istorii Russkoi literatury i obrazovaniya*, 13–25.

The accession of Catherine II in 1762 brought a break with the past and saw a flood of new influences. The story of Catherine and her literary contacts with western Europe is too well known to need repetition. By a miraculous turn of events this petty German princess became the consort of Russia's heir apparent and finally was acclaimed Empress of all the Russias as Catherine II. The way was open for the complete breaking down of Russia's isolation. The woman who had found delight in the works of Beccaria, of Voltaire, and of Rousseau and had caught something of the new spirit of criticism and of freedom of thought then sweeping Europe could not but despise the narrow nationalism, the ecclesiastical bigotry, the despotic discipline by which the intellectual forces were cramped. She longed to free Russia from these confining fetters. Her own words, written between 1759 and 1762, embody the hopes she entertained for the future: "Freedom is the soul of everything in the world. Without it everything is dead. I should like obedience to the laws; but I do not want slaves."[35]

Catherine's words may or may not be taken at quite their face value. But there can be little doubt that, as far as was compatible with the Empress' rather tenuous hold on her throne, she did show a marked tolerance during the early years of her reign and extended her patronage to ideas and practices imported from western Europe. This gave encouragement to a number of movements hitherto held in check by the official coldness toward things of alien origin. Perhaps the most significant of these trends that profited by the government's benevolence was the Masonic movement, which now began to spread rapidly through the higher ranks of Russian society and to add its quota to that of education in the spread of general Enlightenment.

[35] *Ibid.*, 8.

IV

Freemasonry

❦❦❦❦❦❦❦❦❦❦❦❦❦❦❦❦❦❦❦❦❦

IN Tolstoi's *War and Peace* a strange interlude is provided by
Pierre's chance meeting at a wayside station with a Freemason,
Bazdyev, whose intense mystical appeal stirs the troubled mind
of the young man and through whom he is eventually induced to enter the Masonic Order. To the casual reader it is merely
an incident in the great drama that is being enacted, but to the
historian its introduction into the story serves a vital purpose. It
reveals at once the confusion of mind and the deep unrest of polite
Russian society in the early nineteenth century. It reveals a society
that had lost its religion and was casting about for a new faith in
which it could take refuge. Masonry, which tried to fuse mystical
concepts with something of traditional Orthodox faith, was admirably calculated to attract the questing soul, and the movement
gathered into its ranks scores of ardent but disillusioned and be-
wildered youths who saw in it some peace for their souls and a
promise of fulfillment of their frustrated hope for a new world.

Freemasonry as a fraternal order originated in England. The
definitive act of parturition was the formation of the Grand Lodge
in London in 1717. Of course, Masonic tradition is fond of boast-
ing a far more ancient lineage, but such claims are not taken seriously by historians. The prototype of the movement were the
guilds and, in particular, the guilds of masons that came into
existence in the Middle Ages and flourished mightily while the
cathedrals were building. These guilds undoubtedly were a closely
knit organization of craftsmen, banded together to preserve and
transmit the secrets of their calling, to exact proper standards of
workmanship, and to exercise a certain amount of discipline over
the conduct of their members. They might also distribute charity

among them when needed. But a guild of persons drawn together by the bond of a common vocation is one thing, and a fraternal order whose members are associated for cultural and social but not economic reasons is another. There is no proof that there was a continuity; it may be that after the decline of the great era of cathedral building the guilds were kept alive for other than professional needs and came to include in their numbers persons of all callings.

At any rate Masonry as we know it emerged in England in the wake of the great political convulsions of the seventeenth century. There groups of men, or "lodges" as they came to be called, were formed in various towns, at first without any common center. The formation of the Grand Lodge in 1717 gave the movement just that unity and cohesion needed for its further progress in England and for its spread beyond the limits of that island to the Continent and even to America.

The goings and comings involved in diplomatic and commercial intercourse probably carried Masonry abroad. Germany and Sweden seem to have been the two countries where it was first introduced and where it spread with some rapidity. Despite her traditional hostility to things English, France gave it a welcome, and a native French Freemasonry developed. In each country, however, it took diverse forms. As it developed in England, Freemasonry had been comparatively free from elaborate ritual. Its purposes had been moral, and it had exacted a severe standard of conduct. There were but three degrees. On the Continent the ritual became complex; its aims and purposes were far beyond the original. In Sweden the Swedish system embraced ten degrees; the three original English (or Johannine) degrees, the two degrees of St. Andrew (Scottish), and the five so-called knightly degrees.[1] In Germany there was grafted on to the original English degrees a number of orders that had little in common with the parent movement. Such was the order of the Rosy Cross or the Rosicrucians, which came into existence in Berlin in the eighteenth century and put forth a rank growth of higher degrees. This peculiar cult clothed itself in extravagant language. It was the most mystical of the group of

[1] Georgii Vladmimirovich Vernadskii (Vernadsky) *Russkoe Masonstvo v tsarstvovanie, Ekateriny II*, 42.

Masonic orders and came under severe criticism for that reason. It thrived at the court of Frederick II, protected by one of Frederick's most powerful ministers, Wöllner. Still another development in Germany was the order of the *Illuminati* founded by Weishaupt, an unfrocked Jesuit. In France there were the Martinists, followers of St. Martin, as well as a group known as the Knights Templars that claimed to hark back to the Crusades.

It is difficult to establish the exact time or place of the origin of Russian Freemasonry. Freemasonry had spread to Germany by 1739. There were certainly Masons in Russia as early as 1741, when James Keith was named provincial Grand Master for Russia at a meeting of the Grand Lodge in London in that year (this authority probably extended only to the lodges of foreigners living in Russia).[2] These had been started by the English and the Germans for the benefit of their countrymen living in Russia, and their ritual was usually English or German.[3]

But while the existence of the first lodges in Russia will probably, for lack of conclusive evidence, be difficult to fix in time, most writers are agreed that lodges in which Russians actually participated as members were not formed until the middle of the century. There is a report on the Masons submitted on the request of A. I. Shuvalov to the Empress Elizabeth. This report, undated, describes the Masonic Order, its ritual and the various objects used therein, and attached a register of members. Among the members listed were Roman Ilarionovich Vorontsov (Grand Master) and Prince Mikhailo Dashkov. It is also known that Nikolai Golovin, who had been in the service of Frederick the Great, on his return in 1747 was suspected of being a spy in Frederick's service and was subjected to severe examination. He admitted having been a Mason, naming others who had also been members of the order.[4] The in-

2 S. V. Yeshevskii, "Moskovskie Masony vos'midesyatykh godov proshedshago stoletiya, 1780–1789," *Russkii Vyestnik*, 1864, T. 52, 362. The James Keith mentioned left Russia in 1748 and, entering Prussian service, became a field marshal under Frederick the Great. He met his death at Hochkirk in 1758.

3 A. N. Pypin, *Russkoe masonstvo XVIII i pervoi chetverti XIX vyeka*, 89.

4 Nikolai Tikhonravov, *Lyetopisi russkoi Literatury i drevnosti*, IV, 49–52. The author refers it to the year 1747. Pypin, *Masonstvo*, 89, apparently relies on this same source, but on page 92 he appears to refer this to a later date (1756), when at the request of Count A. I. Shuvalov, a certain Mikhail Olsuf'ev submitted a report on the Masons to the Empress. Count Shuvalov

volvement of Russia in the Seven Years' War and the strong anti-foreign feeling that we find under Elizabeth did not favor an institution of alien origin; hence for the full flowering of the Masonic movement in Russia, we must look to the reign of Catherine (1762–96).

As far as we can discern from the paucity of documents, the great development of native lodges in Russia must be referred to the seventeen seventies, with the beginning of an era of an unprecedented tolerance for Russia. The Freemasonry now introduced was of several types. One group was the so-called Strict Observance (of which the Duke of Brunswick was the chief figure, centering in the lodge of the Three Globes); a second group was the so-called Zinnendorf, named for a certain Dr. von Zinnendorf who had been expelled from the Lodge of Strict Observance. A third group, the lodge Royal York de l'Amitié, had split off from the above group and had applied to the Grand Lodge of London for its charter. These three competing types of Masons had long departed from the original English simplicity and had multiplied degrees, decorations and ribbons and become imbued with mystical characteristics not present in the original Masonry.

The second of these types had reproduced itself in Sweden and from Sweden descended on St. Petersburg during the seventies. Here its cause was championed by Baron Reichel. But the order of Strict Observance (sometimes called Rytsarstvo-knighthood) had been imported also from Germany; its recognized leader was Yelagin, who later became one of the most significant leaders in Russian Masonry. Some obscure consideration led them to merge their two organizations in 1776 with Yelagin as provincial Grand Master, but there was great dissatisfaction among those lodges of Baron Reichel. They took advantage of the embassy of Prince Alexander Kurakin to Stockholm in 1777 to announce the betrothal of the heir apparent Paul to the Princess Sophia Dorothea of Würtemburg in order to establish liaison once more with Swedish

was at that time head of the Secret Chancery. The list of members almost seems to be a roster of future intellectual and political leaders of the age of Catherine. Whether 1747 or 1756 is the proper date, native Russian lodges had sprung into existence under Elizabeth and had become important enough to draw the attention of the government. See also Petr Petrovich Pekarskii, *Dopolneniya k istorii masonstva v Rossii v XVIII Stoletie*, 170.

Masonry. Kurakin and Gagarin were inducted into the highest degrees, and on their return an agreement was reached for the establishment of a Russian *Kapitul* on the Swedish system. The first new Swedish lodges came into existence in 1778. Gradually the old national lodge, formed in 1776, ceased to function; and Yelagin finally moved to Moscow, where apparently toward the end of the seventies the Swedish system had come to predominate. But even in Moscow there was still some dissatisfaction, and with the arrival in that city of two key figures in the history of Russian Masonry—Novikov and Schwartz—the whole situation was changed. The cause of this was the increasing competition among lodges for the higher secrets, which it was believed some of them possessed. This led to a strange and interesting development.[5]

To get a perspective of developments in Masonry after 1780, we have to go back some years to pick up the career of Nikolai Ivanovich Novikov, a member of the lesser gentry who had come to St. Petersburg and there had started, with some encouragement from the Empress, between the years 1769 and 1774 a series of satirical magazines. Gradually imperial displeasure caused the toning down of their original bold and caustic wit. This new and insipid diet was little to the taste of their metropolitan readers. A slump in satirical journalism drove Novikov out of business. At this time he was drawn to the Masonic movement and in 1775 was received into the order. In 1779 he removed to Moscow where he shortly engaged in publishing in connection with the University of Moscow.

For the next few years Freemasonry in Moscow was identified with an intense burst of publishing activity, behind which stood Novikov and his associates. In Moscow, Novikov became acquainted with Johann Schwartz, at that time an instructor in the University of Moscow.[6] Schwartz had also identified himself with Masonry, which at that time had suddenly deeply concerned itself with the secrets which it was alleged some of the higher degrees had. The members of the Reichel-Elagin lodges who had

[5] Vernadskii, *Russkoe Masonstvo*, 34–48. A list of the lodges established in Russia during the seventies is given in Yeshevskii, "Moskovskie Masony," *Russkii Vyestnik*, 1864, p. 363.

[6] See Chap. VI for a fuller account of Novikov's publishing activity in Moscow.

put themselves under the Swedish *Kapitul* were disappointed in not having received any of these alleged secrets.[7] This sudden interest in the alleged mysteries of Freemasonry may have been not unconnected with the visit of Cagliostro to Moscow in 1779. At any rate we find even Novikov beginning to question the true meaning of Masonry; it was this feeling of dissatisfaction that led to the dispatch abroad in 1781 of Professor Schwartz to attend the Wilhelmsbad conference of German Masons and to get in touch with the currents of Masonic thought abroad. At this time Germany was witnessing the growth of two of the higher branches of Masonry—the Rosicrucians and the *Illuminati*. The immediate result of this dissatisfaction was the decision of the Moscow Masons to break away from Sweden and to form an independent province of their own. This determination was approved by the congress, and Russia thus became the eighth national province of the Masonic order in Europe.

An even more striking result was the sudden and extravagant development of mysticism among the Masons. This development is usually credited to the new impulses imparted by Rosicrucianism, the cult of the *Illuminati*, and the cult of the Martinists imported from France about the same time; but in reality it was merely a part of a general reaction against the hitherto dominant materialistic philosophy of the Enlightenment. It is hardly surprising that the coterie of intellectual idealists in Moscow should have been attracted to mysticism when it is remembered that such men of great minds as Goethe and Herder passed through a similar phase. In Russia, the movement took various forms and, despite its crude extremes, it had its better side. Besides dabbling in this cult, both Novikov and Schwartz plunged into altruistic activities, too frequently misrepresented. Besides his publishing activity, which was extensive, Novikov promoted various educational enterprises; he established hospitals, and furthered a number of humanitarian causes; he also gave help to students in completing their university studies. He tried to inspire his associates to service, to self-perfection, and to furthering the general good.

A summary of this period of intensive activity of Novikov and

[7] Vernadskii, *Russkoe Masonstvo*, 50–52; M. N. Longinov, *Novikov i Moskovskie*, 100 ff.

the Masons in Moscow is all that is possible here.[8] Novikov's publications embraced periodicals, books of general cultural nature, and religious and Masonic and even mystical works. But his influence was personal as well as literary. He had come into the Masonic movement with some reluctance and on his own terms.[9] Not only did he take a lofty view of the Order, but it was to him a religion of service to humanity. He gathered around him a number of Christian mystics such as Lopukhin, Krayevich, Karneyev, and Repnin. His associates studied Böhme, Johann Arndt, Thomas a Kempis, and Madame Guyon. They talked of the "Inner Church" and in all things they regarded themselves as Christians. They were devoted readers of the Bible, but they showed a certain weakness for alchemy and other psuedo sciences.[10]

Service to humanity consisted of a wide variety of activities. Loans were made to members, their relatives, and friends in case of need, and money was raised for helping the poor. In the province of Yaroslavl a home for the poor was established; a special school was founded for the children of the poor; in the region of Novorossiya, the Masons founded public schools (afterwards taken over by the state).[11] They also started a drugstore in Moscow.[12] Some of the Masons, notably Lopukhin, were munificent benefactors of the poor; another, Gamaleya, freed his serfs and declined a gift of some 300 serfs from the Empress.[13] In 1786–87 during a widespread famine in Russia, some of the Masons bestirred themselves on behalf of the peasants. One Grigorii Podkhodyashin offered a large part of his considerable estate for relief; and Novikov, both in Moscow and on his own estate, personally saw to the distribution

[8] For a fuller account of the work of Novikov and the Masons in the field of education, see Chap. V below.

[9] Longinov, *Novikov i Moskovskie Martinisti*, 99.

[10] Vernadskii, *Russkoe Masonstvo*, 127, 150, 158, 191. The activities of this group show a striking similarity to those associated with the Bible Society under Alexander I. Can it be that there is a direct continuity? See Stuart R. Tompkins, "The Russian Bible Society; a Case of Religious Xenophobia," *American Slavic and East European Review*, October, 1948.

[11] G. V. Vernadskii, *Russkoe Masonstvo v ego proshlom i nastoyashchim*, 198 ff.

[12] Vernadskii, *Russkoe Masonstvo*, 211.

[13] V. V. Sipovskii, *N. M. Karamzin*. See the *Prilozhenie* (appendix): "Novikov, Schwartz i Moskovskie Masony," 12. See also Semevskii, *Krest'yanskii Vopros v Rossii v XVIII i pervoi polovinye XIX Vyeka*, I, 176.

of food. But even this praiseworthy benevolence brought them under some criticism, perhaps owing to the fact that it brought out into sharp relief the heartlessness of Catherine's own conduct in persisting in her plans for the triumphal progress through the Taurid province when famine was at its worst.[14] It is impossible not to be struck with the failure of ideas of tolerance and benevolence to make headway against the universal suspicion and distrust in Russia. Of the critics of freemasonry, I. V. Lopukhin had this to say:

> These persons cannot understand that there might be people of honest intentions, benefactors, serving their neighbors; and because these books which we [i.e., the Masons] published were to help those who read them, all this seemed to them a plot and something suspicious; and in all this they ascribe to us what appears to them probable (which is what they prefer); accustomed to act from motives of money, rank, decorations, or fear, they cannot believe that there are people who, without selfish motives, wish to perform the duties of a Christian, of a loyal subject, of a son of the fatherland, or a fellow human being.

> Deny God, display astuteness in deceit, ruin, slander, and calumniate your neighbor, betray innocent young girls, and in their eyes you will be a respectable and honest citizen. But refrain from these fashionable pursuits and invariably you will deserve the name of a Martinist or of an enemy to society.[15]

The exuberant growth of Freemasonry during these years in Moscow, however, seemed to demonstrate the spread of ideals of humanity, of benevolence, and of Enlightenment. This growth, however, was shortly destined to be struck with blight—a blight

[14] Longinov, *Novikov i Moskovskie Martinisti*, 278. This perhaps illustrates how unresponsive the public mind in Russia could be to generous and disinterested acts. Podkhodyashin is described as a *myeshchanin* who first engaged in Masonic activities in Berlin and afterward became a close associate of Novikov. He seems to have been the son of a former carpenter and *izvoshchik* who engaged in some industrial activities in the Urals and acquired a fortune somewhere near the Demidov works. He apparently acquired peasants (possessional) whom he ill treated. See Semevskii, *Krest'yane v tsarstvovanie Ekateriny* II, I–*Vvedenie*, xxiv. The younger Podkhodyashin seems to have lost all his money in Novikov's *Tipograficheskaya Kompaniya*.

[15] Vernadskii, *Russkoe Masonstvo v ego proshlom i nastoyashchim*, 246–47.

that shriveled much that was promising in Russia. This was official distrust and ill will. Its origin is to be found in many diverse factors. The Empress' distrust was kindled by the extravagancies in which the Masons had become involved. Some Russian writers make the claim that Masonry was bound to rouse the hostility of Catherine by its mystical trend.[16] This was bad enough; but when Cagliostro, the famous charlatan, managed to worm his way into the Masons and exploited his connection on his visit to Russia, the scandal he was involved in was bound to create the worst possible situation for that organization. Catherine's views on Masonry, whatever they may have originally been, were henceforth, owing to the open scandal of Cagliostro's life, to become unfavorable. We find her writing on July 9, 1781, to her confidant Grimm:

> Freemasonry is one of the greatest aberrations that has ever been displayed by the human race. I have had the patience to read all their nonsense, both printed and in manuscript, by which they advance their case; and have seen with disgust that no matter how much you poke fun at people, they refuse to become wiser or more enlightened or more prudent for this. Masonry is sheer humbug, and one wonders why a sensible person, after having been laughed at by everyone, could fail to be disillusioned. If I had my way, I would consign all this rubbish to oblivion. I cannot see how people can tolerate such nonsense or why, when they meet, Masons can refrain from laughing. . . . I have waded through their stupid nonsense, which has furnished me with abundant material for making merry at their expense a hundred times a day in conversation.[17]

[16] This is the view taken by M. N. Longinov in *Russkii Vyestnik*, 357 ff. and by M. Dovnar-Zapol'skii, "Pravitel'stvennoe Gonenie na Masonov," in *Masonstvo v ego Proshlem i Nastoyashchim*, S. P. Mel'gunov and N. P. Siderov (eds.), II, 123. The latter author defended this persecution on the ground that governments are justified in taking what steps they deem necessary to safeguard themselves.

[17] V. A. Bil'basov, *Istoricheskie monografii*, IV, 166–69. During his sojourn in Russia, Cagliostro was involved in various scandalous escapades. He first had a quarrel with the Spanish chargé d'affaires over his claim to rank in the Spanish service. He later accumulated enormous debts and evaded his creditors by taking refuge in the residence of Yelagin. The latter, disgusted at the quantities of food and drink which he consumed at the expense of his hosts, finally ejected him.

The reference in the above quotation to the Masons laughing when they

Catherine reacted to Cagliostro's antics in a characteristic way. She wrote a play—*Obmanshchik*—which was performed in 1786. The handbills distributed on this occasion said:

Although our century has received from all sides the compliment of being called the philosophical century, and although we are ordering in advance the mighty word ENLIGHTEN-MENT as an inscription for its monument, nevertheless, everywhere a great many heads are dizzied by so enduring a swindle that the Goddess of Wisdom found it necessary to beg the Comic Muse for a remedy for this disease. A humorous comedy suffices to heal the dizzy heads and to preserve forever those that are sound. The enchanted castle against which Justice and Philosophy are marching from all sides, with catapults and ballistas, will here be blown to pieces by the explosive of wit.[18]

But a factor hardly less important was the deeply ingrained prejudice of the official class against spontaneous movements of any kind among the people. Catherine at the time of her rise to power and at the meeting of the Commission in 1767 had given her people a clear lead in the exercise of this right of spontaneous initiative and of freedom of thought. But events had made her pause. The Pugachev revolt in 1773–74 had clearly shown that not all self-activity on the part of the people might be beneficent. She had grown increasingly cold to these manifestations and had already given the satirical journalists in the capital to understand that there were limits to the freedom of thought and expression.[19] And when the Masons in Moscow entered a field which the government had taken for its own, viz., that of education, she showed her displeasure by moving in and taking these schools under government supervision.[20] Freemasonry and journalism were inextricably mixed up

came face to face is undoubtedly a veiled reference to the well-known comment ascribed to the elder Cato, who remarked that he did not see how two *flamens* who met on the street could fail to laugh, presumably at the fraud they were engaged in perpetrating on the Roman people.

At the end of the above passage Catherine makes veiled allusions to sterner measures that might be applied to the Masons, since they have failed to profit from the raillery to which they had been subjected.

[18] Francesco, *The Power of the Charlatan*, 233.

[19] See Chap. VII below.

[20] See Chap. V below.

in the activities of Novikov in Moscow. Masonic periodicals and Masonic books appeared cheek by jowl with translations of Milton's *Paradise Lost*, Bunyan's *Pilgrim's Progress*, the works of such mystical writers as Böhme, St. Martin, and Pordedge, and with Golikov's *Deyayniya Petra Velikago, A Dictionary of Russian Writers*. It would have been hard for the eighteenth century to decide where the good left off and the evil began. But by 1785 it was apparent that while the Empress looked askance at the Masons, her distaste as yet had given her no grounds for restraining them. The activity of Novikov's private presses in Moscow not only alarmed the Empress and the authorities, but gave them the pretext they needed for action. The publication of a history of the Jesuits, which put that order in somewhat of a bad light, allowed the government to proceed against Novikov.[21]

A new governor, Count Yakob Bruce, a haughty, overbearing official with the training of a police officer, was found for Moscow. Henceforth, Novikov's activities were more and more sharply scrutinized. The harassment to which he was subjected curtailed his business. Then in 1789 the full force of the French Revolution broke on Europe, bringing in its train a violent reaction. In 1790 came the arrest, trial, and condemnation of Radishchev. Two years later Novikov and the Novikov publications fell under official displeasure. Novikov was arrested and questioned and after admitting his guilt was by official *ukaz* confined to the Schlüsselburg prison. The death of Catherine in 1796 released him.

The incarceration of Novikov rang down the curtain on the activities of the Freemasons under Catherine. There was no formal suppression, but most of Novikov's associates felt the official displeasure. Prince Trubetskoi and I. P. Turgenev were sent to their estates. Prince N. V. Repnin received an honorable exile in the post of governor general of Riga. I. V. Lopukhin, one of Novikov's closest intimates, for the same reason was spared.[22] It is not

[21] The Jesuit Order had been suppressed by Pope Clement XIV in 1774. Catherine, on the other hand, not being a Roman Catholic sovereign, somewhat ostentatiously refused to recognize the dissolution and granted the Jesuits asylum. Their work in the field of education was what recommended them to her protection. They continued their labors with great success down to 1822 when they were expelled from Russia.

[22] Vernadskii, *Russkoe Masonstvo*, 242; see *Prilozhenie* (appendix), 257 ff. (Information on this is also contained in Pypin.)

probable that the lodges entirely ceased to function, but such of their activity that persisted must have been in secret.

It is quite probable that the factors that led Catherine to take action were political rather than intellectual. As early as 1777 when Gustavus III of Sweden visited St. Petersburg and openly flaunted his Masonic ties, Catherine could hardly have been otherwise than affronted, in view of the recent rebuff she had experienced at the hands of Gustavus in the *coup d'état* of 1772.[23] But the taint of cosmopolitanism hung over Freemasonry; and involved as she was in a series of tortuous and complicated diplomatic maneuvers, Catherine could scarcely look with complacency on the going and coming of Masons across the frontiers and particularly their close association with German rulers, including Frederick the Great. After Catherine made her *volte-face* in international affairs, swinging from the Prussian to the Austrian alliance in 1780, she looked with jaundiced eye on the subordination of Russian to German Freemasonry. Even the setting up of an independent Russian province in 1782 at Wilhelmsbaden only partly reassured her. She began to suspect (as was the case) that the Masons were making advances to the heir apparent. She had always been morbidly sensitive on this point, perhaps from a guilty conscience for having robbed her son of his birthright. She interpreted any advances made toward the Grand Duke as a blow directed against herself. She could not but realize that there was much disappointment abroad in the land with her failure to introduce far-reaching reforms, and that many were already looking forward with hope to the accession of a new sovereign. It was inevitable that these complications should involve Novikov and his followers in trouble, and the disclosures at the trial of Novikov could not but confirm her worst fears.[24]

It is difficult to make any accurate estimate of the influence of the Masons on Russia in the eighteenth century. It is true that merchants and *myeshchane* were not welcomed into the Order,

[23] Longinov, *Novikov*, 100 ff. Longinov believes that Gustavus at this time inducted the Grand Duke Paul as a Mason, but there seems to be no direct evidence of this.

[24] Sipovskii, *N. M. Karamzin, Prilozhenie* (appendix), "Novikov, Schwartz i Moskovskie Masony," 12. Not only did the Masons lend the Grand Duke Paul Masonic books, but Novikov submitted to him a project for constitutional reform.

but, as we have seen, there were some who belonged. There is at least one case where a priest of the Orthodox church joined. In general, however, the membership was restricted to the land-owning nobility and the bureaucrats recruited largely from this class. Vernadskii has tried to establish exactly how large a proportion of the bureaucracy were at one time or another members of the Order; and he finds on the basis of his calculations that there were not less than 2,500 Masons in Russia, almost all of them either in the military or civil services. The total number of officials varied from 6,000 in 1777 to 12,000 in 1787. On this basis from one-sixth to one-third of all those in the government service were Masons. If these figures are correct, the impact of Masonry on Russian thought and life must have been prodigious.[25]

While Novikov and others were released on the death of Catherine in 1796, there is no evidence that Masonry revived under Paul. The times were too uncertain and the temper of the monarch too unpredictable, even had he shown special favor. Paul had probably been inducted into the Masonic Order in 1776.[26] He had shown some interest in it. But whatever his interest had been, it cooled, perhaps, as Shumizorskii suggests, under the influence of Rostopchin. He may possibly have concluded that its principles were not to be reconciled with the principle of absolutism to which he was so devoted. In any event his reign was too short and his own originality and that of his intimates so limited that there were not many marked departures, except in externals, from the policies of his mother. The lodges that had suspended operations on the arrest of Novikov in 1792 remained closed, even though a number of their former members were advanced to high rank. But it was to the Order of the Knights of St. John of Jerusalem that Paul's ardent devotion was drawn, and Masonry ceased to attract him.[27]

In 1801 with Alexander I on the throne things took a slightly different turn. It appeared that Alexander, not being a Mason and

[25] Vernadskii, *Russkoe Masonstvo*, 83–90.

[26] Shumizorskii, "Imperator Pavel I i Masonstvo," S. P. Mel'gunov and N. P. Sidorov (eds.), *Masonstvo v ego proshlom i nastoyashchim*, II, 135–52. Also S. V. Yeshevskii, "Moskovskie Masony desyatykh godov proshedshago stoletiya, 1780–1789," *Russkii Vyestnik*, No. 8, 1864, 371.

[27] A. N. Pypin, *Obshchestvennoe Dvizhenie v Rossii pri Aleksandrye I*, 297.

65

having some respect for the views of his grandmother, entertained some distrust at first; this was finally dissipated by a Mason, V. I. Böber, who in 1803 obtained an audience with the Emperor and succeeded in removing some of his misconceptions. The Emperor agreed to allow the Masons to resume their activities and expressed a desire to be enrolled as a Mason.[28] It is interesting to note one significant feature in the composition of the Masonic lodges at this time. As one author says:

> The Masonic lodges of St. Petersburg in the eighteenth century were for the most part made up of the titled nobility, but in the first five years of the revival of Masonry in the nineteenth century, it became noticeable that the charms of Masonry were attracting the middle class of the *intelligentsia* and were filtering down to the more or less well-to-do merchant class and representatives of different trades.[29]

But Russia was shortly involved in war with Napoleon, and after 1805 there was only the comparatively short intermission of peace from 1807–12. (Even this was interrupted by the war with Sweden over Finland in 1809.) It was not until 1810 that the movement began to revive with any vigor.

From the scattered notices we have regarding Masonry during these years, it would seem that the great activity in the order dated from 1810, after which date we have frequent mention of it. We know that M. M. Speranskii, with the approval of the Emperor, attended meetings of Masonic lodges on two occasions and associated with the well-known Doctor Fessler, the Austrian mystic.[30] This would suggest that at this time not only was Alexander favorably disposed toward the Masons, but he actually contemplated taking the decisive step of joining himself.

The intimate association of Masonry with mysticism under Alexander was nothing new, since it had prevailed in the eighteenth century. The relaxation of press censorship by Alexander and the generally milder regime encouraged those who had participated

28 Tira Sokolovskaya, "Rannoe Aleksandrovskoe Masonstvo," in *Masonstvo v ego, proshlom i nastoyashchim*, Mel'gunov and Sidorov (eds.), II, 167.
29 *Ibid.*, II, 158.
30 M. A. Korf, *Zhizn' Grafa Speranskago*, I, 260. He probably was also inducted into the order.

in the earlier movement to resume their activity. In 1806 A. F. Labzin, vice president of the Academy of Arts, himself an ardent mystic, taking advantage of this tolerance, began the publication of the *Messenger of Zion*, whose purpose was to popularize the works of the great mystics, Jung-Stilling, Ekkarthausen, and Swedenborg; but on the orders of the censorship it ceased publication with the ninth issue. Still there was continuous pressure on the censors to relax the ban to allow the resumption of the labors of Novikov in giving such works to the public. Eventually the clamor was silenced by an order that they would be passed only if a sworn statement was obtained from the Minister of Police that the government had granted tolerance to Masonic lodges.[31] The conclusion to be drawn is that, in spite of the fact that Alexander had connived at the revival of Masonry, no general permission had been given Masons to resume activity.

Finally in 1812 a new factor was projected into the situation with the formation under imperial patronage of the Russian Bible Society.[32]

The Tsar, coached by his Minister of Foreign Confessions, Prince Aleksandr Nikolaevich Golitsyn, embraced a vague kind of evangelical Christianity and entered on a period of religious exaltation, of which his earlier life had given no inkling. He was persuaded to encourage the establishment of what at first was the St. Petersburg Bible Society (shortly to become the Russian Bible Society) for the distribution at a nominal cost of the Holy Scriptures translated into the various languages of the Russian Empire. This organization made some headway during the war; and after the restoration of peace, it became the center of a whole group of activities that went beyond the original purpose of the society. Alexander was passing through a phase in which we see Madame de Krüdener flitting in and out of the imperial anteroom, in which we catch glimpses of Alexander kneeling in prayer with Quakers. This phase culminated in that document compounded of evangelical religion and lofty phrases, the Holy Alliance, which its enemies

[31] A. M. Skabichevskii, *Ocherki istorii russkoi tsenzury* (1700–1863 g.), 98–99.

[32] Stuart R. Tompkins, "The Russian Bible Society: A Case of Religious Xenophobia," *The American Slavic and East European Review,* October, 1948, pp. 251–68.

took for sheer hypocrisy. In 1817 the Emperor was so carried away that he formed the new double Ministry of Public Instruction and Ecclesiastical Affairs, whose avowed purpose was to see that the doctrines of primitive Christianity should be taught in the schools, as well as expounded from the pulpits, a step which could not fail to rouse the hostility of the Orthodox church.

From then on the Russian Bible Society grew rapidly and extended its activities into all parts of the Empire. It enjoyed imperial patronage; and its president, Prince Aleksandr Nikolaevich Golitsyn, was at the same time minister of public instruction and ecclesiastical affairs. In this dual capacity he gathered around him persons who, whatever their intentions, went to extravagant lengths. They represented various trends; some were ardent supporters of the efforts of the British and Foreign Bible Society whose avowed purpose was to circulate and popularize the gospels among the common people; others were professional evangelists of the type of Madame de Krüdener; some were simply Masons of the old school, like M. I. Nevzorov;[33] some like Labzin were mystics; others, parading as mystics or Christians of an evangelical form of Christianity, seem to have been time-servers like Karneyev and Magnitskii.[34]

We have already referred to the somewhat uncertain status of the Masons during the early years of Alexander's reign. For this situation many reasons could be advanced. In the first place, they still were under the same cloud as at the close of Catherine's reign. In addition they were now involved in the same shadow of suspicion that lay over all secret societies. It is one of the anomalies of the epoch that, while Europe had never been without its secret organizations, its Eleusinian and Orphic mysteries, its Roman *sodalitates* and *collegia*, its medieval guilds and bands of Albigensian *Kathari*, never perhaps had there been such a burgeoning of secret

[33] Nevzorov had belonged to the Novikov group and had suffered with his leader. He was released from prison on Catherine's death, and under Alexander resumed his Masonic activity, but had little sympathy with the new generation of Masons. See N. Kul'man, "M. I. Nevzorov," in *Masonstvo v ego*, Mel'gunov and Sidorov (eds.), II, 223.

[34] Magnitskii afterward became notorious in connection with the University of Kazan, which he was made curator of by Golitsyn in 1819. See E. M. Feoktistov, "Magnitskii; materialy dlya istorii prosvyeshcheniya v Rossii," *Russkii Vyestnik*, T. 52 (July, 1864), 5–55; T. 52 (August, 1864), 361–449.

Peter the Great

organizations, of societies (some of which claimed to possess the mysteries of magic and alchemy), of *Illuminati* and Rosicrucians, of orders of Knights Templars and St. John of Jerusalem, not to mention quacks and conspiratorial organizations, as at the close of the eighteenth century. Some could plead a serious moral and religious aim, such as the followers of Swedenborg and Jung-Stilling. But in the mind of the undiscriminating, all were lumped together. Thus there still lurked in the minds of Alexander and his advisers the old distrust that we find under Catherine. Indeed, the French Revolution, with its secret and conspiratorial organizations, had served only to heighten this fear all over Europe, and the various sovereigns taking stock of the situation had long since decided to adopt some precautions. Frederick William III of Prussia had in 1798 issued a general decree banning all kinds of secret societies which might in any way direct their activity against the state.[35] Unquestionably, Alexander had discussed the problem with Frederick William (with whom he was on terms of closest intimacy) or his minister Stein and had decided to take a leaf out of Prussia's book.

This Prussian degree forbade the following types of organizations:

1. Those whose principal or secondary business was to pass judgment for any purpose whatever on changes proposed in government administration, or of the means by which such changes might be brought about, or of measures already undertaken to this end.
2. Those in which obedience was promised to unknown leaders, either under oath or by the raising of the hand, either verbally or in writing or in any other way.
3. Those in which obedience was sworn to leaders on matters affecting the state or morality.
4. Those which exacted from their members a promise of silence regarding the secrets disclosed to members.
5. Those which cherished a secret purpose, or which employed secret means for the attainment of any aim, or made use of mystic and secret hieroglyphic forms.

[35] Sokolovskaya, "Rannoe Aleksandrovskoe Masonstvo," in *Russkoe Masonstvo v ego Proshlom i nastoyashchim*, Mel'gunov and Sidorov (eds.), II, 180.

It is easy to see the fears that underlay this bit of legislation. The example of the French Revolution, whose violent excesses were fresh in the minds of the public, and the prevalence among the people of France and its revolutionary armies of Freemasonry and other secret societies ready to join hands across the frontier with their fellows in other countries seemed to threaten the whole existing order, which the governments of the day were not willing to see go down without a struggle. In Russia itself Alexander had already given some countenance to Freemasons, but in 1812 when the battle was joined between the established governments and the revolutionary forces of imperial France, it seemed too dangerous to give them a free hand. Despite his early sympathy, Alexander felt that the issue should be put clearly to the leaders of Free-masonry; either they were to continue their general tasks of Enlightenment and of promoting humanitarian aims and foreswear all political designs, or they must be prepared to incur the risk of the government's displeasure or hostility.

Accordingly, the leaders were summoned to the Ministry of Police and were presented with two alternatives: either to be taken under the protection of the government (which in reality meant submitting entirely to the police) or to be tolerated on the understanding, apparently, that a single wrong step would lead to their suppression. The lodges chose the second alternative. They had to apply for authority to continue activity. In the circumstances of the war now raging with the French Empire, it is quite understandable that the government put all kinds of obstacles in the way of those lodges that belonged to the French system and presumably kept connections with France, while those lodges belonging to the Swedish system were readily granted permission to continue.

Despite the fact that the government had implicitly (in accordance with the spirit of its offer) promised to maintain a policy of "hands off" as long as the lodges refrained from offending official regulations, still official policy could hardly be called benevolent. But for the moment the autocracy was satisfied with the general withdrawal from the French system and entrance into the Swedish system. Moreover, at this time, perhaps in response to the spirit of the times, the Masons quite ostentatiously emphasized the

Mason's duty to his country. For this purpose, they revived the *Constitutions of Freemasons* adopted at the Wilhelmsbad Congress of 1782. While sections 1 and 2 dealt with the Mason's duty to God and religion, section 3 put special emphasis on his duty to his sovereign:

> The Highest Being has entrusted in the most emphatic way his power on earth to the monarch; honor and salute the legal power over that part of the earth where you live; thy first oath is due to God; the second, to thy Fatherland and thy monarch. . . . Honor thy parents. They are the persons who represent God on earth; thy own judgment, partly fallible, cannot free thee from obedience; if they are wrong, they will answer to the court of the Tsar. . . . If thou failest at any time to fulfill thy sacred obligations, if thy heart no longer beats faster at the very mention of Fatherland or of monarch, the Masons will cast thee out of their midst, as a foe to society, as unworthy of the advantages of such a society which deserves the confidence and trust of monarchs, because love of country is one of its chief sources, and with a view to making better citizens, it demands that they fulfill their duty to Tsar and Fatherland.[36]

Masonry made enormous strides during the war of 1812 and the campaigns in Germany (1813) and France (1814) that followed. Frequent contacts of officers with foreign Masons brought in foreign influences and probably furnished added incentive to the growth not only of Masonry but perhaps of other secret societies. The lodges that revived under Alexander were predominantly of the Swedish rite and invoked as the charter of existence of their lodge, the Grand National Lodge, the "Constitutional Patent" received in 1779 from the National Lodge of Sweden. But a flood of new members and new influences came in with the war that were hostile to the Swedish rite; there still lurked in Russian Freemasonry some suspicion of Swedish Masonry and its emphasis on the higher degrees, that is, those above the three Johannine degrees of the original English Freemasonry. These were now enormously reinforced by an influx of German members

[36] Sokolovskaya, "Rannoe Aleksandrovskoe Masonstvo," in *Russkoe Masonstvo v ego*, Mel'gunov and Sidorov (eds.), II, 186–87.

or of Masons with German ideas. A new factor was the arrival of Friedrich Ludwig Schröder, a scholar of note and an ardent Mason, who launched a bitter attack on the higher degrees. Along with Fessler he founded a special group restricted to the three degrees. Eventually a whole series of lodges broke with the old Directorial Lodge (the National Lodge) and formed their own Grand Lodge—Astrea.

For some years there were two rival groups, each competing for members. In general the new lodge, Astrea, flourished at the expense of the older. However, in 1817 this competition and rivalry were terminated by an arrangement by which both agreed on a sort of *modus vivendi* to put an end to this situation. Presumably it was little more than an agreement of mutual toleration. In 1818 there were eighteen lodges in the Union of Astrea; in 1820–21 the number had increased to twenty-four. The Directorial or Provincial Lodge counted in 1815 only six; in 1817 and again in 1819 the number was still six.

These were the best years for the Masonic Order, as well as for the Bible Society. They were also the years that saw the full sweep of those tides of religious mysticism that bore along so many of the thinkers of the time. It would be strange, therefore, if we did not find these elements in Masonry. It would be as unfair to identify Masonry with obscurantism as to equate the Bible Society with cranks and time servers. Both reflected the spirit of that age. They embraced the most diverse elements, but it was the extravagances rather than the normal and the moderate that drew the attention of the world and eventually that brought them under fire. In the roster of names of members we find a sprinkling of persons who afterwards became Decembrists—Pavel Pestel; Sergei Ivanovich Muravyev-Apostol; his brother, Matvei Ivanovich Muravyev-Apostol; Nikita Mikhailovich Muravyev; Sergei Petrovich Trubetskoi; Kondratii Ryleev (the poet); William and Michael Küchelbecker (the close friend of Alexander Pushkin); Alexander Bestuzhev; and a score of others. A sort of exaltation in which yearnings for justice and reforms, a mystical sense of divine immanence, for a short time was fused with the stirrings of the new philosophy in protest against the movement of reaction to oppose which it would pit its strength in vain. By a curious fate the various elements that made up this spiritual and intellectual drive fell apart; forces of obscurantism moved into the Bible Society; the Holy Alliance, created originally to bring religious principles into the dealings of nation with nation, was prostituted by Metternich to base ends; Masonry itself became discredited in the eyes of many when it became more and more confused with other secret societies and when it became associated with the publication of books and magazines on western mysticism. Perhaps most symptomatic of this trend was the revival in 1817 of Labzin's *Messenger of Zion*, suppressed in 1806, which now, under the protection of Golitsyn, minister of public education and foreign confessions, once more began to appear.[37] Since Labzin was a pietist, an honorary member of a Masonic lodge, and head of the Russian Academy of Arts, he had considerable weight in giving a mystical tone to Masonry. But he was only one of the influences. In spite of the decree that all books dealing with the church and matters of faith had to come under ecclesiastical censorship, many of the books of mystical-philosophical trend found their way into print to the consternation of the Orthodox church. In all these matters Freemasonry was usually confused by the public with the new mysticism.

We know little of the exact circumstances that led to the suppression of Freemasonry in Russia. Of one thing we can be sure. External events had much to do with it—in 1820 the mutiny of the Semenovskii Guards and the various revolutionary outbreaks in Europe. At Troppau and Laibach, Metternich was always at hand to warn Alexander of the dangers of radical movements and especially of the secret societies that were swarming over Europe. And it is understandable that the general distrust of all secret societies was extended to include the Masons.[38] According to Sokolovskaya the agreement reached in 1812 bound the Masonic Order to accept in advance without protest any action of the government to regulate or suppress it. Symptomatic of Alexander's growing alarm was the expulsion of the Jesuits in 1820. Finally in 1822 came an *ukaz* suppressing all Masonic lodges and other secret societies;

[37] Under pressure, Golitsyn in 1818 agreed to put this periodical under the ecclesiastical censorship which was equivalent to its suppression. It thereupon ceased publication.

[38] A. N. Pypin, *Russkoe Masonstvo XVIII vyeka i pervoi chetverti XIX vyeka. Prilozhenie* (appendix), 454.

members were also required to sign a promise not to belong to any secret society in the future.[39] The Masons seem to have complied with the order. We know now that other secret societies continued and that out of them grew the revolt of December 14, 1825. The order was repeated in 1826, and all such organizations went out of existence.

No attempt will be made at this stage to assess accurately the contributions of Freemasonry to Russian culture. In origin it was alien, but it had none of the traditions associated however remotely with a guild. It is not surprising, therefore, that it became confused and mingled with elements that had nothing to do with the original Masonry—mysticism, the evangelical religion of the Bible Society, the pseudo sciences, quackery, such as that of Cagliostro and Casanova, and ultimately stark reaction.

The fact remains, however, that Masonry communicated something into Russian life, or perhaps we should say that it provided a means of expression for some normal human aspirations that hitherto had been denied. It sounded a badly needed note of cosmopolitanism when people and governments in Europe were engaged in selfish and ruthless struggles for power and territory. It emphasized humanitarianism and Christian love in a society that had little respect for the underdog or for ordinary social justice. It opened schools and charitable institutions in a country notoriously lacking in them. Originally it had identified itself with the spread of human knowledge and Enlightenment, and Masonry is perhaps not to be blamed that some of its votaries abandoned the cause of learning. It sought to relieve the poverty and distress of those unable to help themselves. Some of its members are to be credited with detecting the injustice that underlay the system of serfdom and for sounding the first, albeit somewhat feeble, note of protest against it. If the humanity and the altruism of a society is to be the sum of all the separate acts of charity and philanthropy of its members, Freemasonry in Russia was a notable beginning. And it is the shame of the Russian system of autocracy that it seemed to prefer that society should dispense with these efforts to alleviate human suffering rather than to have such things undertaken spontaneously by its members. According to the prevailing

[39] *Ibid.*, 454.

theory of autocracy all ameliorative measures of a social or political nature must originate with the state, which can tolerate no rival. There seems little to choose in that respect between the Tsarist autocracy of the eighteenth and nineteenth centuries and the dictatorship of the proletariat of the twentieth.

It has been necessary to digress from the main story of the spread of education in order to give some idea of the temper of the more thoughtful part of society as reflected in the Masonic movement. In a sense it marked an interlude in Russian history, a departure from the hitherto predominant official initiative in all social movements, during which private initiative competed with the government in meeting popular needs. The story will now be continued to show how the period of tolerance of such private participation, after some vacillation, eventually came to an end and how the government resumed its monopoly of all ameliorative social measures.

V

Education under Catherine
and Her Successors

CATHERINE had been well grounded at her home in Stettin in those things which a woman of aristocratic birth could be expected to know. After her marriage and her estrangement from her husband, she turned to books for consolation. She became absorbed in the new French literature of the Enlightenment and while still Grand Duchess had begun correspondence with Voltaire, Diderot, and others. Her letters to these men reveal their influence on her ideas.

On attaining the throne, Catherine invited Diderot to visit her. This visit was postponed on Voltaire's advice until Catherine's position should become secure. When Catherine in 1767 prepared to summon the commission for codifying the laws, the famous *Nakaz* she drafted for its guidance reflected the ideas she had thus acquired.[1] These ideas were of a very general character, but embodied her conviction that true education should be moral as well as intellectual. This shift of emphasis involved nothing less than a revolution in Russian education—a revolution that included a complete change of spirit.

The narrow and jejune diet with which the young had hitherto been provided gave them the merest rudiments of knowledge. The Empress is known to have denounced the existing system by which the children of the gentry were educated at home as, at best, "a muddy stream."[2] In keeping with the spirit of the age, she wished

---

[1] *Ekaterina II, Sochineniya Imperatritsy*, II, 84ff.
[2] V. A. Bil'basov, *Istoricheskie Monografii*, IV, 341; cited from *Zapiski Akademii Nauk*, T. XLVII, No. 2, 33.

through education to give to the young entirely new and broadened concepts of life, such as could not be transmitted by the antiquated system then in vogue. She proposed, partly from circumstances, partly from her own inner convictions, to sweep away much of the old and to lay a broad and comprehensive foundation, which would not only be cultural first and vocational second, but which would provide for the children of the poor as well as of the rich, for children of peasant and landowner, of craftsman and merchant, and which would even be extended to daughters as well as to sons.

The Empress revealed her purpose in education at the start. In 1762, on March 12, a general statute for the education of the youth of both sexes was issued, the period of instruction to extend from five to eighteen years of age. The schools were to be state institutions. This statute remained, however, a mere paper enactment, and its execution had to attend the organization of the proper institutions by which it could be carried into effect. Catherine, however, did not wait for this organization, but proceeded to establish two centrally located schools: Smolnyi Institute started (in 1764) in St. Petersburg for the daughters of the nobility and the Novodyevichy Institute founded also in the capital in 1765 for the daughters of *myeshchane* or townsmen. Both schools imparted knowledge which in those days was thought indispensable for young women; here, the students were taught reading, writing, and arithmetic; and a basic knowledge of the household arts was given. There was some differentiation between the two schools in other respects: girls of noble extraction were taught dancing, painting, and other of the decorative arts; while the middle-class girls were taught such things as they would find useful in their station of life. These two schools had distinguished careers; by 1794 Smolnyi had turned out 440 graduates, while Novodyevichy was only a little behind with 410.

But general education had to await the contemplated revision of the *Ulozhenie* and the proposed reforms in Russia's institutions. In 1767 the Great Congress or Commission, as it was called, for the revision of the *Ulozhenie* was summoned to meet in Moscow. One of this commission's decisions was to name a special commission on education—to consist of Zolotnitskii (as chairman), Ursinus, and Klingstedt. This committee drew up some basic principles for public schools—first, that there should be three types of schools, elementary, secondary, and higher; secondly, that there should be no distinction of class in these schools; and, thirdly, that education should be compulsory.

But the sittings of the main commission were suspended toward the end of the year, and the educational committee's recommendations were stillborn. Catherine's energies were for some years to be preoccupied with the Turkish War and the Pugachev Revolt. Toward the end of the seventies her attention was once more turned to educational matters. A decree of 1775 required that the local boards of public welfare should, in addition to charitable institutions, assume charge of schools which they were to build and maintain. However, nothing came of this order. In 1777 events once again turned Catherine's attention to education. In this year a young prince, to whom the name Alexander was given, was born to the heir apparent, Paul, and his wife. Catherine immediately busied herself with the task of rearing him. This revived interest in education led her to address letters to her correspondents abroad —Grimm, Diderot, and others—for suggestions on the subject of education. They recommended to her the Austrian system, one of the projects which had fired the enthusiasm of the young Emperor Joseph. When Joseph, therefore, paid Catherine a diplomatic visit and the two monarchs met at Mogilev, schools were one of the subjects discussed. As a result, Catherine in 1782 established a commission to draw up a plan for public schools in Russia. This body submitted a project for elementary, secondary, and higher schools, and in 1786 a Board of Public Schools was established.[3] It was proposed to open in the capital town of each province a *gymnasium* on the model of the seminary or *gymnasium* which had been established at St. Petersburg. The governor of the province was to be a curator of schools for his province and was to name a district supervisor and a Board of Public Welfare for the province, which would be responsible for paying salaries. Schools of the three types were to be provided for all. As time went by, the middle or secondary type of school was dropped;

[3] Arkhangel'skii, *Imperatritsa Ekaterina II v. istorii Russkoi literatury i obrazovaniya*, 31.

and since the schools were concentrated in the towns, the peasants were left without schools of their own. In 1783 the *Glavnoe uchilishche* for the empire was established at St. Petersburg. This institution came to be recognized as a training ground for teachers.

The scheme had considerable success. By 1800, 315 public schools with a total attendance of 19,915 students had come into existence. By the end of the century 254 towns had schools, although 250 still had none; there were only 11 peasant schools.[4]

Meanwhile the Empress had invited the Croat educator, Jankovich de Mirievo, to translate textbooks into Russian and to adapt them to Russian conditions. It is noteworthy that the schools were to be to some extent secular, religion being omitted from the upper classes. In addition to Catherine's efforts for the education of the laity, some attention was given toward reforming education for the clergy, a special commission for this purpose being created in 1787. Unfortunately a general wave of reaction at the end of her reign bore even Catherine along. The wars with Sweden and Turkey also diverted her from her tasks in education, while the outbreak of the French Revolution in 1789 brought reform to an end.

Any estimate of Catherine's work must give her credit for broad and humanitarian views and for her belief in cultural, as opposed to professional, education. She sought to have the schools serve moral ends, rather than merely train for service. She also tried to divorce education from its hitherto prevailing class bias. A breakdown of the attendance at thirty-eight of the higher schools illustrates this fact. Of the students in attendance in 1801,[5] the sons and daughters of the gentry comprised 33 per cent; of the *myeshchane*, 14 per cent; merchants, 12 per cent; soldiers (i.e., privates), 11 per cent; serfs, 11 per cent; clerks, 8 per cent; state peasants, 5 per cent; and clergy, 2 per cent. It must be borne in mind that Catherine was forced to make a sharp transition by certain revolutionary changes from a school system which derived its support in large part from the privileged classes (although under state control) to a state-supported one. The secularization of church lands

[4] Nicholas A. Hans, *History of Russian Educational Policy*, (*1701-1917*), 25–26.
[5] *Ibid.*, 30.

had deprived the church of a great part of its property and hence of its ability to support a system of clerical schools. While the nobility, now emancipated from service, kept their children at home for their education, they could not be expected to finance general schools from which their children derived no benefit.

In the field of education the Empress seems to have broken with the hitherto prevailing tradition of Muscovite life that the state should control all public activities. This surrender of the state's exclusive monopoly of public instruction is paralleled by other experiments with private enterprise made by the Empress in the early stages of her reign. In 1765 Catherine founded the Free Economic Society, whose very name is an invitation to personal initiative. When, therefore, Catherine's general encomium on freedom, cited above, was taken as an encouragement to her subjects to bestir themselves and exercise their rights as individuals, there was no protest.[6]

Foreigners were allowed to open *pensions* to cater to the needs of the gentry.[7] The Lutherans had already been permitted to start schools for the children of Germans living in the capital. And in Moscow, when the circle of persons associated with Novikov founded schools and hospitals in addition to their other philanthropic enterprises, the government acquiesced, although this and other of their activities ran counter to the Russian system of state tutelage.[8] In 1783 the Empress allowed the establishment of free printing presses, a measure that at once called into life a score of private ventures. But the liberty that is bestowed as a favor can also be taken away, and hardly had freedom of publication been granted when it began to be curtailed. A play of Catherine's, *Obmanshchik*, presented in 1784, rather ominously singled out the Masons for attack. The followers of Novikov were taken to task for their private philanthropies, including their schools.[9] It did not surprise

[6] Arkhangel'skii, *Imperatritsa Ekaterina II v Istorii Russkoi literatury i obrazovaniya*, 34.

[7] Mikhail Longinov, "Materialy dlya istorii russkago prosvyeshcheniya i literatury v kontsye XVIII vyeka," *Russkii Vyestnik*, February, 1858, 716ff.

[8] A. N. Pypin, *Russkoe masonstvo XVIII i pervaya chetvert' XIX vyeka*, 275.

[9] *Ibid.*, 273–74. The Masons in Moscow also helped poor students to get an education.

the public, therefore, when an *ukaz* of September 5, 1784, placed all pensions and private schools in the capital under the Board of Public Welfare, which was to inspect the schools. No additional schools were to be opened without a verification of the credentials of the instructors. This order was within a year extended to Moscow. Some eleven schools became subject to government inspection; these schools contained 394 students, the greater number of which were members of the gentry class.

But the state schools concerned only a part of the population. The upper class obtained their education in a variety of ways, only one of which was public schools. They had recourse to not less than six alternative methods: (1) tutors at home; (2) tutors abroad; (3) universities abroad; (4) various educational agencies established by the state, e.g., the Lyceum at Tsarskoe Selo, the Cadet Corps, the Marine Corps, the Corps of Pages; (5) various pensions or *Adelspensionats* in the chief cities, such as the Lyceum in Odessa; and (6) Russian universities.[10] Unfortunately the majority of the instructors under whom the young Russians studied, even in Russia itself, were either German or French, so that there was some criticism of this type of education because it was non-Russian in spirit.[11] At the turn of the century foreign influences predominated, especially among the scions of the nobility, in the rearing of the young.

Catherine's son and successor, Paul, can hardly be blamed for the general revulsion against European influences with which the century drew to a close in Russia. But while this revulsion had been kept within bounds by the Empress, under her son it took an eccentric and violent form. Catherine, it is true, was alarmed by the excesses of the French revolutionaries, but she had no faith in military measures as a means of combating ideas. Paul would, according to his own words, have rounded up the Jacobins and made short work of them. His prohibition on the importation of books from abroad and the severe censorship he set up, coming

[10] Eugenie Salkind, "Die Dekabristen in ihrer Beziehung zu Westeuropa" *Jahrbücher für Kultur und Geschichte der Slaven*, 1928 Bd. IV, 285 ff.

[11] This weakness of all Russian education is stressed by Professor Parrot in his letter of February 22, 1825, addressed to the Emperor Alexander. See N. Schilder, *Imperator Aleksandr Pervyi i ego tsarstvovanie*, IV, 557.

after the closing down of private presses already in effect under Catherine, put Russia intellectually in a strait jacket. For his short reign, reform was suspended while educational measures already put into operation by Catherine simply marked time.

The first important act of his successor, the Emperor Alexander, was the naming of a special committee (all of whom were personal friends) to draw up plans for reforms in the government. Some of these reforms went into effect in 1802. The old *collegia* were reorganized into ministries under a single head on the model of western Europe. Among these ministers a Ministry of Public Instruction was to be established. Under it a commission for the organization of schools was to be set up which would have charge of all the lower schools. On January 24, 1803, the "Preliminary Regulations for Public Education" appeared. Its opening paragraph announced that "Public instruction is a special division of the government entrusted to the Minister of this division and, under his direction, subject to the chief school administration."

The commission was made up of six curators of the six areas into which Russia was divided. These curators had charge of all education within their districts (*okrug*), including and chiefly the university, although their place of residence was to be in the capital. Each *okrug* was to include a university. Three universities already existed—Moscow, Vilna, and Dorpat—while three were to be added. The Teachers' Seminary (*Glavnoe uchilishche*) in St. Petersburg was reorganized in 1803 into the Pedagogical Institute. Its main function was to be the training of teachers, but in 1811 certain courses to aid in the preparation of students for the civil service examination (prescribed in 1809) were added to its curriculum. In 1819 the Pedagogical Institute was finally turned into a university. The divorce of this institution from the Academy of Sciences ended the unsatisfactory condition that had hitherto existed in the capital, which, during the eighteenth century, had had an institution that was a university in name but was virtually without students. The other new universities were those of Kharkov and Kazan. All universities were to have, like St. Petersburg, faculties of education. In each of the provincial capitals a *gymnasium* was to to be located. Each county (*uyezd*) was to have a school of its own, which the director of the provincial *gymnasium* was to oversee. At the foot of the pyramid were the parish schools, of which the director of the county school was to have charge.

Some changes were made in the curriculum of these schools. The various institutions were plagued with the recurrent problem of how far they should be self-contained and how far they should merely be stages along the path of the students' progress. The members of the merchant and craftsmen (*myeshchane*) classes preferred to have their children in the county schools take subjects that would help them in making a livelihood. This meant restricting the subjects to reading, writing, and arithmetic; and in some localities the parents refused to send their children if they were taught more. In the *gymnasia* the same thing occurred; the well-to-do had in mind their children's completing their studies so that they might begin their careers; the less well-to-do wished their children to leave school at the earliest possible date to earn their livelihood. Finally, one of the greatest obstacles was that the gentry did not like the universities, preferring to send their children to special schools and pensions where they would receive instruction in keeping with their rank.

It was decided to reverse the policy regarding the *gymnasia* which had prevailed under Paul and to make them a step to the university. The *gymnasium* of St. Petersburg was first reformed to serve as a model for the others. All university subjects, such as philosophy and political science, were to be lopped from the curriculum of the *gymnasia*. Russian and "Divine Law" (religion) were reintroduced, and this addition required the further adding of three classes, making the *gymnasium* a full seven-year course in which Latin and Greek were to have a favored place. Graduates of the *gymnasium* were to have a right to the fourteenth class in the Table of Ranks, while the attainment of a university degree was an easy way of securing priority in the ascent up the official ladder.

On the other hand the county school was to be a complete whole. All the subjects (except languages) taught in the *gymnasium* were taught here, but on a lower level. The number of classes (years) was increased from two to three; the number of teachers was increased from two to five. However, the parish schools for the peasants remained unchanged.

83

Some pruning and grafting had to be done with the schools themselves. The first grade of the town schools (which consisted of two divisions, the lower and the upper school) was lopped off and transferred to the new elementary schools set up in the parishes. Classes three and four of the upper division of the old schools were transferred to the *gymnasia* in the provincial capital, where they became classes one and two. The second class in the county schools now became the first class, to which was added a second (forming the lower school). To these classes were added two more—classes three and four—hitherto nonexistent (these forming the upper school). Thus the student entering the parish school would normally proceed in seven years through the three schools—one year being allowed for the parish school, two years for the county school, and four years in the *gymnasium*.

The parish schools taught the three "r's" as well as an elementary version of what was known as "Divine Law" or religion. The county schools taught arithmetic, geometry, grammar, geography, the elements of physics, natural history, and technology, as well as "Divine Law." In the *gymnasia* more advanced subjects received attention—logic, psychology, ethics, esthetics, natural law, the national laws, and political economy; these subjects were supplemented by physics, mathematics, natural history, commerce, and technology. No formal instruction was given in language or literature. The emphasis was laid on continuity, rather than on each school's being self-contained, as developed under Catherine's system.[12]

It was difficult to maintain this continuity; the nobles disliked the county schools; the merchants and *myeshchane* were in the habit of withdrawing their sons from the *gymnasia* before they finished the curriculum. The government therefore dangled before parents prospects of government posts for those who completed the whole course of study. It was insisted on from the start that

[12] There can be little doubt that Catherine had proposed to provide an education for all with a minimum of class distinction. But circumstances had defeated her. In the tide of reaction that set in after 1785, the trend toward restricting each kind of school for a separate class had come to be recognized as normal. Alexander in his legislation had merely reverted to the original purpose of Catherine in abolishing class distinctions in education.

Catherine II

adequate preparation for all posts required a knowledge of jurisprudence. Finally, in 1809, the definitive step was taken by prescribing service examinations. The *ukaz* that required these examinations noted that the nobility had preferred to rest their prior
claims to admission to government posts on birth and to promotion
on seniority in service and ruled that henceforth admission to the
rank of collegiate assessor—the eighth rank in the service—would
be granted upon passing an examination set by the university. Under this system the support of all schools, down to and including the county schools, now was taken over by the state, partly
from policy, partly by the gradual shifting of the burden by the
local town councils and the boards of public welfare to the shoulders of the government.

From the beginning the *gymnasia*, as organized in 1804, were
unsatisfactory. Latin was taught in the upper classes; since most
of the university professors were from abroad, they had to use
Latin (supplemented by French and German for explanations),
and a knowledge of Latin was a prerequisite. But the teaching of
Latin was most unsatisfactory. Then, despite the efforts to establish
a continuity from the lowest to the highest classes, these attempts
were offset by some overlapping; the *gymnasia* taught university
subjects so that the university courses in these subjects were often
repetitions of what the students had learned in the *gymnasia*.
Courses in medicine sank to a new low; mathematics, history, geography (which were taught in Russian), and philosophical subjects which the student had learned something about in the *gymnasia* were the only courses which could be considered successful.
All students except those bound for the university—future teachers
for the most part—dropped out before completing the curriculum.
It was therefore decided to change the method of education. A
batch of brilliant young gymnasiasts were selected to be sent
abroad for training in order that the language of the universities
could eventually be changed from Latin to Russian.

Finally, in order to meet the reluctance of the nobility to make
use of the *gymnasia*, a reform undertaken in the St. Petersburg
okrug by the curator Uvarov in 1811 pointed the way for complete reorganization of these institutions throughout the empire.
The course at the *gymnasium* was increased from four to seven

years by restoring the lower classes taken from it in 1804. All strictly university subjects, such as philosophy, were dropped, while the teaching of Russian and "Divine Law" was reintroduced in the lower classes. But special emphasis was placed on the classical languages, Latin being started in the third year and Greek in the sixth. The role of the *gymnasia* was thus re-emphasized.

Perhaps at this point mention should be made of two institutions of secondary education founded as lycées on the French pattern to serve as models for the empire. These schools were the lycées founded by the Emperor at Tsarskoe Selo, to which Alexander invited a few of the most distinguished families in the empire to send their sons and which played a memorable role in the education of a generation that attained a high place in the annals of fame. The other school was the lycée started at Odessa on somewhat similar lines by the Duc de Richelieu which performed a somewhat similar function for students of the south.

An earnest effort was made to fill the gaps in the education of the clergy. They had had, since the eighteenth century, their own system of schools, including at this time four academies, 36 seminaries, and 115 lower schools. But there was a total lack of uniformity and system in the organization of the schools and in the curricula offered. In 1807 on the recommendation of A. N. Golitsyn, at this time Ober-Procuror of the Holy Synod, a special committee of clerics and laymen was named to make recommendations. M. M. Speranskii was the most notable member of this committee. The committee's recommendations to the Tsar were accepted and approved. No change was made in regard to the number of academies in existence, but it was decided that henceforth, instead of the rather haphazard distribution of elementary educational facilities, each diocese (in addition to the seminary) would have twenty county (*uyezd*) and thirty parish schools. The financial provision made for these schools by the state was increased from 180,000 assignat rubles to 1,669,450 rubles. In addition, the monopoly of the sale of wax candles in the churches, of which they had recently been deprived, was restored to the clergy in order to supplement the revenue drawn from the state. To undertake the carrying out of these provisions and to draft detailed rules and curricula for the schools, a regular institution was set up to

86

be known as the Commission of Clerical Schools, on which Speranskii served until his retirement in 1811.[13]

The reform in university education proceeded apace. In addition to the new university of St. Petersburg, two others—at Kazan and Kharkov—had come into existence. The enrollment of both of these new institutions was scant for some years, and both went through a period of severe trial. The foreign professors coming to Kharkov from the German universities brought with them the ideas of autonomy as practiced in Germany, according to which the faculty elected their own rector and administered the university. But the authorities soon undeceived them with the result that most of them resigned and were replaced by mediocrities recruited in Russia, under whom the new university made scant progress for the first years of its life. To meet this condition, promising students were sent abroad to be trained for professorial posts. But the new universities disappointed the great hopes raised by their creation.

The efforts of Alexander toward reform were much hampered by the wars with Napoleon and the complications that grew out of them. But a new and significant factor was interjected in 1812. This factor was the newly aroused interest of the sovereign in evangelical religion, which was stimulated by Golitsyn. As distracted as Alexander was by the events of the French invasions, he turned to this new inner religion for comfort. He became a patron and supporter of the Russian Bible Society and during the years that followed was much in the company of mystics and of persons regarded by the Russian world as sectarians.

It was in this mood that Alexander dreamed up his Holy Alliance, which was to be inspired by a spirit of Christian fellowship in the relations between sovereigns, between monarch and people, and in regard to his subjects the relation of loving father to dutiful children. It was this same cast of thought that led him to create the double Ministry of Ecclesiastical Affairs and Public Instruction, which Prince Golitsyn headed. Notice was thus served that all religions, including even Islam, were to be brought under one controlling authority and that their handmaid, education, was to be infused with the same spirit of Christian piety.

[13] A. M. Korf, *Zhizn, Grafa Speranskago*, I, 253–62.

It was at this time that the situation at two of the new universities—Kharkov and Kazan—became acute. Both had been worsted in the struggle for autonomy and, having lost their best teachers, dragged on an unsatisfactory existence. In 1819 the Pedagogical Institute of St. Petersburg had been raised to the rank of a university. But the history of all of the universities was equally dismal. In 1819 the Minister of Public Instruction had dispatched one of his chief assistants, Magnitskii, to inspect the University of Kazan. As a result, Magnitskii was named to the position of curator of the educational district (*okrug*) of Kazan with special responsibility for the university. Thus began a regime that lasted for seven years and soon became notorious. Magnitskii had been a member of the Bible Society and had embraced the rather cloudy mysticism of Golitsyn, which in his case supplied him pious texts and ready cant phrases with which he cloaked his own designs and his fear of anything new. He was a born intriguer and timeserver. The seven years of his incumbency left the university at the end of that time jejune and stripped of all love of learning and all moral aspiration. His friend and imitator at St. Petersburg, Runich, also made the heavy hand of authority felt, and four of the ablest of its staff were brought to trial.[14] Karneyev at Kharkov also brought that university into line. Thus, in the name of public peace and order, higher education had largely been throttled by the end of the reign of Alexander.

The Decembrist Revolt of December 14, 1825, which came on the heels of Alexander's death, shocked the new monarch Nicholas into taking stock of the widespread unrest and the role of the schools, which many were inclined to hold responsible for the revolt. On May 14, 1826, a special committee for reorganizing the educational institutions was set up. Admiral Shishkov as minister of education appeared before it with two proposals. The first principle was for a return to the old idea of each of the schools in the system being self-contained: the parish schools for the peasants, the poorer *myeshchane*, and merchants; the county (*uyezdnye*) schools for the children of merchants, officers, and nobles; and the *gymnasia* for the most part for nobles, but granting permission for other classes to enter them.[15] The second principle recom-

14 Skabichevskii, *Ocherki po istorii russkoi tsenzury*, 140 ff.

mended by Shishkov was that the schools should emphasize moral instruction as well as knowledge.

The changes in the educational system during the early part of the reign of Nicholas I are associated with the name of Count Uvarov. Uvarov had been curator of the St. Petersburg district from 1811 to 1821, when he clashed with the efforts of Runich, a creature of Magnitskii, to destroy the autonomy of the universities and resigned. Whatever he may have been in his younger days, Uvarov's name came inevitably to be associated with the famous slogan "Orthodoxy, Autocracy, and Nationalism," the three principles he proclaimed as the basis of Russian society. When Prince Lieven in 1833 resigned as minister of education, Uvarov succeeded to his post and directed education until 1849, the eve of the great reforms.

One of Uvarov's first acts was the organization of the University of Kiev (rather the University of St. Vladimir at Kiev) to take the place of Vilna (suppressed after the Polish revolt of 1831). His real work was the drafting in 1835 of the "General Regulations of Imperial Russian Universities," which severely circumscribed the autonomy of the universities and inaugurated a system of governmental tutelage for both students and instructors. Its most serious provision was to set up a system of rigid inspection by a so-called Inspector of Students completely independent of the faculty.[16]

The sons of the gentry were to be encouraged to proceed through the *gymnasia* to graduation. Here they were to be at all times under the watchful eyes of the government. In addition Uvarov proposed to establish in connection with the *gymnasia* (as well as some of the county schools) *pensions* for the members of the gentry class. The gentry was also assured that promising students who graduated from the *gymnasia* with good showings would be admitted to the fourteenth grade of the Table of Ranks.

In addition the county schools were now divided into three classes, instead of the former two; their instruction was in the same subjects as the *gymnasia*, save on a lower level. The parish schools were now to be taken on the state's payroll. These changes affecting

[15] Milyukov, *Ocherki po istorii russkoi kul'tury*, II, 323-24.
[16] William H. E. Johnson, *Russia's Educational Heritage*, 96-97.

the schools were approved and became effective on December 8, 1828. A new general charter for the universities came into effect on July 26, 1835, and a new demarcation of the educational districts on June 25, 1835.

To meet the complaint that their students were burdened with useless subjects in the upper classes, the *gymnasia*, beginning with the fourth year, were organized into two parallel and completely separate curricula. Only one of these curricula provided instruction in modern languages, including French.[17]

The needs of the gentry were to be met by a proposal put forward by the committee for setting up, in connection with the *gymnasia, pensions* for those of noble birth, where the nobility might be instructed in subjects appropriate to their station in life and not given in the *gymnasia*—such as French, dancing, fencing, and riding. While it was urged that these *pensions* should merely be in the nature of "finishing schools" for young gentlemen, in order to give them social polish and moral training, the students would also be taught the solid subjects in the *gymnasia;* nevertheless, the *pensions* made such an appeal to the gentry that more and more they usurped the function of the *gymnasia* and in some cases became independent preparatory schools offering shortened curricula designed to "finish" the students for their station in life, rather than to prepare them for the university. While private boarding schools were forbidden in the capitals and discouraged elsewhere by the *ukaz* of 1833, nonetheless, their numbers continued to grow. Thus there evolved in spite of the wishes of the state a privileged school for the nobility.[18]

17 The curious opinion was expressed by the committee that "a knowledge of French fosters presumption (in the student), while a study of the ancient languages tends to modesty and a realization of the limitations of one's knowledge." Milyukov, *Ocherki po istorii russkoi kul'tury,* II, 328.

18 This was apparently recognized by the committee as preferable to taking the alternative course of designing the general schools for the gentry. Prince Lieven thus expressed himself on this:

"In countries where the classes are sharply defined, where it is difficult to pass from one to the other, and particularly from the middle class to the nobility, it is a simple matter to introduce such a system. But in Russia where there is no middle class . . . where the well-to-do peasant at any time can become a merchant and often does become a merchant or something else as well, where the lines setting off the nobility are so vast in extent that they stretch to the feet of the throne, at one end, and at the

The concentric system, whereby the parochial and county schools were under the direction of the director of the *gymnasium* of the provincial capital, was abolished, and the administration was taken over by the officials of the administrative district. Similarly and despite the protest of Lieven, the minister of public instruction, the universities were deprived of all traces of autonomy. While the rector and deans continued to be elected, their powers and those of the academic council were taken away. The curators of the educational districts, now required to live within their boundaries, were responsible for academic discipline; and all the administrative staff functioned under the curator. The inspector ceased to be responsible to the academic council and became a government official. Students also were brought under rigid control in their habits and dress; and a special officer, called the monitor, exercised constant surveillance through his continual presence with them. While Russian became the language of instruction and while courses in Russian and Slavic history were added in the faculty of philology, many of the courses, instead of being educational in their broad aspects, were subordinated to the purposes of training students for administrative needs.

For some inexplicable reason the teaching of the classical languages came under suspicion, apparently as an incitement to revolution, along with such subjects as philosophy and the social sciences. Thus they were crowded out to make way for the natural sciences, which were more appropriate for premedical students and those preparing for other specialized scientific fields. With the exception of Greek—taught in some of the Black Sea ports where the population was largely Greek-speaking—classical languages were restricted to the classical *gymnasia*, seven in number (1851).

After the revolution of 1848 the universities were brought under an even stricter regime. The rector and deans were to be appointed by the state and not elected, and they were required to see that the lectures given did not contravene the teachings of the Orthodox church, the existing form of government, or the spirit

other end are lost among the peasants, where everyone of the middle or peasant class by attaining rank in the army or the civil service enter the nobility, to organize such a school is difficult." Milyukov, *Ocherki po istorii russkoi kul'tury*, II, 330–32.

of the state institutions. To carry this policy into effect, professors were required to submit in advance to the Ministry of Education lithographed, signed copies of their notes for approval, as well as lists of all collateral readings. Deans were required to see that the lectures given followed closely the preliminary notes. The teaching of German philosophers was banned, as was the study of the institutions of those countries shaken by revolutionary disturbances. Constitutional law, statistics, logic, and metaphysics were also stricken from the curriculum.[19] Thus anything that might in any way undermine the beliefs of the students in the established religious, political, and social order was rigidly excluded from courses. The new spirit in higher education was signalized by an order requiring students to wear a uniform and to cut their hair in a specified way.

The history of secondary and elementary education in this period followed much the same lines. *Gymnasium* courses had been extended to seven years, instead of four. Special provision was made at the beginning of the fourth year for students who wished to specialize in some field, thus differentiating students taking the general course from those pursuing more highly specialized fields. The district schools also extended their curriculum to five years. Below this level, education among the common people and the peasants was somewhat sporadic, largely left to local and individual initiative. There is some evidence that a considerable amount of knowledge was imparted in schools established by landlords and others for communicating special skills or sometimes just reading and writing, although it was illegal to send a serf to a *gymnasium* or university unless he were emancipated.[20]

A glance at the figures of attendance at various educational institutions in the St. Petersburg educational area during the first half of the nineteenth century discloses some interesting facts. For the latter part of Alexander's reign and the first years of Nicholas I's reign, the following are the figures for students in the St. Petersburg educational district:

19 William H. E. Johnson, *Russia's Educational Heritage*, 99.
20 Semevskii, *Krest'yanskii Vopros v Rossii, v XVIII v pervoi poloviny XIX vyeka*, II, 564.

Institution	*1810*	*1820*	*1824*	*1828*
Pedagogical institutes and universities	102	85	51	168
Pensions for the gentry		105	68	100
Higher schools (1827–37)			395	386
Gymnasia	458	760	450	431
Private pensions and schools	1,647	2,002	2,027	2,275
County and parish schools	4,043	3,770	4,465	4,689[21]

The distribution by classes for the same area toward the end
of the reign of Nicholas I was as follows:

Institutions	Nobles	Other Classes	Total
Universities	299	125	424
Gymnasia (including those in schools for the gentry)	2,265 (1,099)	566	2,831
County schools	1,814	2,872	4,686
Parish schools	833	6,730	7,613
Private pensions and schools	2,960	3,192	6,152[22]

We have now come to a critical period in the intellectual life
of Russia, wherein many forces, hitherto by themselves almost
imperceptible, began to work together to produce a profound
change in the temper of the country. From the very start of the
eighteenth century, education had come to be looked on as a
preparation for service; even after Catherine tried to substitute
for this end of education the idea of all-round development of
the individual's powers, there still lingered the prejudice that the
only education worth while for a gentleman was a practical one
and, along with this, the belief that a general cultural education
was useful only for those who forswore the life of service. Since
the other classes also had their narrow view of education for their
peculiar station in life, that left the cultural education provided by
the university to those who for various reasons had cut loose from
their original class affinities; this small but rapidly growing class
of "classless persons" came later to be known as *raznochintsy*, a
term variously used by writers and sometimes loosely applied to

[21] P. N. Milyukov, *Ocherki po istorii russkoi kul'tury*, II, 319.
[22] *Ibid.*, II, 329.

persons of other than the serving and privileged classes who wormed their way into the institutions of higher learning with no intention of serving the state. This class increased quickly when the newspapers and periodicals which sprang into life in the thirties and forties began to provide a fairly secure if meager livelihood. They became the "superfluous man" for whom society had no use and who had no attachment to the existing order. They began to give a new temper to the intellectual life of Russia. They were out of step with society, and it is from their ranks that the new figure—the professional revolutionary—now begins to be recruited.

Under Nicholas, successive ministers of public instruction generally conformed to the reactionary trend of the times. This trend in its most extreme form was not merely toward the maintenance of the existing order, but also toward the molding of public opinion to suit the special policies of the government at the moment.[23] It was, however, only after the outbreak of revolutions in western Europe that the government began to bear down on the institutions of higher learning. Almost at once a ban was put on persons going abroad to study with the permission or at the expense of the Ministry of Public Instruction. A limit was shortly placed on the number of persons attending the universities. The universities in 1849 lost their last vestiges of autonomy. The rector and deans became nominees of the crown. The teaching of philosophy in its several branches was for the various universities in Russia proper entrusted to teachers of theology; while in the Baltic states (Dorpat), Orthodox students had to attend the philosophical lectures given by the clergy of their own church. The teaching of public law was stopped. The teaching of the history of the Athenian democracy and republican Rome was eliminated as calculated to unsettle the minds of students and destroy their faith in autocracy. As previously seen, university instructors had to submit in advance out-

[23] Minister of Public Instruction from 1824–28, Admiral Shishkov, was the exponent of this extreme view. We find it embodied in the code drawn up by him and approved by the Emperor in 1826. This so-called "iron code" was found unworkable and superseded by the code of 1828. Nevertheless, this policy of control and direction of public opinion by the state, exercised through the official censorship, though expunged from the law, remained to some extent implicit in the administrative policies of his successors with regard to censorship and education. See Skabichevskii, *Ocherki po istorii russkoi tsenzury*, 214–15.

lines of their course, which had to be followed with scrupulous accuracy, and woe to any instructor who departed from his outline! But the teacher was now to be punished also for equivocal language which allowed students even to guess at his disapproval of the existing order.

One author claims that the idea was seriously entertained of suppressing the universities and of substituting for them special professional schools. There was nothing new in this idea; it was a return to the earlier one, which had been basic in Russian education from the time of Peter, though overlaid for a time by the cultural concept of education imported from western Europe.[24] Tuition was also increased to exclude persons of a lower station in life. But the government followed this action up by efforts to siphon the noble classes away into the service, especially the military service; and when limiting the number of university students, the government had disclosed its motives to exclude those persons "not possessing immovable property, but with an exaggerated estimate of their own abilities and knowledge, [who] are more frequently dissatisfied with the existing order of things and hence a disturbing element, especially if they fail to find satisfaction for their swollen vanity."[25]

It can readily be appreciated that the number of students in attendance at universities showed a marked decline after 1848:

Year	St. Petersburg	Moscow	Kharkov	Kazan	Kiev	Dorpat	Total
1836	299	441	332	191	203	536	2,002
1847	733	1,198	523	368	608	568	3,398
1848	731	1,168	525	325	663	604	4,016
1849	503	902	415	303	579	544	3,256
1850	387	821	394	309	553	554	3,018
1852	358	861	443	321	522	607	3,112
1854	379	1,061	457	366	675	613	3,551

[24] See discussion of the purpose of Petrine education on p. 38–39 of a previous chapter. The above material is given on the authority of Gershenzon, *Epokha Nikolaya I*, 118–24.

[25] In one of the administrative measures introduced at the time, the state went so far as to urge that the children of the noble class should seek pre-eminence as the descendants of the knights of old in military, rather than civil, service. Gershenzon, *Epokha Nikolaya I*, 118.

"Outward signs of attachment to the authorities" (*Caricatures the Russian habit of meek submission to authority. From* Iskra, *No. 8 [1862].*)

It seems fitting here to review the progress of education since the time of Peter the Great, when Russia had first sat at the feet of Europe and European influences had poured into Russia and swept away much that was old and outworn. At first the purpose of educational reforms was purely utilitarian. As time went on and the broader cultural significance began to be grasped, the dam of stagnation was broken, and the new ideas began to lap at the foundations of Russian society. Education then began to be viewed in a new light as something that challenged the main principles of Russian life. These principles were too deeply rooted in the Russian past, in the customs of the people, their laws, their attitudes of mind, and their institutions (especially the church); and it is folly to assume that people are indifferent to what challenges that which is a part of themselves. A long struggle began between the two principles—between that of free inquiry, on the one hand, to which the peoples of western Europe had become accustomed, and the system of tutelage, on the other hand, in which the Russian people had been schooled. The two could not fuse. In this struggle each alternately experienced triumph and defeat. This tension is sometimes represented as a clear-cut issue between reaction and progress. This view is not quite correct. Under the impact of Western ideas and successive political crises, Russia was forced to adjust itself to new concepts. But the great mass of Russians never faltered in their attachment to the basic concepts laid down by the Moscovite tsars that Russia's world mission and their own role as "gatherers of the Russian land" required that all institutions, church and school, should be but instruments in furthering this grand design. The individual Russian, if he were to share in this great world destiny, must subordinate his private interests to those of the state. As Klyuchevsky said, Russia was from the fifteenth century an armed camp, and every Russian was called on to man the ramparts. As an individual, he had no more rights than a soldier on active service. Despite the fact that Catherine and others toyed with the idea that individual self-development was the end of education, she and her successors finally reverted to the idea that the end of education was the service the student could render the state.

VI

The Press

❦❦❦❦❦❦❦❦❦❦❦❦❦❦❦❦❦❦❦❦❦❦❦❦

WHILE education was originally the chief agency for the spread of western culture in Russia, it was at first supplemented and eventually all but superseded in that role. The press from very humble beginnings in the sixteenth century ultimately came to dominate the field of enlightenment. But of far greater significance is the fact that the press has reflected for the past two hundred years the movements of public opinion, to which the government has at all times been extremely sensitive. The activity of the press, therefore, and the resulting reaction of the state together present an absorbing picture of the struggle that constantly went on between a people restive under tyranny and a government whose mission demanded the obedience and collaboration of the members of all classes, even when that obedience entailed the sacrifice of personal interest and the acceptance of a humiliating and degrading subservience.

It is said that the first press was set up in Russia in the reign of Ivan IV. This press was official and existed largely for the printing of ecclesiastical books, since there was little that the government wished to reduce to printed form. Indeed, most written matter circulated in manuscript until the time of Peter. Then it became apparent to that monarch that if Russia were to absorb ideas from western Europe books must be made available. At first he granted to Jan Tessing, a Dutchman, a monopoly for the printing and importation of books through the port of Archangel to Russia. These books were to be printed in Latin or Slavic, and the regular customs duties were to be paid on their entrance into the country. The monopoly was to last for fifteen years.[1]

[1] A. M. Skabichevskii, *Ocherki po istorii russkoi tsenzury*, 5.

In 1703 there came from the official press the first number of a periodical, the *Vyedomosti* or the *Russkie Vyedomosti,* appearing at first at Moscow and later alternately at Moscow and St. Petersburg. In 1727 the ecclesiastical part of the press was moved to Moscow from which all ecclesiastical books henceforth issued. Two official presses were set up in St. Petersburg for secular purposes: one for the use of the Senate in printing official documents; the other belonging to the newly established Academy of Sciences. On January 1, 1728, the latter body began the publication of the *Akademicheskie Peterburgskie Vyedomosti.* As an appendix to the latter there appeared the *Primechaniya,* which in 1754 became the *Yezhemesyachnyye Sochineniya (Monthly Publications),* with the eminent historian Müller as editor, and which had a distinguished career as an independent periodical.[2] Four years later, in 1758, the University of Moscow (founded in 1755) began to issue its *Moskovskie Vyedomosti,* the first university periodical to be published in Russia.

Catherine's accession as empress heralded a new era in the field of literature in general and journalism in particular. Beginning in 1760 in Moscow there began to appear periodicals whose chief purpose seems to have been diversion, and one is impressed with the increasing leisure enjoyed by the gentry.[3] Official sanction was required to print these periodicals on the government presses. After 1764 the *Monthly Publications* of Müller, published by the Academy, and Sankovskii's *Good Intentions* were suppressed, leaving the field to the two editions of the *Vyedomosti* which appeared at St. Petersburg and Moscow. Then in 1769 there was a fresh outcropping of journals—this time satirical—which unquestionably was largely inspired by the patronage of the Empress. There were no less than sixteen of these which blossomed into a short life and then dropped from sight.

[2] A. P. Pyatkovskii, *Iz istorii nashego literaturnago i obshchestvennago razvitiya,* Chap. II.

[3] The titles are significant: *Useful Entertainment,* edited by Kheraskov, with five numbers appearing between January, 1760, and June, 1762; *Free Hours,* also published by Kheraskov, with one issue; *Innocent Distractions,* published by Bogdanovich, January to June, 1763; *Good Intentions,* 1764, published by Sankovskii in connection with the university; *Selection of the best works for the Spread of Knowledge and the Bringing of Enjoyment,* 1762, edited by Professor Reichel.

This initial phase in the development of modern Russian literature is extremely instructive. The new reign had been ushered in with a resounding manifesto in which the new monarch had explained her motives and objectives—to correct abuses that had crept into the government (presumably under Peter III), such as foreign influences and heresies calculated to undermine Orthodoxy. All causes of disorder were to be removed in the belief that order would then naturally assert itself. The suppression of the secret chancery and the notorious *slovo i dyelo* announced to the world that Russia was to be brought into line with the more advanced countries in the enforcement of the law. In this honeymoon period Catherine unquestionably believed that the cure of Russia's ills lay in the rather simple expedient of removing the superficial blemishes that had attached themselves to the body politic and did not call for any drastic surgery. The Empress' idea had largely been absorbed from the reading of French literature. She was particularly fascinated by French satire, in which French genius had found one of its most characteristic expressions, and she was convinced that social ills could best be cured in this way. The new type of journal, therefore, was launched into life with her blessing and looked to the Empress not only for protection but for encouragement. However, official sympathy gradually cooled. The practical problems with which Catherine found herself confronted when she summoned her famous Commission of 1767, the outbreak of the war with Turkey, and the Pugachev Revolt seem to have raised some doubts in her mind concerning the usefulness of satire in the correction of abuses. Her famous *Vremya*, published in 1772 and acclaimed by Novikov in his *Zhivopisets* as a wonderful and salutary influence, was not thoroughgoing enough to call for such encomiums; and though she did not disclose her authorship, she treated Novikov's fulsome praise with some coldness. The satirical phase came and went without that profoundly curative effect on the body politic that was expected.[4]

How sincere was Catherine in apostrophizing freedom and

[4] Perhaps the best-known discussion of this satirical literature is that of N. A. Dobrolyubov in his article, "Russkaya Satira Ekaterinskago vremeni" which appears in Volume I of his works, 108–202. Dobrolyubov assumes that the criterion of satire is its effectiveness in bringing about a change for the better in morals both public and private or in correcting ills, and therefore

encouraging the young writers of the day to attack public abuses? That question has had all kinds of answers, but it is certain that the hand of government was still stretched forth to smite the over-bold. On two occasions in 1764 orders were issued for the public burnings of compositions, condemned as "pasquils," one of them composed as a parody of an *ukaz*. Andrei Krylov was publicly whipped in 1767 for having in his possession a disrespectful "pas-quil" and condemned to exile at Nerchinsk. It is significant that this early flowering of satire came to a rather abrupt end; if the experience of Novikov with the *Truten* is any criterion, it was the general tone of listlessness of the periodicals that ended their popularity; and one is tempted to believe that this in turn came about through official pressure.[5]

The Empress, however, had not lost interest in the press, as evidenced by the grant to a foreigner, Gartun, of permission to print foreign books in Russia, provided he did not in any way enter into competition with the official press and his books were also passed by the Academy and the police. In 1776 two other foreigners, Weibrecht and Schnor, received permission to print Russian

he condemns the satirical literature of the time for its ineffectiveness in improving either the lot of the individual or of the state.

We are face to face here with one of the most fundamental preoccupations of modern Russian literature: that literature is bound to devote itself to analyzing social phenomena and bringing about basic changes in society rather than to discussing questions of private or public morals. To cite significant passages from Dobrolyubov's article:

"It was mighty seldom in the midst of these attacks [i.e. of the satirists] that there was the glimmer of an idea that all these were inevitable consequences of the unsoundness of the social structure. . . . They asserted: one should not fawn on the authorities, one should not take bribes, one should not exploit others. But how is one to get along without flattery or without taking bribes, if the majority of officials cannot make a living on account of their poverty, cannot keep their families, clothe themselves decently, etc. What is one to do if, under present social conditions, everyone who does not exploit some one else is doomed almost to die of hunger?"

This is perhaps not the place to discuss the writer's ideas, but it seems that the author ignored some important consideration, viz., that before practical steps can be taken to eradicate an evil, the evil must be pointed out and the individual conscience roused.

[5] A partial list of these is given in Skabichevskii, *Ocherki po istorii russkoi tsenzury*, 35. A fuller list appears in Longinov, *Novikov*, 22. The factors that caused Novikov to suspend publication of *Truten* in 1770 are discussed in Pyatikovskii, *Iz istorii nashego literaturnago i obshchestvennago razvitiya*, 40.

books, the latter in 1780 moving his press from the capital to Tver.[6]

But the most sweeping changes in regard to the press came with the general break in the policies of Catherine in the year 1780. At this time the Turkish war had receded into the dim past; Russia was enjoying peace; the horrors of the Pugachev Revolt had been forgotten. And now Catherine, having for long kept step in foreign and perhaps domestic affairs with Frederick the Great, began to tire of this association and to turn with hope to the young and ardent reforming Emperor Joseph II. The new liberal movement, which led to the inauguration of reforms in education, inspired Catherine on January 15, 1783, to issue an *immenoi ukaz*, allowing the establishment of private printing presses with a moderate degree of freedom in publication. Almost immediately the newly found freedom led to a fresh outburst of publishing activity unprecedented in Russia's history. Presses were founded not only in both of the capitals but in various remote country homes of the gentry. Perhaps the most striking effect of this wide expansion of publishing activities was to call into life around the university in Moscow a whole group of publishing ventures which continued almost to the end of Catherine's reign. These activities, associated with the name of Novikov, call for somewhat extensive treatment.

Novikov had become a Mason in 1775. In 1779 he had moved to Moscow where he had met Johann Georg Schwartz, a native of Transylvania who had been brought to Russia in 1776 by Alexander Mikhailovich Rakhmanov as tutor of his children. On Rakhmanov's death, Schwartz had been named professor at the University of Moscow.[7] Here Novikov and Schwartz soon became fast friends and the latter was shortly introduced to the Masonic movement and became an ardent participant.

Novikov also formed a connection with the University of Moscow, where he leased the university press and undertook to publish the *Moskovskie Vyedomosti*, the official journal. One of Novikov's first public acts was the formation of the *Uchenoe Druzheskoe Obshchestvo* (Society of Friends of Learning) in 1779; he later

[6] Dobrolyubov, "Russkaya Satira Ekaterinskago vremeni," I, 120.

[7] V. I. Tukalevskii, "N. I. Novikov i I. G. Shvarts," in *Masonstvo v ego proshlom i nastoyashchim*, Mel'gunov and Sidorov (eds.), III.

established a pedagogical seminary, a translation seminary, and an elementary school. In 1783 the *ukaz* permitting the establishment, without the necessity of securing government consent, of private presses was issued. Novikov immediately took advantage of this new decree to start two publishing houses, one in the name of himself and Lopukhin in his own house, the other in the home of Lopukhin in the Armenian Pereulok. In addition, the Masons as a body started their own press in the home of Schwartz near the Men'-shikov tower. In 1784 a *Tipograficheskaya Kompaniya*, a joint stock undertaking of fourteen associates including Novikov and Lopukhin, was also organized. This colossal enterprise, quite in the American spirit as one writer notes, had an establishment representing a capital investment of 150,000 rubles.[8] All of these activities were supplemented by periodicals published by Schwartz on his own account, the *Ekonomicheskii Magazin* (*The Economic Magazine*), *Moskovskaya Nemetskaya Gazeta* (*The Moscow German Gazette*), *Vechernaya Zarya* (*The Evening Dawn*), and *Pokoyushchiisya Trudolyubets* (*The Resting Laborer*).[9] In 1784 Schwartz died, but the work of the Masons and Novikov continued. Through the subsidiary institutions mentioned above, the university was infiltrated and attracted students from all parts of the empire.[10]

The enormous influence of this Schwartz-Novikov group had already aroused the distrust of the authorities when in 1784 Novikov published a history of the Jesuits. Since the Jesuits were then at the height of their power in Russia, they complained to Catherine.[11] The Empress ordered the confiscation and destruction of the whole issue of Novikov's history. But the incident brought all Novikov's publishing activity under surveillance. A commission of three persons, including the Prokuror of the province, the Archbishop of Moscow, and another cleric, was charged to investigate it. The result of this inquiry was the seizure of 461 books, which for

[8] Skabichevskii, *Ocherki po istorii russkoi tsenzury*, 42.

[9] Tukalevskii, "N. I. Novikov i I. G. Shvarts," I, 175.

[10] Skabichevskii, *Ocherki po istorii russkoi tsenzury*, 41. The Masons also promoted charitable work which greatly enhanced their prestige and influence among the people.

[11] *Ibid.*, 47.

the most part were of a religious nature and were alleged to have been published by an evasion of the *ukaz* of January 15, 1783.[12]

The appointment of Count Yakov Aleksandrovich Bryus (Bruce) as commander of the garrison of Moscow foreshadowed an end of the government's complaisance. On January 23, 1786, Novikov was summoned before the governor for an investigation of his publishing activities. Bruce was instructed to inform Novikov that he was supposed to print only what was useful and not that which would disseminate the seeds of a new *raskol'*. At this time all the charitable institutions of the Masons also came under review. Novikov, however, whose orthodoxy was examined by Archbishop Platon, received from the prelate a clean bill of health. Nevertheless, six of Novikov's books were confiscated and burned.[13] With the Moscow garrison now under Bruce's command, many of Novikov's activities were liquidated, including the Society of the Friends of Learning. The "secret" publishing house located in 1784 in the house of Schwartz was also broken up, although some of the books printed in it escaped the general search.[14] These governmental measures led to the issuing of a new *ukaz* on July 27, 1787, requiring that all books of an ecclesiastical character be printed exclusively by the Synod and its presses.[15] This order was followed shortly by another which required that all books of whatever character be examined by a commission of clerics and laymen. These spartan measures brought the Typographical Company to bankruptcy with overwhelming debts. A further provocation to the government was the fact that the Masons had drawn the attention of the public somewhat ostentatiously to the famine of 1786–87 by their wholesale gratis distribution of bread to the sufferers.[16] Then in the following year a book on the history of the Solovyetskii Monastery—a clear infringement of the law of 1787—was published. For the moment this book passed unnoticed, but the tale of the misdemeanors of Novikov and the Masons was piling up.

[12] *Ibid.*
[13] Longinov, *Novikov*, 264.
[14] *Ibid.*, 272.
[15] Dovnar-Zapol'skii in *Masonstvo v ego proshlom i nastoyashchim*, Mel'gunov and Sidorov (eds.), 124, footnote 1.
[16] Skabichevskii, *Ocherki po istorii russkoi tsenzury*, 41.

But it was now that events elsewhere began to have an effect on the affairs of the Russian press. The French Revolution, which broke out in May, 1789, at once sounded an alarm to the monarchs of Europe. The situation in France seemed to justify the most ardent hopes of those who longed for a new and progressive era and the worst fears of those who desired to preserve the institutions of the past. It is probable that the French Revolution merely gave added momentum to a trend already under way. Moreover, the great diplomatic triumphs of the early part of Catherine's reign and the hopes for reform kindled by her good intentions expressed on suitable occasions had turned to bitter fruit. Moscow, the old capital, withdrawn from her influence, seemed to have become a hotbed of opposition and perhaps even of treason. The activity of Novikov and his associates, who had taken advantage of the indulgence granted to them in 1783, had passed all bounds and threatened to shatter the old tutelage in which the tsars had formerly held their subjects. Catherine's insane jealousy of the heir apparent, for whom Moscow had shown a perverse admiration, stung her perhaps all the more because it also pricked her conscience.[17] At first Catherine put a good face on developments in France and, as a child of the Enlightenment, accepted them as the logical outcome of that movement. On one occasion in 1790 she even rebuked Paul for the bitterness he displayed in his partisanship for Louis XVI on reading of the indignities to which he and the royal family were being subjected.[18] But Catherine's firmness soon vanished, and she was as dismayed as any other of the enlightened despots over what was happening. Russia was to experience profound disillusionment in the course of the Empress' reign, which raised grave doubts as to the sincerity of Catherine's original protestations of benevolence and tolerance.

[17] Skabichevskii claims on the occasion of her visit to the old capital in 1775 that Moscow had greeted Paul with a tumultuous welcome while receiving the Empress somewhat coldly. *Ibid.*, 38.

[18] "One day Paul was reading newspapers (about events in France) in the private room of the Empress and suddenly flared up. 'What's all this they are endlessly discussing,' he exclaimed, 'I'd put a stop to it with guns.' 'You stupid fool,' the Empress replied, 'Can't you understand that you cannot fight ideas with cannon. If that is the way you are going to rule, you won't be long on the throne.'" N. Schilder, *Imperator Pavel I*, 248.

This same age, says one historian, which was marked by the birth of an intellectual force in Russia, saw also a complete break in the attitude of the government toward it. The protection, which had gone to the very limit, one fine day came to a sudden end and was never resumed. Having called into existence an intellectual power, the government suddenly took alarm at it, as though it were some spirit rashly called up, and despite the fact that it was an infant that could hardly prattle, the government proceeded to subject it to savage persecution. The outbreak of the French Revolution still further roused governmental hostility. At the end of the last century, things, as we shall see, had got to the point that every man who had anything to do with books for this very reason was dangerous and suspect and was liable to take a journey to more or less distant places.[19]

It was not, however, on the somewhat rash and indiscreet Novikov that the wrath of the Empress was first visited, but on a hitherto little-known official in the College of Commerce. Alexander Nikolayevich Radishchev had been born on August 20, 1749. He had received his early education in the home of his grandfather at the hands of a French emigré, a former member of the Parlement of Rouen. Later, he had attended for some time the University of Moscow. Appointed to the Corps of Pages on the accession of Catherine, Radishchev was sent abroad along with other pages to the University of Leipzig. Returning to Russia in 1770, he entered the service as a protocolist in the Senate and was transferred to the staff of Count Bruce in 1773. He retired in 1775, but reentered the service in 1777 as assessor in the College of Commerce, achieving eventually a post comparable to that of assistant collector of customs at St. Petersburg. Radishchev had written some minor works when in 1790 his *Puteshestvie iz Peterburga v Moskvu* appeared.[20] We are told that a copy of this work found its way into the hands of the Empress, and, after reading some thirty pages, she is said to have summoned an aide and directed that the author be immediately placed under arrest and brought to trial. On July

19 Skabichevskii, *Ocherki po istorii russkoi tsenzury*, 34.
20 In imitation of Laurence Sterne's *Sentimental Journey*, which had appeared in 1768.

15, Radishchev was brought before the high criminal court. His trial lasted ten days. The court found Radishchev guilty of publishing a book "full of the most harmful arguments, calculated to disturb the public peace, to destroy respect for authority, to raise among the people dissatisfaction with the officials and the government, and to lower the dignity and authority of the sovereign through ridiculous and intemperate outbursts."

Relevant passages in the *Ulozhenie* of 1649 were cited (straining their meaning), but the chief reliance appears to have been on what we would call the Articles of War, since Radishchev, as a member of the minor nobility, had taken to the sovereign a solemn oath which required the most unquestioning obedience and the utmost fidelity. On July 25, 1790—within ten days—the court found the author guilty in accordance with Article XXII of the Articles of War (Military Statute), and he was condemned to death by decapitation. The sentence was confirmed by the Senate the following day. On August 10 it was referred to the Empress' Privy Council. The latter body, again stressing the enormity of the crime of violation of the oath of service, confirmed the Senate's verdict. But the Empress commuted the death sentence to perpetual banishment to Siberia. Here Radishchev passed the next six years of his life, at the end of which time the death of the Empress and the accession of the Emperor Paul freed him from his sentence.[21]

The crime with which Radishchev was charged was not the one for which he was condemned. What he really did that alarmed the authorities was to raise questions that were extremely embarrassing to the government. Not the least of these questions concerned serfdom, which had been aired in the commission of 1767 and then forgotten until its ghost was again summoned up by the revolt of Pugachev in 1773. We must bear in mind that the government's harshness was largely dictated by fear, the Empress' own realization of the precarious nature of her tenure, and her fear of having imitators who, like herself, might vault into the saddle.

But the government's concern went far beyond Radishchev. In 1790 Aleksandr Aleksandrovich Prozorovskii was named commandant of Moscow with the avowed purpose of enforcing the

---

[21] A. N. Radishchev, *Sochineniya*, I, Intro.

press laws with greater severity.[22] The police, ably directed by Stepan Ivanovich Sheshkovskii, privy councillor and head of the secret police—whom Radishchev called the Grand Inquisitor—began to second the efforts of the government. Prozorovskii's zeal against Novikov was restrained by the Empress, who warned him that a favorable pretext must be found. A book, published apparently by Novikov, printed in Church script, plentifully sprinkled with quotations from the Bible and even speaking some good words for the *Raskol'niki*, gave the authorities their chance. Prozorovskii was directed personally by the Empress to send an employee to purchase the book in Novikov's bookstore. Curiously enough the police employee failed to carry out his commission exactly; but by a coincidence he bought another book, which, on examination, also seemed to have been illegally published. It appears that either from laxity or with a view to circumventing the laws, some copies of the books which had been seized at the bookshop in the university in 1781 had been in a warehouse and escaped detection. These copies not only were not declared by Novikov, but later were turned over to an agent, Kol'chugin, to be dispatched to fairs to be offered for sale. Thus Novikov's offense caught up with him. He was arrested on the morning of April 22, 1792 and subjected to examination, in the course of which he admitted having sold prohibited books. It does not appear that the offense was sufficient to justify prosecution. The matter was dealt with by the Empress herself in the most arbitrary manner. By a special *ukaz* she directed that Novikov be confined for a period of fifteen years in the Schlüsselburg prison. Here Novikov remained until the death of the Empress.[23]

We must not assume that this period was a time of blind reaction. Events in France had caught the popular imagination, and all well-informed persons were eager to know what was happening and catching something of the spirit of the times. New periodicals began to be issued to meet the popular demand. Professor Sokhotskii started a paper with the high-sounding title, *Zhurnal s poka-*

[22] Potemkin is said to have protested against the appointment, warning Catherine that "blood would stain Your Majesty's name for all posterity." Skabichevskii, *Ocherki po istorii russkoi tsenzury*, 51.

[23] Longinov, *Novikov*, 264; see also Skabichevskii, *Ocherki po istorii russkoi tsenzury*, 51.

zaniem uchenykh i drugikh veshchei (Magazine to instruct the reader in learning and other things), which followed events in France and sounded a daring note of protest against capricious absolutism.[24] Other publications took up the cry—*Rossiiskii Magazin (The Russian Magazine)* of the journalist Tumanskii; the *Zerkalo Svyeta (The Mirror of the World); Lekarstvo ot Skuki i Zabot (The Cure for Boredom and Cares)*, a short-lived publication; and the *Muse*, issued by I. I. Martinov, who was later a prominent historian and a controversialist under Alexander.[25] That the atmosphere continued to be tense and the Empress deeply concerned is well illustrated by an incident that occurred in 1793, when the Princess Dashkova in her capacity as president of the Russian Academy ordered the publication of Knyazhnin's tragedy, *Vadim*, for the benefit of the author's widow, who was in financial straits. The play that dealt with an imaginary hero in the early history of Russia seemed to the Empress' morbid views to contain some slighting references to monarchy and to speak some good words for revolt. The publication of this play brought strained relations between the Empress and her former confidante. The play was confiscated and burned.[26] These events show the drift of the times, but Catherine was too preoccupied with events in Poland to take drastic action, and she passed away before things could come to a head.

However, shortly before her death, an *immenoi ukaz* of the Empress had closed all private presses and had set up a strict censorship in both capitals and ports of entry to pass on books being imported. The Emperor Paul, who succeeded Catherine, redoubled the severity of the censorship and the restrictions on the importation of books from abroad to so great a degree that there was almost complete stagnation in the field of publication and in the intellectual life of Russia during his reign.

However, this situation, which was symptomatic of conditions in Russia under Paul, was too bad to last. Early in March, 1801, the Emperor Paul was assassinated and was succeeded by his eldest

[24] A. P. Pyatkovskii, *Iz istorii nashego literaturnago i obshchestvennago razvitiya*, 47.

[25] *Ibid.*

[26] Princess Daschkaw, *Memoirs of the Princess Daschkaw (Knyaginya Ekaterina Romanovna Vorontsova)*, I, 361 ff.

son, Alexander I, known even at this time for his liberal leanings. The new Emperor's sympathies for a free press were expressed in an *ukaz* issued on March 31, within a month of his accession. This *ukaz* abolished all the restrictions of the recent reign:

> To manifest our solicitude for the welfare of our subjects and our wish to furnish them with all means for the spread of the useful sciences and arts, we decree that the ban on the admission of books, of all kinds, and of music, imposed by the decree of April 18, 1800, be lifted, likewise that the private presses sealed in accordance with the instructions which followed on June 5, 1800, be unsealed, permitting not only the importation of foreign books, journals, and other publications, but also the printing of books within the empire in strict accordance with the *ukaz* of September 16, 1796.[27]

A further *ukaz* of July 14, 1801, however, warned authors that books must continue to b esubmitted to the censor and that if passed by him this fact should be indicated on the title page. On February 9, 1802, matters were restored to the condition that had existed under Catherine; books were to be imported in accordance with the tariff of 1782; and the printing of books by private presses was to be allowed as under the conditions of the *ukaz* of January 15, 1783.[28]

It is not our intention to trace in detail the various changes in censorship which accompanied the progress of the press in Russia, since these are reserved for a special chapter. Suffice it to say that the reign of Paul was quite unfavorable to the existence of a free press, and actually it was not until his death in 1801 and the accession of Alexander that things could be said to have taken a turn for the better. But while the new sovereign was lavish in his promises with the exception of the lifting of the ban on the importation of books, actual concessions were insignificant. Books and periodicals still had to be submitted to the censor before publication. But whatever Alexander may originally have contemplated in the way of reforms, the work was interrupted and largely paralyzed by the vicissitudes of war with Napoleon.

[27] Skabichevskii, *Ocherki po istorii russkoi tsenzury*, 88.
[28] *Ibid.*, 89.

By the time these wars had been brought to a conclusion in 1815, the press had become involved in various crosscurrents. Among them was the new evangelical mystical movement that began in 1812 and later became variously associated with the name of Madame de Krüdener and the Russian Bible Society.

This evangelical mysticism was part of the general movement of European thought that had developed in Europe as a reaction to the rationalism of the eighteenth century. The movement had many phases, but a strong religious tone ran through it. This tone was nothing more than a prolongation of the general impetus that had been given to religious life in the fifteenth and sixteenth centuries by the crises of that age. This urge had been overlaid by the growth of eighteenth-century rationalism and scepticism in religious matters, but had continued to grow. Russia had, of course, not experienced the Reformation and other movements that followed it; but she had not entirely escaped a stirring of religious life, as we know from the great schism of the seventeenth century. One obscure phase of this movement in western Europe was the tinge of mysticism—a term which is usually understood as the individual's direct knowledge of God through personal revelation and intuition. This trend tended to release its devotees from the restraints of the official church or even from the conventions of society. The individual was to be his own guide and imposed his own spiritual and moral standards. This mystical trend had persisted through the century and was perpetuated by a long line of mystics in the spirit of Jakob Böhme, such as Madame Guyon, Emmanuel Swedenborg, Ekkarthausen, Jung-Stilling, and others. As we have seen, this mysticism had penetrated the Masonic movement in the latter part of the reign of Catherine, largely through the Rosicrucian Order, and had become tainted with medieval pseudo sciences, such as alchemy, astrology, and the search for the philosopher's stone. Eventually the excesses that had perhaps been countenanced by Novikov, Schwartz, and others had brought the Masonic Order into disrepute; and the humbug practiced by Cagliostro and Casanova completed its downfall. Eventually the persecutions to which the Masons were subjected and the reaction brought on by the French Revolution temporarily at least brought this movement to a halt.

But the universal tolerance promised by Alexander allowed the mystical movement to come back into the picture, and the troubled times of the campaign of Austerlitz and the East Prussian campaign that followed were not unfavorable to it. Aleksandr Fedorovich Labsin was perhaps the most famous exponent of this revival. In 1806 he began the publication of the *Sionskii Vyestnik (The Messenger of Zion)* to expound these mystical Masonic views. The *Glavnoe Pravlenie Uchilishch* (the Chief Administration of Schools) took the question of permitting this publication under advisement. A certificate was required from Labsin that Masonic lodges were permitted in the empire. In view of the unsatisfactory reply received, permission to continue publication was refused after nine issues had been published.

In general, however, the government pursued a vacillating and uncertain policy. During the campaign against Napoleon there came into existence the Russian Bible Society, an offshoot of the British and Foreign Bible Society. It owed the tolerance granted to it by the government to the personal intervention of Alexander, on whom the events of 1811 and 1812 had made a profound impression, turning his mind into a religious and mystical channel. In consequence, the Bible Society flourished, and to it flocked not only those of an evangelical turn of mind, but dissatisfied and disillusioned souls in search of some form of personal religion in the troubled times. These diverse influences were combined in the person of Aleksandr Nikolayevich Golitsyn, who in 1817 was named to the combined ministries of Ecclesiastical Affairs and Public Instruction. Golitsyn was also serving as president of the Bible Society. Gradually there gathered around Golitsyn and the Bible Society the mystics and many of the Masons who had profited from the era of tolerance to revive the Masonic movement. Enjoying official protection, they revived the *Messenger of Zion* in 1817.

These moves were a serious affront to the Orthodox church and to the Holy Synod, which had been given the right to censor all books of a religious nature. Eventually pressure was brought to bear on Golitsyn to bring Labsin's journal under the ecclesiastical censorship, with the result that it shortly went out of publication. But Golitsyn continued to lend official sanction to the mystical movement and its publications. The Orthodox church, at least the white or secular clergy, was in no position to protest since the Synod, which had formerly enjoyed direct access to the monarch, was now under the new ministry. But opposition grew. Despite the favor which mystics and evangelists enjoyed from Alexander, eventually the church in the person of Archimandrite Photius, as the representative of the monastic orders, secured the assistance of Arakcheyev, then high in the counsels of Alexander. The publication of the Russian translation of a book by Gossner, a German mystic, brought the matter to a head. The book had been authorized by Golitsyn, without referring it to the ecclesiastical censorship. This pretext was used by the enemies of Golitsyn to undermine his influence with the Emperor and bring about his fall. Golitsyn was removed and the double ministry dissolved, the Holy Synod once more becoming an independent part of the administration, enjoying the right of direct access to the sovereign. It was ruled that henceforth all books touching on questions of faith and morals had to be referred to the ecclesiastical censorship.

In general, however, secular journalism continued to enjoy considerable latitude in the articles that it published; and throughout the reign of Alexander there was intense activity in the publishing business. The granting of a free press in 1801 had immediately called into life a flood of new publications and encouraged the younger generation to enter journalism. Some of the first publications took their cue from the official pronouncements on freedom of the press and began the discussion of political questions. Such was the *Vestnik Evropy*, a bimonthly publication founded by Karamzin in 1802. The tone of this periodical was set by the editor in one of the early issues:

Those blessed and ever-memorable times have passed when the reading of books was the exclusive right of a few persons; already reason is active in all stations of life, in all lands, feels the need for knowledge, and demands new and better ideas; all the monarchs in Europe consider it their duty and pride to be patrons of learning. Ministers endeavor in their diction to please the taste of enlightened people. The courtier wishes to have a reputation as a lover of literature; the judge reads and is ashamed of the old unintelligible language of Themis; the young man of the world wants to have knowledge so that his conversation may be agreeable and so that, on occasion, he may philosophize.[29]

Those journals which were frankly political were strongly influenced by the turn of events of this momentous reign. Publications started during the honeymoon of liberalism, 1801–1805, such as the one discussed above, reflect the ardent hopes and the confidence in the light of reason of the period. One journal founded during the East Prussian campaign in 1807—the *Genii Vremen (The Genius of the Times)*—deals largely with the great military campaigns and the sensational diplomatic *volte-face* made at Tilsit. The ordeal through which Russia passed in 1812 called into existence a number of patriotic journals and gave an ultrapatriotic tone to some already in existence. *Syn Otechestva (Son of the Fatherland)*, founded by Grech in 1812; *The Patriot* of V. Izmailov; *Russkii Vyestnik (The Russian Messenger)*, edited by S. N. Glinka from the beginning of 1808; and *Moskovskii Zritel' (The Moscow Observer)*, founded in 1806, are examples of the publications which became intensely patriotic in tone. The great military triumph gave rise to another spate of patriotic journals, this time strongly tinged with conservatism; such was Admiral Shishkov's paper, *Democritus*, founded in 1815. One publication, the *Drug Rossiyan i ikh edinoplemennikov oboego pola (Friends of the Russians and their fellow Slavs of both Sexes)*, was founded in 1816 to work for a rapprochement between Russians and Poles.

One of the outstanding periodicals was the *Dukh Zhurnalov (The Spirit of the Press)*, which began coming out in 1815, edited by Grigorii Maksimovich Yatsenkov. Yatsenkov had had an academic career as an instructor at the University of Moscow and was for many years censor for the St. Petersburg censorship committee. He left this post in 1815 to assume publication of his periodical, in which he openly advocated freedom of the press and a constitution for Russia. Alexander's famous speech at the opening of the Polish *Syem* in 1817 gave Yatsenkov an opportunity to raise the constitutional question. He also broached economic issues, denouncing the middlemen who cornered the market in the necessi-

---

[29] Pyatkovskii, *Iz istorii nashego literaturnago i obshchestvennago razvitiya*, 83.

ties of life and so exploited the misery of their fellow countrymen. Although the examples he cited were from Catherine's reign and he actually quoted the Empress, who had called such manipulators "the worst rascals in the world," he became involved with the censors. When Yatsenkov turned to the peasant question and attacked the greed of the landlords, he became even more suspect.[30] And when in 1819, in a discussion of savings banks, he appealed to class animus, he brought down on himself the wrath of the government, which, after all but reducing him to silence, finally suppressed his magazine in 1820.

One or two periodicals were of an official or semiofficial character. Such was the *Periodicheskoe izdanie ob uspyekhakh narodnago Prosvyeshcheniya (Periodical Publication on the success of Public Instruction)* that was issued by the Head Administration of Schools from 1803 to 1818. A project of Bakharevich to start an official gazette in order to bring to the attention of the public governmental pronouncements was the subject of considerable controversy in official circles and was eventually dropped. Instead, the practice was adopted of subsidizing the *Syevernyi Vyestnik (The Northern Messenger)*, founded in 1809.

But a significant number—perhaps the majority—of Russian journals took advantage of the release of the press from official tutelage and were launched to exploit the newly kindled interest in education, in learning, or in the public taste for *belles-lettres*. Thus they could avoid becoming entangled with the censors on political issues. Some journals, like *Vyestnik Evropy* and *Russkii Vyestnik*, had long and distinguished careers and survived early vicissitudes to continue until the end of the nineteenth century.

One of the most brilliant journalists of the period was Ivan Petrovich Pnin. Educated during the latter part of the eighteenth century, he entered the chancery of the State Council in 1801 and, after the formation of the ministries, took a post in the Ministry of Public Instruction. Pnin was strongly interested in current problems and drew up in 1804 a plan of popular education. On the peasant question, he took advantage of the progressive spirit of the early part of Alexander's reign and wrote a criticism of the peasants' lot in a book which was moderate enough and passed

[30] *Ibid.*, 195.

the censor the first time; but permission for a second edition was refused. Perhaps Pnin is best known for an article called "Author and Censor," a translation allegedly from the Manchurian, a satire on the follies of the famous "preliminary censorship," which was published in *Zhurnal Rossiiskoi Slovesnosti (Journal of Russian Letters)*. This article gives a clearer idea than anything else of the trials of the author (and of the censor) in trying to make an unworkable system work. A selection from this piece of journalism follows:[31]

Author—I have here, my dear sir, a book which I wish to print.

Censor—It must be scrutinized before it can be printed. And what is the title, may I ask?

Author—It is called *Truth*, my good sir.

Censor—*Truth!* Oh! We shall have to scrutinize it pretty thoroughly.

Author—It seems to me you are taking an unnecessary task on yourself. Scrutinize truth! What does that mean? I assure you, my dear sir, that truth is not my creation, but it has been in existence thousands of years. The divine Kun [Confucius] traced its outlines in his sapient laws. This is what he says: "Mortals, love one another, take nothing from one another, instruct one another, and observe justice toward one another, for this is the foundation of social life, the soul of order, and, hence, necessary for your welfare." That is the gist of this book.

Censor—Take nothing from one another, instruct one another, observe justice toward one another! My good man, your book must by all means be scrutinized. [*with abruptness*] Show it to me at once.

Author—Here it is.

Censor—[*turning over the pages of the manuscript, and running his eyes over the pages*] Yes, mmm, that's all right . . . and we can allow this . . . but it will be quite impossible to let this go through [*pointing to one passage in the book*].

Author—Why not, may I make so bold as to ask?

[31] *Ibid.*, 111 ff.

Tsar Alexander I

A. N. Radishchev

N. I. Novikov

M. M. Speranskii

Censor—Because I shall not allow it—and consequently it is inadmissible.

Author—Do you have, Mr. Censor, any more right to forbid the printing of my book, *Truth*, than I have to offer it?

Censor—Of course I have, since I must answer for it.

Author—How is that? You have to answer for my book? My dear sir, you assume a right that is not yours. You cannot be responsible for the form of my thought, nor for the content. I am not a child and do not need a nurse.

Censor—Yes, but you may go wrong.

Author—And do you mean to say that you cannot, Mr. Censor?

Censor—No, because I know what can and what cannot be allowed.

Author—Can that mean we are forbidden to know that? Can that be some secret? I know full well what I am doing.

Censor—If you agree [*pointing to the book*] to cut out those passages, you will be able to give your book to the world.

Author—You want to take the heart out of my book, to rob it of all its beauty, and want me to agree to humor you in mutilating it and making it absurd. No, Mr. Censor, your request is inhuman; am I to blame, if my truth does not please you, and that you do not understand it?

Censor—Not every truth should be published.

Author—Why not? A knowledge of truth leads to happiness. To deprive man of this knowledge is to keep him from attaining his own happiness, means to rob him of the chance to be contented. If we may not allow one truth, we can't allow any, because truth forms one unbroken chain. To take out one of these is like taking a link out of the chain and ruining it. In truth, a great man does not fear to hear the truth, nor demand that he should be believed blindly, but wants people to understand him.

Censor—I tell you, my good man, that your book without my attestation is and will be nothing, because without it, it cannot be printed.

Author—Mr. Censor, allow me to tell you that my truth has cost me untold labor; I have not spared my health in writing it; I have stuck to it day and night. But to oppress property, as the wise Kun says, ought not to be allowed, for that is the way to violate justice and good order. Indeed, more truly, one might call your attestation meaningless, for experience shows that it guarantees book or author nothing. So, Mr. Censor, your explanation is quite inadmissible.

Censor—[*drawing himself up haughtily*] I am talking to you as a censor to an author.

Author—[*with noble feeling*] But I am talking to you as one citizen to another.

Censor—What impudence!

Author—O Kun, beneficent Kun, if you had overheard this conversation, if you had seen how your laws are carried out; if you had seen how justice is maintained, if you had seen how they contribute to your divine purposes, then, indeed, your indignation would have been understandable. But farewell, Mr. Censor, I have so conspired together with you that I have lost all desire to print the book. You may as well know, however, that my *Truth* will abide unchanging in my heart, full of love for humanity, and needing no attestation but my own conscience.

The aversion which the Emperor Alexander began to show after 1820 to the disturbances which broke out in Europe at this time led him to become conservative, if not reactionary, in his internal policies. This induced a mood of bewilderment and disappointment among his contemporaries and has puzzled later generations. What induced this change? The most charitable view seems to be that he had never really assimilated the ideals of constitutional liberty which his tutor Laharpe had endeavored to instill in him. He never really lost his fanatical devotion to autocracy, in which he had been cradled. Moreover, his early friends and associates, whom he had gathered together in his unofficial committee to draw up a blueprint for the new heavenly city, showed themselves quite incapable of translating their ideals into reality. Disillusioned and disheartened by futile or divided counsels and harassed as he was by pressing foreign and domestic problems, he turned to those among his entourage who could take some of the awful burden off his shoulders. That those he turned to in most cases were ruthless timeserving bureaucrats quite out of sympathy with his ecstatic visions escaped him, since he had little discrimination in selecting his tools. Only at the end of his life did he realize that he had been victimized by those who should have served him.

But the nineteenth century was now faced with a problem which had only recently emerged. The press had been seized on eagerly by Peter as a means of spreading that Enlightenment which Russia desperately needed. The press was largely to supplement the regular educational institutions in their task of spreading useful and practical knowledge. But with the emancipation of the gentry and the consequent growth of an enlightened upper class, to whom education was not a training for service but a door to new delights and to dangerous speculation on political and economic problems, immediately a problem arose. How in an autocratic state is enlightenment to be kept within bonds? This was a problem which the French Revolution had pointed up. It involves censorship—an issue with which more enlightened countries had long wrestled. The first halting steps had been taken by Catherine without really facing up to the problem. But the revolution, the vast network of secret societies with which Europe was overrun, the smoldering unrest and violent outbreaks of the opening quarter of the century confronted the government with unprecedented difficulties. To put the press in a proper setting, it is necessary to review the whole question of its censorship by the organs of government—a task to be undertaken in the following chapter.

VII

Censorship

THE control of thought has at all times been assumed to be a necessary function of government in Russia. This function, until the eighteenth century, had been exercised by the church, since religion was the sole intellectual interest of the population. When the government embarked on a program of education in which secular interests predominated, it was only to be expected that such control would be exercised by the state.

Peter's reforms roused opposition among almost all classes of Russian society. Yet it was not on political issues that vigilance was required but in the field of religion. The printing presses already in existence in Kiev and Chernigov had lent themselves somewhat too freely to publishing books suspected of heresy. A warning was issued in 1721 that henceforth their publications must be passed by the Synod.[1]

The question of literary censorship in Russia could hardly arise until presses became numerous, and under Peter they were few in number. The one press not actually under official control was that of the Academy of Sciences, which was declared free from the Synod's control in 1727. But for the next thirty-five years there were signs of the government's nervousness at the increasing circu-

---

[1] Kiev was the battleground for numerous creeds and, having been Russian only for two generations, it was natural that heresies should creep in here. Heretical books named in the *ukaz* of 1720 as having been printed were the Lutheran or those of the *raskol'niki* (or old believers). It must also be borne in mind that Kiev had once been under the Patriarch of Constantinople, deviations in whose favor were as unacceptable as falling into any other religious heresy. See Skabichevskii, *Ocherki po istorii russkoi tsenzury*, 4; also *Istoricheskie Svyedeniya o tsenzurye v Rossii* (published anonymously; ascribed to P. K. Shchebal'skii), 4.

lation of books (many in manuscript) and pamphlets and the evil
consequences that this presaged for the relations between state and
people. A decree of the Empress Elizabeth in 1742 required that
the permission to publish granted by her predecessors be reviewed
once more. A second decree in 1748 provided for censorship by
the Academy of Sciences wherever mention was made in a book
of prominent persons of the last two reigns. A further decree in
1750 forbade the importation of such books from abroad. The
powers of censorship exercised by the Academy were enlarged to
include maps and other publications (presumably of a scientific
nature) which were not suitable for publication.[2]

Under Catherine II there was at first a general relaxation of
restrictions on printing and an increase in the number of presses
engaged in work for the government. During the early part of
Catherine's reign the only unofficial press was one established in
1771 for the printing of foreign books. But even this press had to
secure the permission of the Academy of Sciences and of the police
for its publications.

In 1783 when the desperate exertions of the Turkish War and
the Pugachev Revolt were over and Russia seemed to have entered
on a period of tranquility, Catherine saw fit to gratify her people
by issuing an edict which permitted the establishment of private
printing presses on the same basis as other commercial enterprises.
The sole safeguard retained was that all publications were subject
to review by the *Uprava Blagochiniya* (Office of Police).[3] But

[2] The extravagant lengths to which the government carried its precautions against the indiscriminate dissemination of knowledge of even a quasi
scientific character is illustrated by the Bering expedition of 1733-41. The
participants were forbidden to publish in Russia or abroad any details of the
expedition or to communicate them to persons living abroad. The records
might still be collecting dust in the archives had not Joseph de l'Isle, the
geographer, smuggled some of them abroad and published his map and
comments in defiance of the Russian government. This move, in turn, forced
the Russian government to release their material; see S. R. Tompkins and
Max Moorhead, "Russia's Approach to America," *British Columbia Historical
Quarterly*, April–June–October, 1949. Yet the demand for books was so
slight in the eighteenth century that it does not appear that there was any
immediate danger of such information becoming common property. One
writer records that in 1752 the Synodal press had such a great accumulation
of books remaining unsold that orders were issued to burn them. See P. P.
Pekarskii, *Nauka i literatura Rossii pri Petre Velikom.*

[3] Skabichevskii, *Ocherki po istorii russkoi tsenzury*, 37.

since there were no regulations for guidance, this informal censorship remained for the most part a dead letter.

The government seems shortly to have repented its decision. Various administrative measures that followed forecast a return to the traditional Russian attitude of hostility toward the free expression of opinion. The publication of Radishchev's *Puteshestvie iz Petersburga v Moskvu (Journey from St. Petersburg to Moscow)* and the punishment meted out to the author did not augur well for freedom of the press. In addition, the harsh and arbitrary administrative sentence received by Novikov and his group for their publishing activity at the University of Moscow served notice that freedom of the press was definitely at an end.[4]

In 1796, some weeks before her death, an *imennoi ukaz* of the old Empress had closed down all the printing presses. Alarmed by the excesses of the French Revolution, Catherine had soon lost her early enthusiasm for freedom and was stampeded into undoing much of what she had already done.

Her son and successor, Paul, continued her policy by requiring censors in both capitals and in ports of entry to scrutinize books imported into Russia. This rule must have proved difficult to enforce, for on July 4, 1797, a second decree appeared by which all censorship was brought under the control of the state council. On May 7, 1798, boards of censorship were established at all ports of entry; all cargoes before being discharged had to be searched for printed literature; even passengers had to have their baggage examined for hidden publications.[5] Doubtful cases had to be referred to the state council. Finally in 1798 the importation of all foreign books was forbidden; the port censors were done away with; and a book could not be published in Russia without the permission of the censors in the capital. Thus, for the present, the country was closed to all influences from abroad. Everything that could remind Russians of more fortunate times in which freedom had flourished or more fortunate lands in which freedom was still to be found was now denied entry.

[4] For a fuller account of these events, see Chap. VI above.

[5] These incidents are not so remote from the experiences of persons traveling to the Soviet Union within the past generation. Any person seeking entrance to the Soviet Union in the years prior to World War II if his baggage contained printed literature was exposed to grave consequences.

Censorship

The *ukaz* of March 31, 1801,[6] held out to writers and publishers a promise of complete relaxation of the censorship to allow full discussion of public questions. This *ukaz* was intended only as a provisional measure. For two years hints of further legislation continued to be heard. Yet in spite of the freedom of thought of which the new regime boasted, censorship was not to be abandoned, for in 1804 a new law was issued, providing for censorship in advance of all material proposed for publication:

The censorship is to take a relative view of all matters submitted to it for publication to see that they contain nothing contrary to Divine Law, the state, morality, and the personal honor of any citizen. The censor who approves a book or a publication that violates this injunction, like any transgressor of the law, is accountable to the law in proportion to the seriousness of his offense.

If the censor finds in the manuscript submitted to him any passages which violate the injunction in the above-mentioned fifteenth section, he is not to make any corrections himself in them; but he is to send the manuscript back to the publisher, marking such passages so that they may be changed or omitted altogether. On the return of the manuscript thus corrected, the censor will approve it for publication.

Of course, the censorship, in banning the printing of books and various publications or their issue, is to be guided by reasonable prejudice in the author's favor, avoiding every arbitrary interpretation of works or of passages in them which for any alleged reason might be subject to being banned. When a passage is open to doubt, is capable of two interpretations, in this case it is to be taken in a sense most favorable to the author rather than the opposite.

A modest and reasonable search for every kind of truth that has to do with faith, humanity, civil condition, legislation, administration, or any other branch of the government not only is not to be subject to even the most moderate severity of the censorship but is to enjoy that complete freedom of printing which raises the level of enlightenment.[7]

[6] See Chap. VI above for the wording of this decree.
[7] *Istoricheskie Svyedeniya o tsenzurye v Rossii*, 15. See also Sukhomlinov,

These regulations, prescribing censorship in advance within somewhat modest limits, governed censorship for the first ten years of Alexander's reign. After 1805, Russia was almost continually at war, and legislative changes were halted. But after the conclusion of the war with Sweden in 1809, Alexander resumed his program of reform. The first fruit of this program was Speranskii's thoroughgoing plan of reorganization of the administration. Censorship was, however, dealt with in a haphazard manner and without a clear-cut policy. In 1811, for example, a ministry of police was established, and the new minister was instructed to see that books considered prejudicial to public order and tranquility should not circulate in the capital, even though permission had been issued by the minister of public instruction to print them. Thus, over the protest of Minister of Public Instruction Count Razumovskii, the committees of censorship were now subject to two branches of the administration, resulting in friction and misunderstandings.[8]

After the defeat of Napoleon the reign of Alexander was somewhat darkened by the shadow of reaction that fell over the country. This reactionary trend brought in its train, especially after 1820, cases of suppression of various books and periodicals.[9] But it was not until the fall in 1824 of Golitsyn, minister of public instruction and ecclesiastical affairs, that conditions really became oppressive. To the new minister, Admiral Shishkov, all that was Western was suspect; and his ardor for all that was native Russian led him to labor unceasingly for the suppression of the Bible Society, which was finally closed down by Nicholas in 1826. The new monarch signalized the return to a stricter regime by instructing Shishkov to draw up in the summer of 1826 the most exact and complete regulations for the guidance of censors. This new code laid down the principle that it was the business of the government to direct public opinion along lines suited to the needs of the moment. It

"Materialy dlya istorii obrazovaniya v Rossii v tsarstvovanie Imperatora Aleksandra I-go," in *Izslyedovaniya i Stat'i*, II, 414. The author claims (II, 404) that the precedent set by Denmark in the restoration of censorship in 1803, after experimenting with a press free of all restraints, strongly influenced Russian policy.

[8] *Istoricheskii Svyedeniya o tsenzurye v Rossii*, 20–21; Skabichevskii, *Ocherki po istorii russkoi tsenzury*, 116–17.

[9] See Chap. VI above.

established a further significant principle—that, in contrast to the code of 1804, doubtful passages were to be taken in a sense unfavorable to the author. Henceforth, equivocal language was to expose the author to serious penalties. But Shishkov undertook to go further; he decreed that critics must observe appropriate objectivity in passing judgment on any piece of literature. Moreover, in accordance with Shishkov's well-known conservative taste for pure Slavicism, writers were warned not to sin against the rules of grammar or against the purity of the Russian language. But this attempt to prescribe the whole literature of a people required the services of innumerable censoring authorities—such as the Synod for religious books, special censors for foreign books, censors for theatrical plays, censors for affairs of the Roman Catholic church, for the Protestant churches, for medical books, for textbooks, for the kingdom of Poland, and for the Grand Duchy of Finland. Finally, nothing could be printed about any branch of the government unless it had first received the approval of that ministry or department.

This censorship program was the "Iron Code" of Admiral Shishkov, designed to reduce the press to an instrument of state policy. The supreme authority in the field of censorship was to be a board consisting of the minister of public instruction, the minister of the interior, and the minister of foreign affairs. Local committees of censors were to be established in St. Petersburg, Moscow, Dorpat, and Vilna who would subject all censorable material to scrutiny before publication. Censors at St. Petersburg were to be responsible for the censoring of foreign books, and the committee of censorship was to be staffed with the necessary linguists. The other committees (much smaller in personnel) were to examine books printed in their locality and were to function under the curator of the educational district. All censors were to be guided by instructions emanating from St. Petersburg and approved by the monarch.[10]

The basic principle on which this code was founded—that people were to think what the government wished them to think—was an outright challenge to the whole scheme of modern civilization. It was a bold experiment with official control of public opinion,

[10] Skabichevskii, *Ocherki po istorii russkoi tsenzury*, 214–16.

destined shortly to be abandoned. Still it is perhaps questionable whether the unsoundness of Admiral Shishkov's code was the reason for replacing it with a milder one. It is more likely that the code proved unworkable. Official Russia in the early nineteenth century had not yet attained that degree of omniscience possessed by the Communist party today. Perhaps modesty made the bureaucrats hesitate to prescribe for the public what constituted truth and what was in conformity with the dogmas of their own faith.[11]

In 1827 the method prescribed for the censoring of foreign books was found unsuitable, and the Minister of the Interior was instructed to review these arrangements. When he asked whether he should regard the general code of Shishkov as outside his competence, he was told that the "Iron Code" was to be embraced also within the scope of his investigations and recommendations. The result of his probe, therefore, was a drastic revision of Shishkov's code. A special commission was set up and, following deliberations that went on all through 1827, the draft was ready for submission to the Emperor. On April 22, 1828, the document received Nicholas' final approval and became law.[12]

In general the new law was liberal. It gave up the task of prescribing what the public should believe and confined itself to more practical aims. As one writer says: "In the draft of the new code, they [the censors] are not set up as the judges of the merits or usefulness of a book. They merely answer the question: Is the book under review harmful?"[13]

The final authority in censorship was to be the Chief Administration of Censorship, which was to be set up as a branch of the Ministry of Public Instruction. In addition to representatives of that ministry, the Administration was to include the presidents of various learned societies and lay members of the Holy Synod, as well as the director of the Third Section of the Imperial Chancery. Under this body were to be established local committees in St.

---

[11] Of course the modern state exercises a degree of monopoly in the field of publicity undreamed of in earlier ages—that it is possible for a modern state to reach down into the secret recesses of the soul and induce unquestioning faith not only in its doctrines but in the most fantastic distortions of fact with which states seek to buttress this belief.

[12] Skabichevskii, *Ocherki po istorii russkoi tsenzury*, 220–21.

[13] *Istoricheskie Svyedeniya o tsenzurye v Rossii*, 44–45.

Petersburg, Moscow, Riga, Vilna, Kiev, Odessa, and Tiflis. The censoring of foreign books, hitherto under the Ministry of the Interior, was now transferred to the Ministry of Public Instruction. In addition to abandoning the aim to instruct public opinion along lines in conformity with the government's wishes, the new law returned to the older views of the law of 1804, particularly to that part of the old law which declared that in case of doubt in regard to the author's meaning the author was to receive the benefit of the doubt. The censor was instructed to refrain from expressing any personal views regarding the correctness of the author's opinions or judgments and from questioning the correctness of the author's diction. The sole criterion was to be, "Is the book harmful?" Within reasonable limits all sorts of questions of public interest were open to discussion in the press. No publication could be absolutely banned except with the Emperor's approval.

Yet despite this generally enlightened legislation, censorship began almost immediately to encroach on liberty of expression. There had been a slight limitation on complete liberty of the press in that news of court functions and the movements of the Imperial family could be printed only with the Emperor's approval. But within a matter of weeks a process of further whittling down began. Edicts were issued that ecclesiastical books had to go before the clerical censors. Then special arrangements were made in the Department of Posts for censoring books coming from abroad. Textbooks were the next exception; they were withdrawn from the competence of the board and put under the authority of the Chief Administration of Schools. Medical works were to be censored by the Medical-Surgical Academy or by the medical faculties of the universities. In the frontier provinces of the West the provincial authorities were made judges of periodicals published within their province. Military books became subject to the General Staff; the Administrative Senate was made responsible for the Senate's official gazette. In the same way, the Ministry of Foreign Affairs was to be its own censor of the political portions of the St. Petersburg *Vyedomosti*, published in French and German. It was decided that posters should come under the scrutiny of the minister of the interior. All kinds of dramatic presentations were to be reviewed by the Third Section of the Imperial Chancery. Exceptions to the law continued to multiply; ministry after ministry clamored for the right to censor all publications that mentioned or discussed the work of these ministries.

Not long after the creation (in 1826) of the Third Section of the Imperial Chancery, its first director, Count Benckendorf, demanded in 1830 that he receive from publishers copies of all journals and almanacs. On his insistence he himself in 1832 was named a member of the Chief Administration of Censorship. Benckendorf thereupon advised Uvarov, the new minister of public instruction, that he must have submitted to him a list of all books or artistic productions showing any trend toward atheism or any tendency toward undermining faith. He insisted that articles henceforth must be signed. Benckendorf was also responsible for the ruling that the Imperial theaters could not be discussed by the press without the approval of the court.

Successive changes in the incumbents of the post of Minister of Public Instruction further complicated government policy in the matter of censorship. In 1828, indignant at the repeal of his censorship law, Shishkov had resigned, and Prince Lieven had been named to replace him. Lieven held the post until 1833, when he in turn was succeeded by Sergei Semenovich Uvarov, who remained in office until 1848. Uvarov had shown under Shishkov some signs of independence and moderation in the case of the four professors in 1824; but his regime is frequently identified with the worst period of Russian reaction.[14] An example of Uvarov's narrow point of view is seen in his proposal to the Board of Censors that they take under their consideration the question of cheap books and periodicals for the people. The Board, after taking the matter under advisement, came to the conclusion that "to rouse discontent among the lower classes by any means and to keep them, as it were, in a state of excitement is not only unwise but harmful."[15]

Despite Uvarov's keen interest in literature, he was forced continually to yield ground to trespassers on his special domain—the censorship. The strong-minded and aggressive Benckendorf, di-

[14] "The regime of Privy Councillor Uvarov was one of the most trying for himself and most distressing for both censors and writers." This is the opinion of the anonymous author of *Istoricheskie Svyedeniya o tsenzurye v Rossii*, 54. For the case of the "four professors," see Chap. V above.

[15] Skabichevskii, *Ocherki po istorii russkoi tsenzury*, 311.

rector of the Third Section of the Imperial Chancery, again interfered in matters of censorship which he thought touched upon his own sphere of activity, and in case he received an unfavorable or evasive answer he did not hesitate to take the matter directly to the Tsar. But other ministers, Kankrin, the minister of finance, and Nesselrode, the minister of foreign affairs, were not far behind; and their example was taken by lesser lights in the government. In 1845 Count Stroganov drew attention to the fact that "In recent times, there have also been issued instructions of His Majesty forbidding the publication of information concerning other branches of the government without obtaining previously the concurrence of their responsible heads; in the matter of the theaters, the Caucasus, the peasants, and various government measures of the time."[16]

Two significant incidents in the history of the censorship were the suspension in 1834 of Polevoi's *Moskovskii Telegraf* and two years later the suspension of Nadezhdin's *Teleskop*.[17] There had long been a feud between Uvarov, the minister of public instruction, and Polevoi. Perhaps Polevoi's bourgeois origin may have been responsible for some of the acrimony, with the studied tone of independence of the Moscow press as a whole adding its bitterness. Accounts differ concerning the exact occasion of the ban, for Polevoi was not without friends; but in 1834 the periodical passed off the stage forever.

The case of the *Teleskop* was more clear cut. Nadezhdin had secured the manuscript of the *Philosophical Letters* of Chaadayev, a series of private missives which the author had penned for the sole edification of his correspondent, a young woman of his acquaintance. These letters were translated from French into Russian and appeared in Nadezhdin's periodical in the autumn of 1836. The features of Chaadayev's letters that gave most offense were perhaps his slighting remarks about the Orthodox church and his extolling of its Catholic rival. Adherents of the official church were not

[16] *Istoricheskie Svyedeniya o tsenzurye v Rossii*, 59.

[17] Explanations of the reasons for this official ban differ, but frequent clashes of the editors with the censors certainly foreboded them no good. At the last Benckendorf seems to have defended Polevoi. Skabichevskii, *Ocherki po istorii russkoi tsenzury*, 240–44; see also *Istoricheskoe svyedenie o Tsenzurye*, 54–55.

lacking to draw the attention of the hierarchy to this bold assault on the sacred institution. The inevitable result was that the magazine was suspended.[18]

The sensational developments of the early years of Nicholas' reign—the Decembrist rising, the wars with Persia and Turkey, the July, 1830, revolution in Paris, the Polish rising of 1830–31— hardened the mind of the Emperor against new progressive movements everywhere and set the tone for the censorship. In 1833 the comparatively mild regime of Prince Lieven as minister of public instruction was succeeded by that of Uvarov with whose name was long associated the characteristic abuses of the censorship of Nicholas—arbitrariness and capriciousness. It was not so much, however, the harshness of the regime as the want of a clear objective and the conflicts within the censorship itself, conflicts which bred intrigue and the worst feature of the Russian police system, the *donos* or secret denunciation—the readiest weapon for the journalist or even the public servant to undermine his rival.[19] It was a time of increasing intellectual ferment, centering to some extent in the universities, despite the handicaps under which they worked, and growing interest in German philosophy—especially that of Hegel and Schelling—and the increasing appeal of the new French socialist writers—Prudhon, Saint Simon, Fourrier—not to speak of the political unrest abroad. Added to these influences was the degree to which the mind of the public was becoming absorbed in the evils of serfdom and in the various projects of reform. The brilliant writers who, however imperfectly, reflected the diverse currents of Russian thought and whose names were to become illustrious later—Pushkin, Griboyedov, and Lermontov—could scarcely avoid the many pitfalls in their path. One after another they became involved in this intricate game of denunciation, suspicion, and intrigue, from which there was no escape if they were to continue

18 Skabichevskii, *Ocherki po istorii russkoi tsenzury*, 244–49. Byelinskii was acting as editor at the time of the periodical's suspension.

19 As mentioned above, the duties of censorship were distributed among the Minister of Public Instruction, the boards of censors that were responsible to him, the Third Section of the Imperial Chancellery, and the ecclesiastical censorship which passed on all books that dealt, however slightly, with faith, morals and religion. In addition each branch of the government claimed the right to pass on anything that appeared in print that touched on matters of that department.

writing. It is understandable that Pushkin, who had been intimate-
ly connected with the revolutionists of December 14, 1825, could
not shake off the odium of this association. But in his case, to the
evils of ordinary censorship were added the personal censorship of
Nicholas and the strict accountability to the Emperor to which,
after 1826, he was held in all his movements and his creative work.
The poet's escapades, his eccentricities, and his indiscretions exposed him to humiliation and exasperation; but when to these an-
noyances were added the role of mentor, which Uvarov assumed
toward his poetry and his very diction, and the petty persecution
at the hands of Benckendorf, it is little short of a miracle that Pushkin was not driven to the extreme limits of endurance.[20]

The experience of Gogol in submitting his *Dead Souls* in 1841
to the censors for their approval deserves more than passing comment. In a letter of January 7, 1842, Gogol gives this account of
the banning of his book:

> The blow was not an unexpected one for me: they are for-
> bidding the whole manuscript. I submitted it first to the censor,
> S., who is somewhat more reasonable than the others, on the
> condition that if he found in it any passage that raised any
> doubt in his mind, he would let me know directly that I might
> send it on to St. Petersburg. Within a couple of days, S. an-
> nounced triumphantly that he found my manuscript quite ir-
> reproachable both in its purpose and in the impression made
> on the reader and that with the exception of one unimportant
> page—the alteration of two or three names (to which I at once
> agreed and made the necessary changes)—there was nothing
> that might call for a single censor's mark. He made the same
> statement to others. Suddenly something disconcerted S., and
> I realized that he was submitting my manuscript to the com-
> mittee. The committee received it just as if preparations had
> long since been made and the stage set for a comedy; for the
> criticisms were all, without exception, comedy of the highest

[20] For an account in English of Pushkin's relations with Nicholas, see
Henri Troyat, *Pushkin* (New York, 1950), an abridged edition of the author's two volume work in French, *Poushkine* (Paris, n.d.). More detailed
accounts are given in Skabichevskii, *Ocherki po istorii Russkoi tsenzury*,
260–68.

order. As soon as G. (who was acting as chairman) heard the name, *Dead Souls*, he cried in the voice of an ancient Roman: "No, I shall never allow it; the soul is immortal, there cannot be a dead soul, the author is attacking immortality." Finally with great difficulty the wise president got a word in, saying that the author was talking about "revision souls." As soon as he had intervened in the discussion and other censors had supported his claim that "dead souls" meant "revision souls," a still greater commotion arose. "No," exclaimed the president, and he was echoed by half the censors, "that has long been banned even though there was nothing in the manuscript and though only the one word 'revision' appeared in the manuscript. That is an attack on serfdom."

Finally, G. himself saw that the matter had gone too far. He began to assure the censors that he had read the manuscript and that there was no mention of serfdom in it; that there were also none of the usual slaps at serfdom which appear in many stories; that here something quite different was under discussion; that the story was based on farcical misunderstandings of those who were selling, and the sharp tricks of the purchaser, and the general mix-up occasioned by this strange transaction; that this story portrayed a number of characters, gave a description of the internal conditions of Russia and some of its inhabitants, and contained a collection of sketches of the least disturbing kind. But it was no use. "The enterprise of Chichikov," they all began to shout, "is a criminal offense. Of course, he does not justify it, but he does represent it here and others will follow his course and buy dead souls."

Such arguments. These are the arguments of the Asiatic censors, the old folks who have completed their service and are sitting at home. Now come the arguments of the European censors, who have returned from abroad, the young folks. Whatever you say, the price which Chichikov pays (said one of such censors, K., to me), the price of two and a half which he is willing to pay for a soul is disturbing. Human feeling cries out against it, even though in the last resort the price is given for one name, written on paper. But even that one name is a soul, a human soul; it lived; it existed; this would not be allowed in France, in England, or anywhere else. After this no foreigner will come to Russia.

These are the principal reasons that led to the banning of the manuscript. . . .[21]

The motivation of censorship regulations in Russia up to this time had been the disquiet engendered by the July Revolution in France in 1830. To some degree the memories of that uprising were fading away and the censorship was becoming lost in mazes of red tape and endless recrimination. The recession of revolution into the past had dulled the sense of urgency; and censorship had come to be a matter of personal feuds, intrigues for power, and professional rivalry. But the outbreak in Paris in February, 1848, at once revived all the old fears and uncertainties. The Tsar, ever on the alert against "dangerous ideas," had in the Convention of Münchengratz of 1833 brought the three Eastern powers—Russia, Prussia, and Austria—together in an alliance which came to be known at that time as "An Intellectual Dam" against the new and dangerous ideas of liberty and equality. He had also in implementation of that agreement stubbornly disapproved of the attempts of Frederick William IV of Prussia to grant his people a constitution—however innocuous. He assumed the role of "gendarme of Europe" or at least of that part of the Continent that he looked upon as his sphere of influence. The news from Paris in February was like the trumpet of battle to the charger, and the Tsar braced himself anew for the struggle.

The first immediate result was the naming of a special committee to review the whole question of censorship. The idea was due to the prompting of Baron Korf, a conservative who shared many of Nicholas' views. The new committee was under the chairmanship of Prince Menshikov and included among its members, Buturlin, Baron Korf, Degai, Count Stroganov, and General Dubelt. The committee did little more than explore the ground and issue warnings to the periodical press that they would be held accountable for the publication of anything not in the public interest. Exactly what was the function of the new committee was left somewhat uncertain; and this fact may explain why it was super-

[21] Skabichevskii, *Ocherki po istorii russkoi tsenzury*, 282.

seded on April 1 by a permanent committee, consisting of Buturlin (chairman), Baron Korf, Count Stroganov, Degai, and Dubelt.

The general attitude of the administration was clearly revealed in a communication of April 25 of the committee to the Ministry of War with reference to an article appearing recently in *Russkii Invalid*, an official publication of that department:

The Emperor has deigned to draw attention to the fact that while contemporary events in western Europe rouse in the body of thoughtful and reasonable people merely proper disgust, yet it is necessary to shield the lower classes from the spread among them of a circle of ideas which now, thank God, are quite foreign to them. Yet in this connection we must be on our guard since Russian newspapers are read by all the lower functionaries, in their own homes, in lackeys' quarters, and in inns, and spread in this way among hundreds of thousands of readers to whom all this is as sacred as the law since it has appeared in print. In this sense, doubtless, there is no purpose or need for these numerous readers, of whom the majority are on the lowest level of education and of the social ladder, to know, for instance, that in Paris the throne has been hurled out of the window and publicly burned or to read the communists' tirades, those dangerous fabrications in which foreign newspapers now abound.

Meanwhile His Majesty has been pleased to remark that in the political columns of our newspapers there sometimes appear articles which, although they contain nothing contrary to the existing code of censorship, yet it would be more expedient and safer that under these special circumstances which transcend the general law they should not appear in Russian newspapers.[22]

The activities of the committee of April 2, as it was called, afford considerable insight into the currents of Russian thought at the time. The committee itself was unofficial and its working was veiled from the public. Nevertheless it had the ear of the Emperor and thus, through its mysterious operations, made itself felt not only to journalists but to the censors; one of its sharpest weapons, that of official reprimand, was reserved for any of these custodians

[22] Lemke, *Ocherki po istorii russkoi tsenzury i zhurnalistiki XIX stoletiya,* 210.

of public morality who proved faithless. The committee thus became, as Baron Korf said, a sword of Damocles that at all times hung over the heads of writers and censors alike. It was not only a sort of a barometer of opinion of the official world, but also of those conservative elements in society that were appalled at the events that seemed to be shaking the very foundations of European society. It will be instructive to look for and to list what seem to have been this committee's chief aims and methods.

Its first objective was to screen the news arriving from abroad and to prevent its reaching the masses in such form as to incite them to emulate the example of the revolutionary mobs of western European capitals. But this precaution was far from enough. The committee sought also to prevent such incitement's reaching the people even indirectly through parallels drawn by historians from early Russian history. One of the first cases dealt with an article published by the historian S. M. Soloviev in *Sovremennik*. In this article on the "Time of Troubles" Soloviev had said:

We have seen what was the nature of the rising in the north country and who followed the banner of Bolotnikov; arriving under the walls of Moscow, Bolotnikov at once proclaimed the purpose and character of his revolt; in the capital, there appeared leaflets from him with appeals to the very lowest stratum of society. "We direct," writes the Muscovite hierarchy to the local clergy, "the boyars' serfs to kill their masters and their wives, to plunder their *votchiny* and *pomyestiya;* and we direct beggars and nameless thieves to kill the merchants and all trading people and to loot their property; and we invite them—thieves— to us and we will give them the titles of *boyars* and *voyevody* and *okol'nichi* and *dyaki*."

After this result, the pretender and Lisovskii advanced toward the capital and everywhere they found allies; they found them among the common people, proclaiming to the peasants that they were free to seize the land of their lords, who had served Shuiskii, free even to marry their lords' daughters.

The comments of the committee on the above passage were as follows:

Such particulars, which are the body of history, may of course in this sense be included in special works in this connection which have their own special circle of readers; but their insertion in a journal which circulates widely among all classes must be recognized as harmful and not in keeping with the purposes of such publications. In accordance with the will of the monarch which follows in this connection, we beg you to convey the appropriate reprimand to the censor who passed it.[23]

The Emperor's arbitrariness and caprice continued to clog the censorship. An article apparently written by Buturlin himself and appearing in *Biblioteka dlya Chteniya* contained reminiscences of Bulgarin who had been an active figure for many years in the administration of both Alexander and Nicholas. Bulgarin quoted Speranskii's comments on his (Speranskii's) dismissal by Alexander in 1812 on the eve of the invasion of Napoleon: "If I had been related to one of the noble families, doubtless things would have taken a different turn. Whoever wishes to retain his place in the world should use a marriage ring as a sheet anchor." The Emperor was furious when he read this article. His reasons were that such a statement, which implied criticism of the government, even if the words had actually been uttered by Speranskii, had never been intended for publication. Its appearance so shortly after the death of Speranskii touched on affairs that were all but contemporary and too fresh in people's minds to be allowed to become common knowledge.[24]

But if the discussion of contemporary or recent affairs were to be banned, it might be assumed that events which had long since passed into history were a safe topic for discussion. Indeed, a clause of the code of censorship expressly permitted discussion of events of a period prior to the accession of the Romanovs (1613). Acting on this assumption, Count Stroganov had personally authorized the publication by *Obshchestvo istorii i drevnostei* (the Society of History and Antiquities) for the first time of a Russian translation of Giles Fletcher's *Of the Russe Commonwealth*, which had first appeared at London in 1591. This time it was Uvarov who intervened to bring the matter to Nicholas'

[23] *Ibid.*, 222.
[24] *Ibid.*, 216. Speranskii had been dismissed early in 1811 from his post as imperial secretary and exiled to Nizhnyi Novgorod.

attention. It was enough that the Englishman had given a grim picture of Russia and its monarchs in the sixteenth century to induce Nicholas to stop publication and to issue instructions that a personal reprimand be administered by the Governor-General of Moscow. The secretary of the society was sent into exile at Kazan. No Russian translation of Fletcher's famous book appeared until 1905.[25]

The Stroganov-Fletcher affair seems to have been one of the last official decisions in which Uvarov had a hand. His influence continued to decline; and although he intrigued actively to have the committee dissolved, the Emperor came more and more to repose his full confidence in it. When the Minister saw that his office had ceased to have a voice in final decisions in matters of censorship, Uvarov requested that he be retired. He was succeeded by Prince Shirinskii-Shikhmatov, who had for some years been his assistant.

One significant incident of this period was the disciplining of Yu. Samarin, the Slavophile, for an indiscreet article in *Moskvityanin* which attacked the so-called "German" policy of the government. This policy was one of the long-standing grievances of native Russians against the government's seeming predilection for foreigners in the service, especially in the army. The Russians had had in the past only themselves to blame that so few of them were qualified for military posts, but it was a sore point nonetheless. Samarin was arrested and confined in the Prison of Peter and Paul and after some ten days was summoned to the Emperor's presence and delivered a severe homily on disrespect for the government, ". . . You have attacked the government and me, for what the government is, that I am; we are one and the same; although I have heard that you draw a distinction between me and the government, I do not recognize it. You write 'if we are not to be masters in our own house etc., etc.; if the Germans do not become Russians, the Russians will become Germans'—surely this was written in delirium."[26]

It would be idle to assume that the government was alone in

[25] Skabichevskii, *Ocherki po istorii russkoi tsenzury*, 349–50; see also *Fletchera Sochinenie O gosudarstve russkom*, intro., by A. A. Titov.
[26] *Ocherki po istorii russkoi tsenzury i zhurnalistiki XIX Stoletiya*, 223–24.

supporting a rigorous censorship. The journalist and historian Pogodin wrote in 1849 to Kireyevskii somewhat disheartened about the severity of the censorship to which their journal *Moskvityanin* was being subjected. Kireyevskii took a different view, and there was much in Russian history to support him: while censorship was hurting literature, the harm was but temporary and literature would recover; an appeal to the government against such censorship would render the government distrustful, if not hostile. The present alarming situation in Europe should be allowed to clear up. The great thing was that the government should not be stampeded into doing anything hostile that would create a panic and lead the country into war. Moreover, Kireyevskii concluded in a characteristic vein, the government should not be induced to embark on some foolish program in regard to the peasants that would raise false hopes of freedom.[27]

The fate of the Petrashevskii circle in 1849 is too well known to be treated in detail. Petrashevskii had drawn to himself the notice of the government for the publication of the *Pocket Dictionary of foreign words that have entered the Russian language*, which had given expression to certain liberal ideas. The first part had been printed and sold; the second part—M to O—was printed in 1849, but was confiscated by the government. Indeed the censor who had passed it was severely censured. Later in the year the Petrashevskii circle was raided at one of its meetings. The unfortunate members, including the future novelist, Dostoyevskii, were arrested, brought to trial, and some of them sentenced to death. Final preparations were made for the execution, and the prisoners were led to the scaffold and blindfolded. Only at the last minute was their reprieve read to them. Their sentences had been commuted to banishment to Siberia.

A curious illustration of the temper of the times is to be found in a remarkable article appearing in the *Otechestvennye Zapiski*, a periodical which had long been under suspicion and had more than once received a warning from the censor. Apparently to turn away the wrath of the government and to give proof of its "trustworthiness," the periodical printed an article from which the following excerpts are taken:

[27] *Ibid.*, 221.

Russia in its youth was an independent state which repelled all the attacks of the West, but in the strength of its manhood it is a mighty colossus. World annals offer no example of such strength and power, and the good fortune to be a Russian is a patent of nobility among the peoples of Europe. As in antiquity the name Roman signified a man *par excellence,* so, in our day, the name Russian has the same significance. We take no pride in our glory, in our might, or in our national virtues, but, in themselves, they inspire the respect of all peoples. We do not look askance at other nations, but, on the other hand, we do not settle in colonies among them, while they do migrate to our country. Russians in Europe are mere visitors or guests; at times, they have been emancipators from slavery; more than once they have paid off scores with their foes in their magnificent capitals; but their actions have always been characterized by magnanimity, and Russian munificence has inspired the confidence of many peoples. We stand in need neither of goods nor of grain, for which they come to us, and it never occurs to a Russian to leave his country to earn a livelihood in the way that foreigners swarm into Russia for this purpose. We are rich in everything and so are always ready to help and not to seek charity. They seek to divide us . . . fools! They do not see that we are already sundered from them by walls—by our historical development, by our moral principles, and by the structure of all parts of our state organization.

They fancy that we learn from them how to live at the same time that we have long lived our own life. Peter the Great learned from the carpenters and ship-builders of Saardam, talked with Leibniz, but did not copy the Dutch form of government and did not study the religion of Soren or other preachers. So in our days as we need their Watts, their Fultons, their Burnetts, and their Leverriers, but not their Prudhons, their Cabets, their Ledru-Rollins, with their followers, we stand in need of the fruits of their education and enlightenment, but we reject their corrupt teachings as poison, and our strong moral bulwark guards us from this calamity. We are ready to lavish our gold and all material advantages on any scholar or artist; but we strongly urge French demagogues not to come here; they will die of hunger because no one will welcome them. Let them root in their own rubbish and not hope to come to us as teachers, since our wise monarch has closed the door to this trade with French charlatans.

Russians! our country is dear. Leave the flowers that bloom in the shadow of their autocratic monarchs, flourishing on the basic principles of thy might and wisdom. Storms from without will not affright us; we are sundered from them by the indestructible bulwark of our Orthodox faith and our whole moral and historical development.[28]

This curious mixture of Slavophilism and official nationalism appears to have been in part an effort to conciliate the censors and to cultivate official tolerance. We have no means of knowing how it was received, but it seems highly significant that it should have appeared in a journal that had long been known for its "liberal" leanings and had been kept under close official scrutiny.

That the censors did not look with too great favor on the Slavophiles is shown by the difficulty experienced by a proposed publication, *Moskovskii Sbornik*. It was to be a series of four volumes, the first to contain articles by I. S. Aksakov, I. V. Kireyevskii, and K. S. Aksakov. One of these articles, concerning the life of the ancient Slavs, maintained that communal life had been their distinguishing feature. In a long memorandum the committee of censors challenged this assertion of the primacy of communalism with the claim that autocracy had been and continued to be the most characteristic institution of the Russian. The committee refused to pass this article and forbade its publication. Ivan Aksakov was deprived henceforth of the right to edit any magazine.[29]

It is interesting to observe that there had been throughout the whole reign of Nicholas two trends in government policy which in general had been discredited, but which nevertheless kept cropping up. Some of the more thoughtful officials had adhered to the view that the proper function of censorship was entirely negative and should be limited to preventing the publication of what was harmful to the state; and that, in doubtful cases where two

[28] *Ibid.*, 213–14.
[29] *Ibid.*, 285–86.

interpretations of a passage were possible, the passage should be interpreted in a sense most favorable to the author. Both of these principles had been emphasized in the code of 1828.[30] But while there was no abandonment of these two principles, the first of them seemed to run counter to the views of Uvarov, judging from the memorandum he submitted to the monarch on December 4, 1832, just after his appointment to the post of deputy minister of education and the completion of his first inspection of the University of Moscow in that capacity:

> ... but I firmly hope that there remain for us means ... having gradually got control of the minds of the youth, to lead it imperceptibly to that point where it ought to shine for the solution of one of the most difficult problems of the time, proper basic education indispensable to our time, deep convictions, and an ardent belief in the genuinely Russian principles of orthodoxy, autocracy, and nationalism, which constitute the last anchor of our security and the truest guarantee of the strength and greatness of our country.[31]

It is plain to be seen therefore that, whatever might be provided by the code of 1828 which was in force at this time, the negative role of the censors had been abandoned for a more positive one.

On the other point the committee of April 2 definitely and arbitrarily went back on the generous provision of 1828 and instructed the censors that they should keep a sharp lookout for all attempts to evade the censors by "writing between the lines." This order intensified what had already become a war of wits between the censors and the authors. There came into existence in the thirties and forties what was known as "Aesopian" language, in which the writer veiled his thoughts with devices more or less transparent, e.g., the substitution of a remote or even a mythical country for Russia; of fictitious names whose reference to real

---

[30] Shishkov's "Iron Code" of 1826 had emphasized two principles: first, that it was the business of the censorship to give a decisive lead to public opinion; secondly, that in doubtful cases, the author should not be given the benefit of the doubt. These two principles had been ostentatiously scrapped in the rather liberal code of the regime of Prince Lieven.

[31] *Ocherki po istorii russkoi tsenzury i zhurnalistiki XIX Stoletiya*, 186–90.

persons would be readily understood by the reader; symbolic terms for real institutions. Thus there developed the apparatus of conspiracy through circumvention of the laws without incurring the penalties of open violation.[32] The Decembrists had tried to elude the police by secrecy with some measure of success. But their conspiracy had ended in a bloody climax, and the establishment of the Third Section had definitely closed this avenue. The younger intellectual generation, harassed by the censorship, now turned to Aesopian language to outwit the censors. Conspiracy now exchanged secret organization for figurative language to veil criticism of the existing order and proposals for reform.

The reign of terror, as it has been called in retrospect by Russian writers, was unchallenged from 1848 to 1855. As the international horizon darkened and Russia braced herself for war, the censors redoubled their efforts to bring about a closing of ranks among all classes. Moreover, even some of the journals under suspicion for liberalism joined hands with the government, as the article quoted above from *Otechestvennye Zapiski* testifies. But while the old regime might enjoy some respite from the barbs of its enemies, its ultimate security hung on the issues of war. As one writer says, "English and French cannon shot away the regime of Nicholas."[33] The impact on Russian society of the fall of Sevastopol can hardly be understood in the West where the Crimean War has usually been regarded as a mere check administered to Russia's Balkan policy. In Russia it was regarded rather as a judgment on the whole existing order; and with the Emperor's death and the accession of a new monarch, society turned hopefully to the new Emperor and his confidants in the belief that they would find some way to remove at least the grossest abuses of government and of its social system in order to bring Russia into step with the rest of Europe by relaxing the old system of distrust, suspicion, repression, and fear that made many ashamed of their national heritage and fearful of the future.

[32] *Ibid.*, 209; for methods used in "Aesopian Language," see S. A. Nikitin, *Istochnikovedenie Istorii S.S.S.R.*, II, 156–57.
[33] A. Brückner, *A Literary History of Russia*, 245.

VIII

The Decembrists

THE reign of Alexander I (1801–25) was the culmination in Russia of the influences of the Enlightenment of the eighteenth century, while the reign of Nicholas I (1825–55) saw the rise of entirely new modes of thought which were to dominate Russia through the whole of the nineteenth century. Between these two reigns lies the Decembrist rising of 1825.

The long story of the Russian revolutionary movement may be said to begin with the Decembrist rising of 1825. Yet the scene that was enacted on Senate Square in St. Petersburg on that winter's afternoon was in a sense but the culmination of a long series of changes which had been leading up to that dramatic episode. The historian is tempted to see in this event the germ of the political and social upheavals which have shaken the foundations of the Russian state and of Russian society within our own time. Whether this is or is not the case, the rising does illuminate with startling clearness the condition of Russia in 1825 and the forces which were then at work in that country.

Before attempting to gather up the actual threads that were drawn together in this conspiracy, one may make certain broad generalizations in regard to the half-century preceding it. Russia had, despite all efforts to the contrary, remained backward. Her social and political structure seemed to be taking on more and more of a medieval form. The bonds of serfdom were being drawn still tighter. Catherine, after a feeble beginning, had definitely forsworn any effort to introduce constitutional government and had settled down into the traditional role of the Russian autocrat. Yet it was an age of Enlightenment for Russia as well as for the rest of Europe. The ripple of philosophical and political thought that began in the Paris *salons* washed even the banks of the distant Neva. Schemes of reform (far removed from the sphere of practical politics) became the subject of drawing-room conversations. Young men who had read the works of Montesquieu, Rousseau, Voltaire, Mably, Helvetius, d'Holbach, and other French writers, as the fashion of the time, became armchair statesmen for the entertainment of polite society in the *salons* of the capital.[1]

The French Revolution put an abrupt end to the open discussion of such dilettante proposals. These conversations had to be postponed to a more convenient season. The accession of Paul— a definitely reactionary monarch—went still further to make such subjects taboo.

A new era seemed to dawn in 1801 when the Tsar Alexander came to the throne. Brought up carefully by Catherine, he had early come in contact with Western thought and associated with advanced intellectuals at court. Under his favor liberal thought flourished in the highest circles, and Imperial patronage was sufficient to awake to renewed life the vogue for constitutional and social reform.[2] Alexander's secret committee submitted various schemes of reform; but while the Emperor might toy with advanced ideas, he was restrained by some consideration from giving these ideas objective reality. What this consideration was, we are in some doubt; but it is significant that at this time the stream of forward-pointing political thought was reinforced by a current from an entirely different quarter. Russian armies had taken part as early as 1799 in campaigns in western Europe under Kutuzov; but after 1805, some units of Russian military forces were almost continually beyond the frontiers. The results of this contact with Western life and thought can hardly be exaggerated. Soldiers are usually of an age most likely to receive vivid impressions from their experiences. Moreover, the excitement of service and return to Russia produced a feeling of almost exaltation which was well calculated to break down the most ingrained habits of thought. Pushkin has graphically described the enthusiasm of these times in his short story "The Snowstorm":

[1] *See* instances quoted by Semevskii, *Byloe*, Vol. III (January, 1906), 8.
[2] *Ibid.*
[3] Alexander Pushkin, *The Snowstorm*.

Meanwhile the war had been gloriously ended. Our regiments were returning from abroad. The people were running to meet them. The bands were playing songs of victory: "Vive Henri Quatre," Tyrolean waltzes, airs from "Joconda". . . . The soldiers talked gaily among themselves, continually mingling German and French words in their conversation. A never-to-be-forgotten time.[3]

The whole atmosphere of Tolstoi's *War and Peace* bears witness to the epic character of this wonderful period. To this inrush of new customs and ideas no emperor, however powerful he might be, could set bounds.

The intellectual ferment was naturally greatest among the officers who were as a rule the best educated class in the army. They were probably the most intelligent also. The dossiers of the Decembrists contain the personal records of scores of these young men, which reveal the mentally stimulating effect on them of their sojourn abroad. For example, one of them recorded the following incidents in his career:

In 1813 on the entry of the Russian armies into Prussia, at the crossing of the rivers Niemen, Vistula, Oder, and Elbe, on the twentieth of April in a general engagement; Saxony, before the city of Lutzen, in action the eighth and ninth of May before Bautzen, for which he was rewarded with the order of St. Anne of the Fourth Class; on the entry of the Russian armies into Bohemia and at the crossing of the defiles of Giezkeubel and of Holenburg in Saxony, the sixteenth of August before the city of Pirn and on the retreat through the defiles of Giezkeubel and Holenburg in active engagement, on the seventeenth of August in resistance to the hostile corps of General Vandame before Kulm and on the eighteenth in the defeat of that corps in active engagement, for which he was also rewarded with the Order of St. Vladimir of the fourth class with the Prussian Clasp for merit and with the Iron Cross; on October 4th before the city of Leipzig where he was wounded by a gunshot in the thigh.[4]

[4] Russia (R.S.F.S.R.–1917) Tsentrarkhiv—*Vosstanie Dekabristov; Materialy*, Tom. 1 (hereinafter cited as *Vosstanie Dekabristov*).

Another such record was this:

From the fourth of March, 1814, in Switzerland, France, Bavaria, Württemburg, Saxony, Prussia and the Grand Duchy of Warsaw to the day of the return to Russian territory, the third of December; in 1815 from the twelfth of April abroad in Russian Poland, Prussia, Saxony, Bavaria, and France to the day of his return to Russia the fourth of December of that year.[5]

These are extracts from the military records of two of the most prominent of the Decembrists—Trubetskoi and Ryleev; but these records are typical of scores of others associated with them in their activity. It is safe to say that all Russian troops set foot in some of the countries of western Europe—and those the most advanced and cultured nations of the Continent. What more natural than that the institutions and customs of these countries, in such striking contrast to those of Russia, would leave indelible impressions on the minds of the young soldiers, impressions destined in later years to produce profound results?

The one institution of western Europe which caught the imagination of the Russians of this time was the secret society. Already Freemasonry had made some progress in Russia. Tolstoi in *War and Peace* has portrayed the activities of this order in Russia during this time which must have reflected conditions in western Europe; but the revolutionary epoch had produced an astonishing crop of new ones—the Carbonari in Italy, the Hetairiai in Greece and in the Balkans, and the Tugenbunde of Germany. All these were typical examples of the most nationalistic and revolutionary societies. Others were purely cultural.

In the years following the war Russian officers who had seen service abroad felt impelled to transplant these alien institutions to their native soil. Some of the transplanted societies were the Green Lamp, the Russian Knights, the Free Gardeners, the United Slavs, the Little Russian Society, and the Caucasian Society.[6] These societies and similar ones represented the varied aspirations of the new era. There can be little doubt that, while many of them were

[5] *Ibid.*, 151.
[6] N. Pavlov-Sil'vanskii, "Pestel Pered Verkhovnym Ugolovnym Sudom," in *Byloe*, 25.

not political, all of them tended to foster revolutionary ideas. They were relatively safe from interference by the government as long as constitutional ideas were affected by Alexander and his court. But as the Emperor became more conservative, there was a tendency for the societies to come under suspicion. After 1821 some effort was made to regulate their activities.

But our concern is with one particular order which appears to have been organized at St. Petersburg in 1817. In 1816 Alexander Muravyev proposed to his brother Nikita, a captain of the Guards' general staff, the organization of a society having for its purpose the introduction of representative government into Russia. A meeting was held at which Sergei and Matvei Muravyev-Apostal, Yakushkin, and Nikita Muravyev were present. Shortly afterward Nikita Muravyev brought into the circle Paul Pestel and Prince Trubetskoi. Organization was not completed until the eighteenth of February, 1817, when a constitution drawn up by Pestel was adopted. The name given to the society was the Union of Salvation. It was to be a secret order with three degrees— brothers, men, and boyars—and provision was made for a careful selection of candidates and a period of novitiate. An oath was demanded of the novice not to divulge any of the society's secrets, and as he proceeded from one degree to another, still stricter oaths were required of him. Elections were held once a month to fill the offices of president, overseer, and secretary. The real power, however, was in the hands of the boyars who constituted the Duma.[7] The leading members of this organization were members of the higher nobility and regimental officers in the army. The transfer of officers from one station or regiment to another naturally interrupted in some degree the activities of the order in St. Petersburg, but the officers so transferred in many cases became the nuclei of similar groups throughout the country. This factor is very important as it explains the spread of the movement in an age when communication was poor. The movement of the court to Moscow in September, 1817, was the first of a series by which numbers of officers were transferred in this way to distant stations.

[7] *Vosstanie Dekabristov*, I, 305–306; see also Ludwig Kulczycki, *Geschichte der Russischen Revolution*, I, 86 ff.

The purpose of the organization does not appear to have been clearly defined in the constitution. The members subscribed to certain vague humanitarian and ethical principles which were safe enough as long as no one endeavored to cast them in a positive framework; but as soon as an effort was made to define more specifically the purpose of the order, dissension arose and two parties formed—those who wished to keep the organization "safe" and those who wished to make it definitely political. In 1819 the latter tendency triumphed, with the result that a number of secessions took place, the more conservative elements withdrawing. Complete reorganization followed.[8] The spread of the rumor that the Emperor proposed to add to the new kingdom of Poland the land formerly embraced in the Grand Duchy of Lithuania roused the members to such a pitch of national feeling that one of its members, Yakushkin, offered to assassinate the Emperor, but abandoned the plan out of deference to the wishes of his associates.

We have rather full information about the new order, as it was described in detail by Pestel in 1826 before the Examining Commission.[9] Pestel appears to have opposed the change in the order; but although he was no longer in St. Petersburg, he seems to have been active in his station in the South. The various branches of the new society probably were similar in form as the members kept in touch with one another. The new organization was even more elaborate than the original Union of Salvation. The new name was the Union of Welfare. The founders occupied a privileged position; from their numbers was drawn the council which formed the executive; this executive, together with the founders, exercised the final authority, accepted new members, made regulations, and so forth. The actual administrative head was the president (one of the founders). An official called an overseer was named to act as a check on the president. The members were pledged to bring in other members. New members were organized in groups of ten under the lead of a member who was instrumental in enrolling them. There was strict supervision of the novices, and severe discipline was enforced. While there could be no state-wide

8 Kulczycki, *Geschichte der Russischen Revolution*, 92, 93. At Poltava the order was closely identified with Freemasonry.
9 *Vosstanie Dekabristov*, IV, 108, 110, for the evidence of Pestel.

Fatal shooting of Count Miloradovich, December 14, 1825. *From the painting by Charlemagne*

national organization, the society did grow, and eventually there appear to have been seven or eight different branches. Not all were active. Apparently there were three different degrees of activity among the branches—the chief branch, the active branches, and the associate branches. Owing to the dispersal of officers, Moscow, Kiev, Tultchin, and Poltava became centers of the movement.[10]

The spread of the new gospel to the provinces brought greater latitude and permitted development along novel lines in accordance with the individuality of the more forceful local leaders. The Tultchin branch in the neighborhood of Kiev was particularly active under Pestel. It must, of course, be understood that these branches were continually changing in personnel as the members moved from place to place. The center of interest began to shift definitely to the South, where political and revolutionary color was given to the movement. It is significant that the leaders opened up negotiations with the Poles in these provinces. The so-called Patriotic Society had been created as a protest against Alexander's policy of Russification in Poland.

The year 1821 was a critical one in the history of this movement. It was at this time that the Tsar can be said to have definitely abandoned his schemes for constitutional reform, and the change of policy was reflected in the Union of Welfare. The more moderate members and those who were prone to follow the fashions in their thinking began to draw away from the movement when they saw the danger of conflict with the government. At a conference of the delegates of the Southern societies, held at Moscow in 1821, the fainthearted gained the upper hand and resolved on dissolution. But this action was not recognized by Pestel and his associates at Tultchin. Two other branches followed the lead of the Tultchin organization in refusing to recognize the action of the Moscow congress. These branches were Vasilov and Kamensk. There appears also to have been a branch in the army of the Caucasus, although it is not known whether it was associated with the others mentioned. This group of organizations came to be known as the Southern *okrug*, which, although a continuation of the older Union of Welfare, claimed complete autonomy, not only from Moscow but from St. Petersburg, and developed along

[10] Kulczycki, *Geschichte der Russischen Revolution*, I, 86.

its own lines, unrestrained by moderating influences. Its activity became definitely revolutionary.

The government was not uninformed on these developments within the regiments of the guards. In 1822 Adjutant-General Vasil'chikov was apparently apprised of the existence of such an organization, probably by his brother who was commander of the Guards' Division. He found a suitable occasion to convey the news to Alexander, who showed himself strangely indifferent and is said to have remarked only: *"Mon cher Wassiltshchikoff! Vous qui êtes à mon service depuis le commencement de mon règne, vous savez qu'j'ai partagé et encouragé ces illusions et ces erreurs."* Then after a pause Alexander added: *"Ce n'est pas à moi de sévir."*

Shortly afterward a full-scale report on secret societies and particularly on the Union of Welfare was submitted to the Emperor by A. K. Benckendorf, then chief of staff of the Guards. Benckendorf was apparently informed by someone on the inside, and his report gave a full history of both the Union of Salvation and the Union of Welfare up to 1821, with the story of the supposed extinction of the organization in 1821.

While nothing would appear to have come from this document immediately, it was probably not unconnected with the general order of August 1, 1822, by which all secret societies in the empire were ordered closed. This decree included, of course, the Masons, who immediately disbanded. But the political societies continued to function. Why tolerance was shown them remains a mystery, but they were either overlooked or forgotten until 1826 when the order suppressing secret societies was repeated for their benefit and enforced.

In 1823 the revolutionary tendency of the Southern *okrug* was much accelerated by the admission to its membership of two men of strong character and uncompromising temperament—Sergius Muravyev-Apostol and Bestuzhev-Riumin. They soon came into conflict with Pestel over the question of the proposed assassination of the Tsar. The former members were anxious to begin the revolt during the summer while the maneuvers were in progress at Bobruisk. The Tsar was to be seized, the fortress to be occupied, and the troops moved on to Moscow. Apparently the controversy continued all that year. At a meeting held at Kamionka it was finally decided that the Imperial family was to be destroyed as the first step in the proposed revolution. A conference was held the following year at Kiev at the annual fair.[11]

In the meantime what was happening at the capital? The news of the dissolution of the Moscow organization caused consternation in St. Petersburg. Turgenev summoned the members to a meeting and suggested the organization of a society to continue the activity of the old one. The new society was finally organized in the autumn of 1822.[12] There is no evidence that there was a break in continuity. Much the same thing happened here as occurred in the South. The personnel was purged of its fainthearted members, and the work continued.

It became customary to speak of the St. Petersburg organization as the Northern *okrug* of the society. In 1823 there was a flutter of excitement among the members when it was learned that Pestel was coming up from the South as a delegate. He reached St. Petersburg in January, 1824, and met the members of the Duma— Trubetskoi, Obolenskoi, Turgenev, Ryleev, Matvei Muravyev-Apostol, and Semenov. Pestel carried matters with a high hand and reproached the members with their lethargy, their lack of unity, and their failure to maintain as effective an organization as had been done in the South. He proposed, therefore, first, to unite both societies; second, to recognize the chief members in the North as boyars with both organizations to be placed under a common executive, consisting of the boyars of both orders; and, third, to require implicit obedience to the will of the majority. His projects met with a cool reception.

Pestel, who was dominant in the South, could not extend his personal ascendancy to the Northern organization. It was decided to leave matters as they were until 1826. This policy of drifting explains much of the confusion that arose later on. How much out of hand the members were getting was seen in May, 1825. Yakubovich announced his resolve to make an attempt on the life of the Tsar at the time of the summer maneuvers. As no preparations whatever had been made to stage a revolt, Ryleev and others did

[11] *Vosstanie Dekabristov,* IV, 104; Kulczyski, *Geschichte der Russischen Revolution,* I, 98.
[12] *Vosstanie Dekabristov,* I, 307.

their best to dissuade him, and Yakubovich consented to postpone the action for one year.[13] It is apparent from the evidence quoted that, while the members of the organizations in both North and South contemplated a revolution, it was relegated to the future at a time not earlier than 1826. What led them to change their plans we will see later on.

Exactly what did the leaders of the movement actually propose in the way of revolutionary action? On their general aims they have themselves shed a good deal of light, as several members of the organizations drafted constitutions which they hoped to put into force. Pestel embodied his scheme in a fragmentary book of 250 pages, which he called *Russkaya Pravda*. A somewhat grandiloquent subtitle describes it as the "Official Constitutional Charter of the GREAT RUSSIAN PEOPLE to serve as a Covenant for the Completion of the governmental structure of Russia and containing the true instruction for the People and for the temporary Supreme Government."

Space does not permit us to give more than a passing notice to this highly important publication, but its outstanding features may be stated briefly. First, its intense nationalism, as seen in the defining of the boundaries of the Russian state and the treatment of non-Russian races, is important. Of the latter the Poles were the only ones to whose national aspirations any concession was made. Poland was to be allowed her independence, and here we see quite definitely the price at which Polish support was bought. The other national groups were to be retained in the Russian state on the grounds that never having formed a separate state they could not claim their independence. Russia was to be divided for administrative purposes only into districts, but local autonomy was definitely rejected in favor of a highly centralized government.[14] Here we see the French influence on Pestel. Secondly, we note Pestel's purpose to establish complete liberty of all classes before the law and in economic relations. He dealt with the various classes in

[13] *Ibid.*, I, 308.
[14] Pavel Pestel, *Russkaya Pravda*, 13–19. The independence of Poland, however, was to be conditioned on two things: first, entering into a perpetual alliance with Russia; secondly, adopting the same form of government as Russia—republican.

turn, the peasants requiring the most elaborate treatment. He advocated emancipation, to be carried out in various ways according to the status of the serf, but all under the direction of the government and with a general provision for the peasant's ownership of the land.[15] With regard to the form of government, the sovereign power was to be a representative body modeled on the English Parliament. The *Sobranie* or lower house was to be chosen by indirect election by the legislatures of the provinces. The upper house or *Sobor* was to act as overseer and would review and revise the decisions of the lower house. The *Sobor* consisted of 120 members chosen for life. The administration centered in the Duma of five members, who held office for five years and were under the control of the upper house. Care was taken to insure that deputies in the house should not hold civil positions and also that the house should control the army, except in times of war when it named a commander in chief for this purpose.

A distinction was drawn between ordinary and constitutional laws. In the case of constitutional law the people must be consulted by means of a plebiscite. It is to be noted, however, that the franchise was not to be limited to those possessing property qualifications.[16] Of still greater interest is the way in which Pestel proposed to provide a bridge between the old and the new political parties. Before the supreme commission Pestel testified that, while he recognized the injustice of the existing social and political order and the pressing need for a change in Russia, he was also appalled by the terrible suffering that might ensue in the chaos which would follow the destruction of the present form of government, as demonstrated in the French Revolution. This had suggested to him the idea of a provisional government to maintain order until a constituent assembly could be called. He had come around to the republican point of view and apparently was not willing to leave to the constituent assembly the question of whether Russia should have a republican or monarchical form of government.[17] It is noteworthy that it was the strongly pronounced republican views

[15] *Ibid.*, 82–92.
[16] *Ibid.*, 92.
[17] Pestel discussed this subject quite frankly in his answers to the examining commission. See *Vosstanie Dekabristov*, IV, 102–103.

of Pestel which brought him under the ban of the supreme commission.

Another constitutional project was drawn up by Nikita Muravyev along much the same lines, but different in details. There were to be two chambers in this legislative body, the lower to be elected directly by the people, the upper indirectly by the provincial assemblies. Ministers were made responsible to the lower house, which was supreme also in money matters just as is the English House of Commons. Muravyev limited the franchise to owners of property. He wanted to give the government the form of a constitutional monarchy, and this was the principal point of disagreement with Pestel.

A third proposal for a constitution was found among the papers of Trubetskoi and is given in Dovnar-Zapol'ski.[18] Trubetskoi laid down the principle that the Russian people must be free and independent of all control except their own. Equality of all before the law was also fundamental, and the emancipation of the serfs followed from this principle as a matter of course. The serfs' claim to some share of the land of the landowners was recognized. This scheme was distinguished by an elaborate system of federal government, the state being divided into fourteen provinces and two districts. The provinces were to be self-governing with an elected body of two houses, a chamber of deputies, and a Duma. A National Assembly or *Vyeche* and a Supreme Council would form the national government. The government was to be a constitutional monarchy and was to be federal in organization.

In addition to these three constitutions one other effort was made to formulate and popularize the underlying principles of the movement. This fourth effort was the famous catechism of Sergius Muravyev-Apostol, read to the Chernigov Regiment on that fateful morning of the fourteenth of December. It begins with the words, "Why has God created Man?" and it preserves the ecclesiastical tone throughout. Nevertheless, it advances in strong language the claims that the Russian people had been robbed of their liberty by the Tsar and that it was their duty to strike a blow for freedom. This document was apparently the only effort made by the conspirators in the way of a popular appeal.[19]

[18] M. V. Dovnar-Zapol'ski, *Memuary Dekabristov*, 96–116.

To resume once more the thread of our narrative, communication between the Northern and Southern societies took place only intermittently after Pestel's visit at the beginning of 1824. We have Pestel's own evidence that he lost interest in the society during 1825, and one cannot escape the feeling that there was a lull at this time in the South as well. It was possibly as a protest against this lull that Yakubovich announced his purpose to kill the Tsar. As 1826 was set as the probable date of the rising, it became necessary to set on foot preparations to that end. As a result of the prolonged discussions of the years 1821–24, the conviction had spread, particularly in the South but also in the North, that it would be necessary to put the Emperor Alexander out of the way. Violent action, however, was not to extend to the Imperial family, who were to be removed across the frontier. Ryleev, in his evidence, tells of the preparations which were made during the summer of 1825. What spurred the Northern members to action was the return of Trubetskoi from the South with the news that the organization there was very active and contemplated revolutionary action in the near future.[20] Trubetskoi's judgment in this connection seems to have been at fault; and if in his conversation with the Southern members, he misled them too, the causes of mutual misunderstanding are laid bare. The threat of Yakubovich did not precipitate matters, since he was induced to put off his attempt indefinitely. Ryleev set about winning over the officers at the naval base at Kronstadt to secure a frigate to convey the Emperor and his family abroad. He was also responsible for the only effort made to recruit members from outside the nobility. The proposal was received with consternation. "Our merchants are boors," Baron Steingel said to him; and Ryleev dropped the scheme.[21]

Further information on the conspiracy under way seems to have come to the Emperor in the summer of 1825. An Englishman, Sherwood, serving as a noncommissioned officer in one of the military colonies, had as early as 1823 had his suspicions aroused regarding the existence of some sort of a plot against the Emperor. But it was not until 1825 that his suspicions were confirmed. He immediately

[19] *Vosstanie Dekabristov*, VI, 128–29.
[20] *Ibid.*, I, 162.
[21] *Ibid.*, I, 179.

applied to the Emperor directly for an audience. The matter was turned over to Arakcheyev, who took it on himself to interrogate the young soldier and, when convinced of the genuineness of his story, sent him on to St. Petersburg, where he saw the Emperor and repeated his story. Sherwood was given some sort of leave to seek further confirmation of his suspicions, which he did during the course of the autumn. Further information was given the Emperor by Count Witte during the course of October, and Witte was authorized to continue his investigations among the Southern military colonies. But before any countermeasures could be taken, Alexander died at Taganrog on November 19.

Alexander's death threw all plans into confusion. To the conspirators in the North it seemed that they must act now if ever, and meetings were called at once to secure definite action. The events that followed the Tsar's death gave the conspirators every hope that they would be able to bring their plots to fruition. As is well known, the crown would naturally have gone to the Grand Duke Constantine, who was next in line; but the Grand Duke had a violent dislike for court and official life, partly as a result of a *mésalliance* and partly owing to his unpopularity in the highest circles. In 1822 he definitely renounced the throne, and the act of renunciation was deposited in the Metropolitan Cathedral at Moscow. Nicholas probably knew of this fact, but it was not communicated to the officials; and on the death of his brother, Nicholas probably felt scruples about accepting the throne without consulting Constantine. The Grand Duke, unfortunately, was in Warsaw acting as governor general; and the exchange of communications occupied some three weeks. In the meantime the officials, before learning of Nicholas' purpose, had instructed the officers of the St. Petersburg garrison to have their soldiers take the oath of allegiance to Constantine. It was not for some days that the officials and the public had any inkling of the true state of affairs; and even after it became generally known that Constantine had renounced the throne, there was a dangerous interlude before action was taken to administer the oath of allegiance the second time. Of this uncertainty, the bolder members of the conspiracy decided to avail themselves. It was decided to raise the whole of the garrison in so far as possible. This would be done by means of the officers serving in the regiments who were also members of the society.

In the meantime Trubetskoi had been chosen to co-ordinate all measures of the conspiracy, and in this capacity he apprised the branch at Tul'chin of their contemplated action. It was finally decided to take advantage of the swearing in of troops to start a revolt; and the officers charged with this, if successful, would lead the troops to a central point of the city—the Senate Square. One officer was given the task of taking into custody the Imperial family; but beyond this step, their plans do not seem to have gone. The purpose apparently was to allow events to determine their later action. Word came that the fourteenth of December was the day set for the swearing in of the troops. Everything seemed to promise fair, and the conspirators spent three anxious days and nights completing their plans. Early on the morning of the four-teenth an eleventh-hour conference took place. It appears that the favorable reports of the previous days had now to be heavily discounted and that there was no longer any possibility of united action on the part of the garrison troops. Only individual com-panies here and there could be counted on. Trubetskoi claimed that he refused point blank to go any further, although in this case his evidence is contradicted by Ryleev. At any rate Trubetskoi left home and could not be found for the rest of the day, while his fellow conspirators went ahead relying on his co-operation and leadership.[22]

The first act of the drama was played about seven o'clock in the morning when Bestuzhev delivered a violent harangue to his company of the Moscow regiment and prevailed on them to refuse to take the oath to Nicholas. The example was followed by other companies and practically the whole regiment fell into line behind Bestuzhev and Shchepin-Rostovskii and marched toward the Senate Square. Here they formed up in an orderly manner, cheering from time to time for Constantine. Yakubovich joined them, but he was of little assistance. No additional troops arrived for nearly two hours although the crowds gathered in great numbers. The Gover-nor-General of St. Petersburg, Miloradovich, attempted to expos-tulate with the troops and was shot down. Eventually other troops

[22] *Ibid.*, I, 2, for evidence of Pestel; *ibid.*, I, 152, for evidence of Ryleev.

joined the mutineers until there were parts of three regiments on the square.

In the meantime Nicholas had put himself at the head of the Finland Regiment at the Winter Palace and moved to the center of interest on Senate Square. He was warned away from the point of danger and had to content himself with drawing up his troops in the streets leading to the square. As reinforcements for the loyal troops arrived, one after another of the approaches were occupied. The troops in the square remained entirely passive and contented themselves with cheers for Constantine, except when the Metropolitan of St. Petersburg attempted to prevail upon them to return to their allegiance. His priestly garb saved him, but senior officers who approached with him were not so fortunate, two of them being shot down.

The day was now wearing on toward afternoon. It was nearly two o'clock and darkness comes early in St. Petersburg in winter. Inaction was telling on the loyal troops, and it was noted that communications had passed back and forth between the Life Grenadiers and the rebels. But no leader appeared to break the deadlock, and no effort was made to replace the absent Trubetskoi until later that afternoon. The approach of darkness warned Nicholas that something must be done. It was decided to use the artillery, all of which, along with the cavalry, had remained loyal and so deprived the revolutionaries of the means of resistance. A last ultimatum was issued to the mutinous troops to lay down their arms. The crowd was urged to disperse, but they stubbornly refused. Some replied that they would die with the revolutionaries. The ranks on the square stood defiant and firm.

The first salvo from the guns thundered over their heads. The shells tore gaping holes in the buildings surrounding the square, inflicting casualties on some bystanders. This first salvo was soon followed by a second and a third directed at point-blank range into the troops who stood in mass formation. No need to describe the havoc. Utterly unprotected and unable to reply except with small arms, the soldiers moved back and forth in an effort to escape the devastating fire. Finally they broke; and taking advantage of the only exit that was not blocked, they rushed wildly in the direction of the river and hurled themselves over the parapet on to the ice, straggling away as a disordered mob in search of safety.

Their leaders endeavored to rally them and might have done so, but the flying shells that pursued them broke the ice and many sank into the holes thus opened. All order vanished, and the troops scattered to safety or were swallowed up in the dark currents of the river. That night the troops bivouacked in the streets, while patrols moved hither and thither throughout the city picking up the stragglers who fell into their hands by the hundreds. The orders of Nicholas to clear the street were followed to the letter. The dead were picked up on the square and thrown into the Neva, and with them, it is said, many of the severely wounded. By daybreak of the fifteenth the quiet of death reigned in St. Petersburg.[23]

In the meantime what was happening in the South? Some months before the death of Alexander, a warning had come to him of the activity of Pestel. This message apparently was conveyed to the police by an officer in Pestel's own regiment. Alexander took no action; but when his papers were opened, the communication apprising him of this situation was found, and orders were immediately issued to take Pestel into custody. He was arrested on the thirteenth of December by command of General Dibich. Instructions were also issued to arrest Sergei Muravyev-Apostol and Bestuzhev-Ryumin. Both, however, eluded arrest and struck off first for Byloe-Tserkov and afterward for Vasilkov, where they hoped to raise some of the troops. The commander of the regiment at Vasilkov was on his guard and forestalled this move by arresting the officers who had left camp to meet Muravyev-Apostol, but Muravyev-Apostol procured a detachment of troops and, returning, took possession of the barracks and freed the officers. On the next morning a mass parade was held of all troops for divine service, and on this occasion the catechism was read to the assembly. Muravyev-Apostol then harangued the troops and induced them to follow him to Masnoviluvka. From here they went to Kologi. Enthusiasm, however, waned; and some of the officers deserted. But Muravyev-Apostol pressed on and met the first loyal troops near Kovaluvka. Here his columns were scattered, and he was taken prisoner. Thus, on the third of January, the revolt was put down.

[23] Levin and Pokrovskii, "Dekabristy," *Istoriya Rossii v XIX Vyeke*, Vol. I.

The conspirators who were taken prisoner were at once hurried to St. Petersburg, where, along with those seized in the capital, they were questioned with a view to ascertaining the ramifications of the plot. Nicholas was astounded at its extent, as more and more names were added to the list. It was finally decided that a commission should be appointed to make a far-reaching investigation. Early in the year this commission began its work under Levashov, minister of war, with Golitsyn and the Grand Duke Michael among its members.[24] Sessions were held almost continuously at first, later at less frequent intervals, and in June the commission's report was ready. This report, which contained a vast amount of evidence, was submitted to the Emperor, who decided to appoint a special court to try the accused. The trials followed at once and were fairly brief. Five members of the conspiracy were condemned to death—Pestel, Ryleev, Kachovskii, Sergei Muravyev-Apostol, and Michael Bestuzhev-Ryumin. (They were to be executed by the barbarous method of being quartered, but the sentence was later commuted to hanging.) Others whom the court recommended for death were sentenced only to imprisonment. The sentences of the five leaders were carried out early on the morning of July 14. They remained firm to the end, mutually drawing support from one another's courage.

The rest of the condemned dragged out their lives in various prisons throughout the length and breadth of European Russia or in Siberia. In 1855 at the coronation of Alexander II most of those remaining in prison or in exile were released.[25]

The part played by the Emperor Nicholas in the investigation of the revolt has long been the subject of criticism. During the critical moments of the revolt he remained firm; in the aftermath he was not so steady. Urged on by him, his officers put down the rising with ruthless severity. In some cases the rebels were hunted down like animals. In the investigation Nicholas took a personal share. He was present at the sessions of the commission and interrogated the accused. Some he visited in prison. This participation brought in some cases unexpected results. Almost all of the conspirators made the fullest confessions. Indeed, numbers of them,

[24] "Letters of M. D. Nessel'rode," *Kraznyi Arkhiv*, Vol. X (1925), 261–85.
[25] Kulczycki, *Geschichte der Russischen Revolution*, I, 199.

urged by the Emperor, recklessly incriminated themselves and their associates.

The ones who showed themselves pliable were rewarded by attentions to their families, while the others were put in close confinement. Yet among those treated with the utmost consideration was Ryleev, who was later hanged. It is difficult to reconcile the emotional appeals to which Nicholas had recourse to worm the secrets out of these unfortunate men and the callousness with which he left them to their fate. The conspirators themselves seem to have believed in his magnanimity and responded to his advances. The virtue of consistency, of which so much is made, was noticeably absent. Ryleev treated for his life. Pestel offered to devote himself to the Emperor's service for the rest of his days. Sergei Muravyev-Apostol, stouthearted to the end, was not above addressing the Emperor on his own behalf in a letter which concludes: "As for me personally, if I were permitted to express to Your Majesty a single wish that I now entertain, it is to employ in a suitable way in behalf of my country, the gifts that heaven has granted me, especially if I might hope to inspire any confidence in Your Majesty, I should take the liberty of petitioning to be sent on some dangerous mission such as the vast empire of Your Majesty so frequently offers, in the South towards the Caspian Sea and Lake Aral, on the Eastern front of Siberia, still unexplored, or lastly in our American colonies. Whatever the task might be that was imposed upon me, Your Majesty would see in my zeal to discharge it that one can rely on my word.

"The only favor which I dare to ask of Your Majesty as a kindness which will remain indelibly imprinted on my heart is my reunion with my brother. Pray, Sire, to hear with favor the petition of he who signs himself at this moment—Your Imperial Majesty's faithful subject, Sergius Muravyev-Apostol."[26]

The liquidation of the revolt was a curious human drama. Cowardice and heroism, self-seeking and unselfish devotion were to be found side by side. The tragic consequences of their years of plotting had overtaken the conspirators, and they felt their awful isolation and weakness. They were probably no better nor worse than the average of mankind the world over, but at least the five

[26] *Vosstanie Dekabristov*, IV, 261–62.

who paid the supreme penalty atoned for their weaknesses. The case of the others was hardly less tragic.

When one considers the extent of the plot, the Decembrist rising is of supreme significance and interest in the history of Russian revolutions. According to Kulczycki, the number of prominent persons involved from first to last was not less than six thousand. It made a profound impression upon Russia at the time. The high rank of the conspirators and the severity with which they were treated were a sufficient guarantee that revolution would not raise its head again as long as Nicholas occupied the throne.

Had the movement any chance of succeeding, and if so, why did it fail? These two questions are interesting subjects of speculation and ones to which no decisive answers can be given. With regard to the first question, if we limit ourselves to the actual revolt, it can be said that the conspirators were within a very little distance of succeeding on December 14. The possession of artillery, determined leadership, the accession to their ranks of the Life Guards, almost any stroke of fortune might well have given them possession of the Winter Palace and the city. Whether that would have meant ultimate success is another question. Their scheme provided for the calling of a provisional assembly, which would have had to decide the question that was insoluble for the society, namely, whether Russia was to have a monarchical or a republican form of government.

And while this question was being debated, who was to guarantee that power might not slip from their grasp? The hold of the officers on the army was purely personal and uncertain. Under the leadership of determined men they could easily be brought into line, but of the real issues of the conflict the rank and file had no conception. To the soldiers on the Senate Square the revolt was merely an issue between Constantine and Nicholas, while to the conspirators it was autocracy versus constitutional government. Intelligent support of the army therefore was not to be counted on. One is constrained to find in this event a curious portent of what happened a hundred years later when a provisional government, having seized power in 1917 with the support of the army, found that support withdrawn six months later, and their purpose of deciding the country's destiny by an academic discussion thwarted by an appeal to the rule of the sword. Might not a sudden change of allegiance have robbed the conspirators of the fruits of victory in 1825 as in 1917?

The revolt in the South never had a chance. Here there was no central point from which, when seized, the country could be dominated. There was no concentration of troops, and hence the leaders had to content themselves with what scattered detachments they could raise. Communication was uncertain, and the few bold spirits found themselves isolated in a vast region where physical obstacles were insuperable. It was simply a case of hunting down the remnants of the movement, which was merely a matter of time.

But whether the movement had the chance of ultimately succeeding raises more fundamental questions. The weaknesses were those inherent in Russian history. As pointed out above, the movement was confined to the Russian nobility. An abortive effort of Ryleev to recruit from the bourgeoisie was regarded with horror even in the army. It was only among the senior officers that the members were found. No provision had been made for organizing among the junior officers or noncommissioned officers. This meant that the revolution could have no hold on the common people and, indeed, as we know from reading the evidence, the rising was purely an intellectual movement, inspired partly by the literature of the Enlightenment and partly by the experience through which the officers had gone while abroad.

However real to them, these experiences abroad could not be communicated to or shared with the mass of the people. It is probable that the emancipation of the serfs, which was one of the most important planks in the Decembrists' platform, would have been accepted passively by the peasants; but the introduction of representative government would have created a condition little short of chaos. Representative government would have been understood only in the towns and could have aroused little interest in the country districts. It is extremely likely that the revolutionaries would have found their schemes unworkable. The truth is that many of these men were great landowners who felt that their class did not have the power in political affairs to which their rank and wealth entitled them. The franchise was to be limited to men of property. By this limitation the revolutionaries were attempting to reproduce under Russian conditions representative institutions as they existed in England at that time, where power was in the hands of the wealthy and the highborn. A pure democracy was the last thing in the world that the revolutionaries intended to found.

Is this rising evidence that the Russian mind had by the year 1825 attained the intellectual maturity reached by western Europe? If our criterion is to be the immediate practical results achieved, then, of course, the Decembrists were children. Yet in a larger perspective, the movement had tremendous repercussions, although many of its results were long delayed. It is a striking evidence to the vitality of the ideas of justice, of humanitarianism, of freedom, and of equality imported from western Europe that for the first time educated Russians could break through the iron fetters fastened on them by prejudice and tradition and conceive of a new order that would satisfy the very natural yearnings of the human heart. But to what extent did they break with the past? They used the jargon that was drawn mostly from the French writers of the Enlightenment and worked incessantly in turning out ideal constitutions and creating on paper new institutions modeled on those of France or England or the United States. They took up the cause of the peasant and of the soldier and proposed to solve the old problem of the corruption and arbitrariness of official justice as administered by the courts. But they were constrained to adapt these causes to a number of basic Russian ideas. In the adaptation of them many became unrecognizable.

How far were these men really followers of Voltaire, Helvetius, Adam Smith, and Destutt de Tracy, and how far did they merely follow Russian tradition? On the surface in the evidence taken by the examining commission, one finds few references to Russia's past. Pestel, under examination, testified that part of his opposition to the constitution proposed by Nikita Muravyev was that "it resembled the former appanage system and could not help but be vicious."[27] But there are few passages to suggest that the revolutionaries were able to rise above the narrow circle of Russian ideas. An ancient philosopher said that the gods of the Ethiopean were black, while the Thracians gave their gods blue eyes

[27] Ibid., IV, 86.

The Decembrists

and red hair, and that if horses and cattle had gods, they would be in the form of horses and cattle.[28] In forming conceptions of ideal beings, men necessarily do so on the basis of their experience. The same principle applies to ideal societies which are conceived as something to satisfy a yearning that grows out of men's life. In the words of Omar Kháyyám: "Heaven but the vision of fulfilled desire."

It is depressing to have to record that Pestel believed it necessary to have a secret police to keep citizens from subversive activity.[29] In this belief he found many Russians to agree with him. In the eighteenth century Shcherbatov in his *Journey to the Land of Ophir* depicts his concept of an ideal state and pictures a society whose basic principles are little removed from Russia, with the exception that the government concerns itself with the welfare of all citizens; but in return all citizens are brought under strict control and subjected to the most meticulous regulations in regard to what they eat, wear, and how they employ their time, such regulations to be enforced by a numerous and powerful police.[30]

In other respects few of the Decembrists seem to have risen above the prejudices of Russian society of the time. Owing to the necessity to collaborate with the Poles, the Decembrist leaders were committed to the independence of Poland, but seem to have done so grudgingly only out of regard for the sympathy that the cause of the Poles commanded abroad and the difficulty of holding the country in subjection.[31] But Poland's claims to the so-called "con-

[28] Xenophanes (fl. ca. 530 B.C.)—"Yet if oxen and lions had hands and could paint with their hands, and fashion images, as men do, they would make pictures and images of their gods in their own likeness; horses would make them like horses; oxen like oxen . . . Ethiopians make their gods black and snub-nosed; Thracians give theirs blue eyes and red hair." Charles M. Bakewell, *Source Book in Ancient Philosophy*, 8.

[29] Kulczycki, *Geschichte der Russischen Revolution*, I, 160, and Pavel Ivanovich Pestel, *Russkaya Pravda* (ed. by P. Shchegolev), 112. See also Chap.: "Dvoryanskii publitsist Ekaterinskoi epokhi—Knyaz M. M. Shcherbatov," in V. A. Myakotin, *Iz istorii russkago obshchestva etyudi i ocherki*.

[30] Vernadskii, *Russkoe masonstvo v tsarstvovanie Ekateriny II*, 177.

[31] See the evidence of Pestel, *Vosstanie Dekabristov*, IV, 83, 117–18; see also that of Borisov, *Vosstanie Dekabristov*, V, 30–31. The intrigues of Stratford Canning, English minister in St. Petersburg, are mentioned by Pestel more than once. See *Vosstanie Dekabristov*, IV, 117–18 and IV, 289–90.

165

quered provinces" of western Russia were bitterly resented, and the rumor that Alexander was to gratify Polish wishes brought strong reaction from the leaders of the society to any such move.[32] Neither Pestel nor Zavalishin contemplated granting any of the other subject races the right to self-determination. They were to be satisfied with the status of "Russians" in the new order.[33]

On two questions the Decembrists had pronounced progressive ideas and a certain measure of agreement—the need for constitutional government and for the emancipation of the serfs. As we have seen, however, they were divided on the issue of whether the form of government should be a republic or a constitutional monarchy. But in both cases the Decembrists drew from the political theories and forms of western Europe rather than from the native. They might very well have harked back to the attempted constitutional revolution of 1730 in their own country; but few, if any, of the conspirators knew about it. They preferred to draw their models from abroad.[34]

On the question of the peasants, especially those in bondage to the landlords, the members of both societies were agreed that they must receive their freedom, although they might differ concerning the conditions under which freedom should be bestowed. On this topic Russian society had been somewhat sensitive since the days of Radishchev and Novikov. But it seems prob-

[32] *Vosstanie Dekabristov*, IV, 277. For evidence of Pestel see V, 256–60; evidence of Sergei Muravyev-Apostol: Borisov thought that none of the others could profit from independence, *Vosstanie Dekabristov*, V, 30–31.

[33] Zavalashin believed that means would be found to keep them in the empire, *Vosstanie Dekabristov*, III, 341–45. Most of the Decembrists were at one with Nicholas I who said, "Where once the Russian flag has been raised it must never be lowered." G. V. Vernadskii, *Ocherk istorii prava Russkago Gosudarstva XVIII–XIX vv*, 157.

[34] On the death of the Emperor Peter II, in 1730, on the initiative of the two powerful families, the Golitsyns and the Dolgorukiis, the crown was offered to the Duchess of Courland, Anne, a niece of Peter I, on the understanding that she govern as a constitutional monarch. Although she accepted the terms, she afterward repudiated them and resumed the traditional role of autocrat. Gilbert H. Lincoln, unpublished manuscript of dissertation submitted for master's degree at University of Oklahoma, 1951, "The Russian Constitutional Crisis of 1730," 34.

able that the Russians were influenced more by the French writers of the Enlightenment than by any of their own countrymen. What roused them against serfdom was the sense of shame they felt when they returned from a sojourn in western Europe, where many either were educated or had served in the Russian armies, to find a great part of their countrymen in bondage. They felt that they could not hold up their heads before Europe where serfdom had now vanished. But here they had the landowning class (to which they for the most part belonged) solidly against them. The native-born Russian of the upper class who had never been abroad looked on the mass of the peasants as *Chern'*, the "black people" or rabble, beings of a lower class than they who had been born to rule and exploit. Serfdom was taken for granted, and no question of moral or legal justification could arise.

While informed native Russians might be roused to indignation at serfdom's abuses or excesses, few questioned the institution. Only when it was brought into sharp contrast with the lot of the peasants in enlightened countries, through travel abroad, could this prejudice be broken down. But those who experienced this revulsion were the exception and not the rule; so the scales of justice were weighted against the peasant. The great mass of the land-owners and finally even an enlightened monarch were on the side of the existing order. The Decembrists were voices crying in the wilderness. For the moment they were half a century ahead of their time and for this they suffered. But their martyrdom was not quite in vain.

One naturally hesitates to scan with too critical an eye the motives and conduct of men who gambled their lives in a great cause. There was, of course, rank cowardice as well as self-sacrific-ing courage in the conduct of the Decembrists before and after the revolt. Many broke down in prison and cringed before and flattered the new Emperor in an effort to escape the consequences of their act. Many were lukewarm or indifferent to the cause they professed. There was treason and duplicity, and what is even worse, many turned renegade at the last. But we must admit that there was a hard core of sincerity and self-sacrifice to be found among the conspirators. The real question is, what is the verdict of history on these young madmen?

One may blame the failure of the attempted coup on the inexperience of the conspirators (which was great) or on their complete failure to give the movement a broad base by bringing in members of other than their own class. From a military point of view, the Decembrists' chief neglect was not informing the very soldiers who were to be the instruments of their policy about the nature of the cause. Even had the move been successful, however, it would have to many borne a striking resemblance to the various palace conspiracies of the eighteenth century by which most of the sovereigns were raised to the throne.[35] But even admitting that idealistic motives were lacking in these earlier revolts, one may doubt whether the end result would have been far different. Was not Pestel's mother right when she decried the futility of any violent change in government, protesting that it would be only to exchange one set of masters for another? The Russian habit of submission to constituted authority was too deeply rooted to be suddenly shaken off. Pushkin and Ryleev might both apostrophize freedom and pray for a regime of law to be substituted for that of autocratic and arbitrary power. The Great Russian people had taken the decisive turn long ago when the rights of the various classes had been sacrificed to the state in order that it might be great and expand. There had never been a Magna Carta, a Bill of Rights, or a habeas corpus. Poland, the only country in eastern Europe that had experimented with such *palladia* of freedom, had succumbed to Russia, whose might was built on absolute power. It is significant that the only previous attempt in Russia to attain constitutional government, the abortive revolution of 1730, made little appeal to even the broad masses of the nobility, who quite readily put their heads back into the yoke. The middle class, traditionally the bulwark of freedom, was despised and all but non-existent; the peasants had no conception of it, being more concerned with their more immediate problem of food and their oppressive burdens of taxes and of labor dues to landlord and state. Freedom to the Russian mind meant freedom from the things most hated and was not related to responsibilities. Nor did the

[35] This seems to have been all that Nicholas saw in the movement; and well he might, since both his father and grandfather had perished in such tragic events.

Russian have any realization that freedom must be secured by safe-guards.

The Decembrists might indulge in rhetoric about the great heroes of antiquity or might echo the sentiments of Rousseau, of Voltaire, or of Locke and discuss the social contract and natural rights; but these were abstractions that had little, if any, relation to life. Without some effective means to curb the exercise of arbitrary power or to secure the rights of the individual against the state, the dream of freedom was illusory. The revolutions of 1917 have demonstrated how ill prepared the Russian world was for any form of free government, even after the lapse of one hundred years.

Even had the Decembrists succeeded in getting rid of the Emperor and shipping the Imperial family abroad as contemplated, it is doubtful that they could have set up a free government. There is no reason to believe that the Decembrists had done much more than was done in 1730 or in 1917. Russia would have plunged into anarchy, at the end of which she would have submitted to a new tyranny imposed by some group more powerful than the others. It is quite possible that Russian society would have been purged of the drones and that corruption might have been reduced and inefficiency replaced by efficiency. The cry of most Russians would have been in 1825 as Denikin's was in 1918—that Russia must be united and great—and in the interests of greatness the Russians would have almost necessarily submitted to some strong power. The utmost that would have been attained would have been a stronger and more efficient form of despotism.

It was long the practice to refer to the revolt of 1825 as a "bourgeois" revolution. It is difficult to see how that term can be applied to it with any accuracy when we know that none of the so-called bourgeois elements of society were allowed to participate in it. It was chained to the nobility; and, in addition, practically every member of the society either was or had been an officer in the army. As we see from Pestel's evidence before the commission, it was intended definitely to be a military revolt, copied after the military risings in Naples and Portugal. The army was to bring on the revolt, to take charge of affairs, to call a Constituent Assembly, and to take steps looking toward the formation of a permanent government. This was to be achieved by forcing the

169

Senate to issue the necessary manifesto which had been prepared in advance by Trubetskoi.[36]

Certain vital reforms were to be introduced in this hurried fashion, apparently without leaving it to the discretion of the Constituent Assembly. It may not have seemed incongruous to the revolutionaries to have made the attempt to bring freedom to the country in this forcible way, but the average western European would find that it does violence to common sense. But recent history in Russia would indicate that there is nothing incongruous to the Russian mind to have freedom brought on the point of a bayonet. Perhaps the revolutionist does not trouble to be consistent.

How does the present generation of Russian revolutionaries regard their revolutionary forebears? In 1925 the Soviet authorities arranged the celebration of the centenary of the Decembrist rising and proceeded to publish all the documents connected with the investigation and the trial. No doubt in the speeches and publications of the time every care was taken to ensure that young Communists would be given the "correct" view of this earlier manifestation of the revolutionary spirit. Nevertheless, the Communists did hasten to pay tribute to the Decembrists. Lenin's own words quoted in the introduction to the *Vosstanie Dekabristov* are worth repeating:

We see clearly that three generations, three classes, have contributed to the Russian revolution. At the beginning, there were the nobles and the landowners, the Decembrists and Herzen. The circle of these revolutionaries was narrow. Far removed were they from the people. But their work was not lost; it was the Decembrists who inspired Herzen, it was Herzen who spread the revolutionary agitation.[37]

[36] M. V. Dovnar-Zapol'skii, *Memuary Dekabristov*, 94–95. Project of a manifesto found among the papers of Trubetskoi. See also *Vosstanie Dekabristov*, I, 108–32.

[37] V. I. Lenin, *Sobranie Sochinenii*, T XII, Chap. 1: "Pamyati Gertsena."

The Press under Nicholas

❧❧❧❧❧❧❧❧❧❧❧❧❧❧❧❧❧❧❧❧❧

"OUTER slavery and inner freedom" is the way Herzen describes the reign of Nicholas I.[1] Actually Herzen's characterization applies only to the first part of that reign—from 1825 to 1848. Even that "inner freedom" was greatly abridged after the February Revolution in Paris, and Herzen himself compared the writers of the period from 1848 to 1855 to the character in Mozart's *Magic Flute* who was forced to sing with a padlock on his lips.[2] Byelinskii, fortunately, died in 1848. The same year, Herzen, losing all hope in the chances for freedom of the press at home, went abroad never to return.

Yet in spite of the gloom and despair in which his reign closed, the time of Nicholas I was one of the most remarkable in the history of Russian thought. It could perhaps be said that the minds of Russians began to attain something like maturity and to move freely in the intellectual atmosphere of western Europe. But the age had a greater significance than a quickening of the Russian spirit. It was a sharp turning point in Russia's history in at least two ways.

In the first place educated Russians turned away from the literature of the French Enlightenment, primarily materialistic, and became absorbed in the new German idealistic philosophy. After all, the Decembrists had been men of the eighteenth century in which they had, intellectually, been cradled; and it was in the spirit of that century that the Decembrists addressed themselves to the task of inaugurating a constitutional regime for Russia. The

[1] M. O. Gershenzon, (ed.), "Epokha Nikolaya I," in *Russkaya Byl*, VII, title page.
[2] M. Lemke, *Ocherki po istorii russkoi tsenzury i zhurnalistiki XIX stolyetiya*, 185.

tepid enthusiasm that this ideal evoked in the great masses of Russians and even among educated classes brought complete disillusionment. Even the intellectually alert sank back into torpor until the new German ideas kindled them once more into life. In another way the reign of Nicholas saw a break with the past. "The year 1826," says Skabichevskii, "is important in our development especially from the fact that this was the year of the shift of the center of our intellectual ferment." As the writer goes on to remark, ever since Catherine's time the intellectual movement had been concentrated in the higher circles of society. But with Nicholas everything changed. The upper ranks of society lost interest in literature and art. The former cultural dominance of this class passed to another.[3]

What was this other class to which precedence in thought passed? If we go back to the Decembrist movement, we are struck by its exclusively aristocratic character. Not only were the leading figures drawn from the upper class of the nobility, but also there was scarcely one of the roster of those arrested who did not come from one or other of the categories of the landowning class. Moreover, as we have seen, there was a violent prejudice against associating other classes with them in the great venture.[4] But after 1825 there appear among the intellectual elite, persons described either as *kuptsy* (merchants) or *myeshchane* (townsmen or petty bourgeois), as well as the sons of priests. Such was Polevoi, editor of the *Telegraf* (suppressed in 1834), not a few of whose difficulties were due to his bourgeois origin and the prejudice of the aristocratic bureaucracy against him. But there must have been dozens of less exalted station. The movement of the center of gravity from one class to another may be in part explained by the demoralization caused in aristocratic ranks by the collapse of the Decembrist rising and the consequent evaporation of their fine idealism. In the words of one writer:

The majority of our so-called fashionable society of that time

[3] A. M. Skabichevskii, "Ocherki umstvennago razvitiya nashego obshchestva 1825–1860 g." in *Obshchestvennye Zapiski*, T. 192, (1870), 294 ff.

[4] See remark of Baron Steingel to Ryleyev when the latter proposed to enlist persons of the merchant class in Chap. II above, cited from *Vosstanie Dekabristov*, I, 179.

were distinguished by their utter frivolity and the absence of all culture, their constant chattering in French, their successful mastery of the external forms of European dandyism, and the reading of the novels of Pol de Coque, which it was impossible to call education. The only exceptions were few; to them belonged Count Mikhail Yurievich Bielgorskii—a man of fine aristocratic character and at the same time unusually well read for a man of the world. The others did not and could not take the least part in the growth of a national literature nor of any human interest and knew of the existence of Russian literature only through Pushkin and others who belonged to his circle. They assumed that all Russian literature consisted of Zhukovskii, Krylov (whose fables they had read in childhood), Pushkin, Knyaz Odoyevskii, Knyaz Vyazemskii, and Count Sollogub, who was then reading his *Serezha* to his fashionable friends, since it was still unpublished. To achieve literary fame in the great world, it was necessary to frequent the *salon* of Madame Karamzin, the widow of the historiographer. This was *the* salon of the great world, *par excellence.*

At a time when the morals of the fashionable society took such a turn for the worse the masses of nonserving landlords, of bureaucrats, and all kinds of substantial and prosperous *raznochintsy* were quite a fruitful seedbed for intellectual development. This group took a fresh and lively interest in Russian literature of the preceding age and was fascinated by the works of Pushkin.[5]

It is not our purpose to explore further here this problem of the respective roles played in the intellectual history of the nineteenth century by various classes, but rather to notice the broad trends of the years from 1825 to 1855.

With the age of Nicholas the universities and journalism became in Russia the chief organs for the development of thought, and it is easy to understand why. Travel abroad and the ordering of foreign books, particularly in the field of philosophy and social studies (upon which the government had begun to look as the

[5] Panayev, *Literatur'nye Vospominaniya*, cited by Skabichevskii, "Ocherki umstvennago razvitiya obshchestva," in *Otechestvennye Zapiski*, T. 192 (1870), 306.

source of all revolutionary movements), became extremely difficult.[6]

Of all literature that appeared during these years the periodical and daily press by all odds quite overshadowed other publications. At the stage Russia had reached there was scant interest in serious and extended works in the fields of history, philosophy, and general literature. Perhaps there were few persons to meet even this modest need. But with the restrictions imposed by censorship, *belles-lettres* was from the first a fairly safe field, and enough native literature had already appeared to foster a taste for writing and literary criticism—immature though both might be.

Some of the periodicals that met the need were simply continuations of periodicals founded under Alexander. Such was *Vyestnik Evropy*, began in 1802 by Karamzin and continued by Kachenovskii and Zhukovskii. This periodical was considered the organ of the classicists and retained its conservative character, although under Kachenovskii it developed a skeptical attitude in the field of historiography. In 1828 there began to appear in *Vyestnik Evropy* a series of articles by Nadezhdin under the pseudonym of Nadoumko. These articles were written in a severely critical spirit toward both classicism and romanticism in Russian literature. The author claimed that romanticism and classicism were the wrong track for Russian writers and that both were alien to the spirit of Russian life.[7]

Another journal was *Syn Otechestva*, founded in 1812 by Grech and continued by Grech with the assistance of Bulgarin, whose chief interest was in foreign affairs and whose spirit was narrowly patriotic. *Otechestvennye Zapiski* (founded in 1820) was a rather conservative, colorless periodical until 1838, when it acquired a reputation for dangerous liberalism under the editorship of A. A. Krayevskii. *Russkii Vyestnik*, founded by N. Glinka in 1808, followed this same trend.

After the accession of Nicholas there came into existence a

[6] Skabichevskii, "Ocherki umstvennago razvitiya nashego obshchestva," *Otechestvennye Zapiski*, T. 192 (1870), 309.

[7] Although Nadezhdin did not work these ideas out and although there was some inconsistency in them, they are a highly interesting anticipation of the new later realism (or naturalism) that was shortly to appear in Russian literature.

number of new periodicals, at first of distinct literary flavor. In 1828 Polevoi received permission to begin the publication of his literary journal, *Telegraf*. It immediately achieved a surprising success, within a short time having 2,000 subscribers. Polevoi was an ardent defender of the new school of Russian writers. Writing in 1846 at the time of Polevoi's death, Byelinskii said:

The *Moscow Telegraf* was an unprecedented phenomenon in every way. A man almost unknown in the field of literature, by origin a merchant, undertook the editing of a periodical, and his periodical, almost from the first number, struck all with its liveliness, its freshness, its novelty, its diversity, its taste, its fine style: finally the fidelity of every line to the policy adopted once and for all and emphasized with great force. Such a journal could not fail to be noticed even among a crowd of good journals, but amid the moribund, colorless, mediocre journalism of that time, it was a striking phenomenon. . . . The first idea which he began to develop with energy and talent, which continually inspired him, was the necessity of intellectual development, of following up contemporary achievements, to progress, to go forward, to avoid decay and stagnation as the chief occasion of the decline of Enlightenment, education, and literature. This idea at the time was a distinct novelty.[8]

Yet Polevoi's success was not of long duration. In 1834 the magazine was suppressed and his condition became tragic. He had a large family to support on his earnings and was forced to assume the editorship of various periodicals whose policies were at variance with those of *Telegraf*. He was associated with Bulgarin, Grech, and Senkovskii. He allowed Senkovskii to edit his articles for *Syn Otechestva*, and when finally he became editor of that organ his humiliation was complete. Polevoi finally died in poverty on February 26, 1846.

Among other ventures of the time were *Moskovskii Vyestnik* (1827–30), promoted by Venevitinov but under the editorship of M. Pogodin. Venevitinov died in 1827 and Pogodin became sole editor. *Everopeyets* (founded in 1831) was edited by I. Kireyevskii.

[8] Skabichevskii, *Ocherki umstvennago razvitiya nashego obshchestva Otechestvennye Zapiski*, T. 192 (1870), 304.

Important contributors to this journal were Yazykov, Baratynskii, A. Khomyakov, Zhukovskii, Vyazemskii, and A. I. Turgenev. In the second issue of *Evropeits*, Kireyevskii published an article on "The Nineteenth Century" which led to the journal's immediate suppression. The *Teleskop*, a purely literary venture, did not publish political articles, but nevertheless came under suspicion of the government because of the distinctly progressive (liberal) attitude it displayed. It finally was suppressed in 1836, as we have seen, for the publication (although with the censor's approval) of Chaadayev's *Philosophical Letter*. Perhaps even better known than these journals was *Biblioteka dlya Chteniya*, an organ with almost a universal appeal, founded by Professor O. Senkovskii of the University of St. Petersburg in 1834, which managed to last for three decades. One innovation this journal introduced was the publication of articles on economics. It was ardently free trader and eventually became one of the most active advocates of railway building. *Biblioteka dlya Chteniya* nevertheless became known as conservative, if not reactionary. A very influential journal was *Moskvityanin* (1841–56), which was widely patronized by the Slavophiles, although not controlled by them. *Otechestvennye Zapiski* continued to have a distinguished career and acquired many notable contributors. In the forties it became the organ of Utopian socialism advocated by the *Zapadniki* or Westerners. In 1836 Pushkin founded *Sovremennik* (*Contemporary*) as a literary journal. In 1846 this magazine was taken over by Nekrasov and I. I. Panayev and at once began to bid for some of the rising young writers— Byelinskii, Herzen, and others. Along with *Otechestvennye Zapiski*, *Sovremennik* quickly came under suspicion for its advanced views; but under the Buturlin committee it, like other periodicals, had to temper its radicalism.[9]

A curious interlude in the history of journalism was the story of *Moskovskii Nablyuditel'* (*The Moscow Observer*). This magazine had originally been founded by Stepanov and had been conducted under Shevyrev, with Adrosov as assistant. In 1838 Shevyrev resigned as editor, and control of the journal was turned over to Byelinskii and his friends.[10] At this stage of his life Byelinskii

[9] For the Buturlin committee see Chap. VII above. Both journals had to make wide use at this time of Aesopian language.

had just returned from the Caucasus and had formed a friendship with Bakunin, with whom he lived. Bakunin introduced him to the philosophy of Hegel, and together Bakunin and Byelinskii proceeded to found a paper devoted to literary criticism. Under the influence of Hegel, Byelinskii accepted the view that the great poet had to be objective and that subjectivity on the part of a poet made him second-rate. Let us hear what Byelinskii has to say on his state of mind at the time.[11] Following is a letter from him addressed to Bakunin:

> I formed a friendship with you; you initiated me into the Fichtean view of life, and I seized hold of it with energy, with fanaticism; but was it the same for me as it was for you? For you it was passing over from Kant, a natural and logical transition; but I, I wanted to write a short article, a review of Drozdov, and with this in view to lay in a stock of ideas. I wanted my article to be good—and this is its history. On returning from the Caucasus I was in a mood of transition—my spirit was weary of abstractions and I yearned for contact with reality. Katkov, as far as he could, slaked my thirst with Hegel, but at that point I needed you, and you again became my proclaimer of truth. This was my second course. It was poor in results—it was just the seed. My third course—you remember the evening at Botkins'. My whole being was shaken to its foundations. For the first time the light of happiness, of content, shone on me through the darkness of deception; for the first time, through happiness, I recognized much truth. A new era had dawned for me. I wept at midnight.

A year later Byelinskii repeats this:

> I travel from the Caucasus to Moscow, Bakunin meets me— we live together. During the summer he perused the philosophy of religion and of law by Hegel. A new world was opened to us; might is right and right is might:—no, I cannot tell you with what sensations I heard these words; this justice of conquerors— I understood that there is no material force, not one bayonet of

[10] Skabichevskii, "Ocherki umstvennago razvitiya nashego obshchestva," *Otechestvennye Zapiski*, T. 194 (1871), 337.

[11] These citations are from Byelinskii's correspondence as cited by D. I. Chizhevskii in *Gegel' v Rossii*, 118–19.

empire or sword; there is no caprice, no chance—and my onerous guardianship of the human race was at an end, and the significance of my country appeared in a new light. In the presence of this, Katkov continued to act as transmitter, insofar as he could; and I, as far as possible, got some results from *Esthetics*. My God! What a bright, new, infinite world! The word "reality" became for me the equivalent of "God."

In another letter he wrote: "I sacrificed little for this thought, or rather I sacrificed only one thing. I had to be prepared to strip myself of all subjective feelings for it . . . by life, at the cost of tears, and much travail of mind, I mastered this idea and it sank deep into my soul."

These ideas did not find favor with the public, and after the publication of five numbers, in 1839 *Moskovskii Nablyuditel'* had to suspend publication. *Biblioteka dlya Chteniya*, meanwhile, had met the competition from Byelinskii's journal with Dickens and Thackeray, translations of Sand, Balzac, and Hugo, and the latest news in science. Byelinskii finally recognized the futility of the struggle and the narrow esoteric character of his message. He got into debt, went to work in a shop, and lived a life of privation. He finally decided to leave Moscow.

One writer says about this incident:

Could society agree with the critic who started to proclaim to it that however base reality was it still was reasonable, because it was a manifestation of eternal reason, and that, therefore, we ought to be reconciled with actuality, whatever it be, and every expression of dissatisfaction with life or desire to improve it—is the conscious yearning to contribute our tiny share to the development of the universal, absolute idea, that, therefore, every suffering or discontented poet does not sing of, we are bound to agree with him that Pushkin only then reached his highest poetic maturity when he renounced lyrical subjectivity, that Gogol does not please us because he brings the whole sordidness of life to a general mockery of all life, but because he is artistically objective and reconciles us with the disagreeable side of life, bringing them to the pearl of creation.[12]

In addition to periodicals, public opinion was served by publications classed as newspapers, although they would scarcely rate with modern newspapers. Many of these papers were subsidized by the government or were closely connected with it; such was the *Peterburgskiye Vyedomosti,* previously mentioned in connection with the eighteenth century.[13] *Moskovskie Vyedomosti,* which had been published originally from 1756 by the University of Moscow, became the organ of the cultural revival under Novikov. Then in 1806 this paper was taken over by the government and after many vicissitudes came into the hands of Katkov (1863), when it lost its official character. A publication of the Ministry of the Interior, *Syevernaya Pochta* (1809–19; 1862–68), gave news of commercial interest. *Sankt Peterburgskie kommercheskie Vyedmosti (The St. Petersburg Commercial News)* (1802–10), subsidized by the government,' also retailed news of the business world. A more important publication was *Russkii Invalid,* a daily, organized originally by private interests, but ultimately taken over by the Ministry of War. Much of this paper's material on international and military affairs was drawn from the foreign press. Although care was exercised to see that such material was trustworthy, at least on one occasion in 1848, the paper drew fire from the censors.[14] Eventually it took on a purely official character, publishing only news from official and military sources. Beginning in 1837 various provinces began the publication of *Guberninskiye Vyedomosti.* These papers contained for the most part official and unofficial news—the unofficial portion consisting of heterogeneous matter on history and geography. The various *Guberninskiye Vyedomosti (Provincial News)* were exceedingly valuable for news from the provinces. *Syevernaya Pchela,* owned by Grech and Bulgarin, both of whom were known for their conservatism, was highly regarded at court, where it was thought to reflect public opinion.

Besides the foregoing publications, there were a number of official publications which enjoyed a wide circulation. Among

[12] Skabichevskii, "Ocherki po istorii umstvennago razvitiya nashego obshchestva," *Otechestvennye Zapiski,* T. 194 (1871), 352–64.

[13] For the beginning of the *Peterburgskie Vyedomosti* in 1728 see Chap. VI above. The founding of the *Moskovskie Vyedomosti* by Novikov is recounted in the same chapter.

[14] See Lemke, *Ocherki po istorii russkoi tsenzury i zhurnalistiki XIX stolyetiya,* 210.

them was *Zhurnal Manufaktury i torgovli* (*Journal of Industry and Trade*), which was devoted to business and industry. Another such paper was the *Gornyi Zhurnal* (*Mining Journal*), part of which was devoted to mining, metallurgy, geology, forestry, and other technical subjects, but part of which contained articles on general economic problems. Another valuable publication was *Trudy Imperatorskago Vol'nago Ekonomicheskago Obshchestva* (*Works of the Free Economic Society*), which had originated in 1765 and continued publication until 1917.[15] It published material on agriculture and especially serfdom, but became more and more devoted to general economic problems and economic statistics from the provinces. This general interest ultimately became dominant. In 1841 the newly formed Ministry of Imperial Domains (established in 1839) began the publication of *Zhurnal Ministerstva gosudarstvennykh imushchestv* (*Journal of the Ministry of Imperial Domains*), which, while official, opened its columns to specialists in the field of agriculture other than those employed by the government.[16] Not to be ignored in summarizing the organs that influenced and reflected public opinion are the publications of the so-called illegal press—periodicals published abroad and smuggled into the country. Such was *Kolokol*, Herzen's famous underground organ published in London.

In addition to the periodicals mentioned above, *Dennitsa* should be included in a list of suppressed publications. Altogether four periodicals were suspended between 1831 and 1836. These harsh acts determined the tone of the Russian press for the latter part of the thirties.

The only publications that prospered during this period were such newspapers as *Syevernaya Pchela* (published by Bulgarin and Grech) and the periodical *Syn otechestva*, the former a very unsavory political publication first permitted by Admiral Shishkov, whose editors circulated everywhere in government circles, enjoying the confidence of high officials which they shamelessly ex-

[15] For the founding of the Free Economic Society see A. I. Kodnev, *Istoriya Imperatorskago Vol'nago Ekonomicheskago Obshchestva s 1765–1865 goda*. Successive occasions on which it intervened in the peasant question (1765 and 1812) are recounted in Semevskii, *Krest' yanskii Vopros v XVIII pervoi polovinye XIX vyeka*, intro. xvii, and I, 46.

[16] S. A. Nikitin, *Istochnikovedenie Istorii S.S.S.R.*, 168–70.

P. I. Pestel'

A. S. Shishkov

N. M. Karamzin

A. S. Pushkin

ploited for their own purposes and for the confusion of their enemies and rivals. One writer compares the journalism of the thirties to a dark and stinking morass. It was an age of disillusionment and emptiness when no vision was vouchsafed. But a regeneration was at hand.[17]

The intellectual trends of the forties which were reflected in the periodical literature were influenced by two factors: the shift in the intellectual center of gravity of that society and the assimilation of a new philosophy. As one writer says:

There was a perceptible change in the class make-up of the thoughtful part of society. In the twenties and thirties the thinking and cultured people belonged to fashionable circles and the strata of persons that attached themselves to them, with some sprinkling of those drawn from other classes. In the forties the center of the intellectual life shifted to the "middle class" of the rich, well-to-do, and poor nobility, with a somewhat larger admixture of persons drawn from the "lower" classes. The general spiritual character of these persons was not the same as we find among representatives of the thoughtful part of the fashionable world. The hereditary traits of the gentry, the mentality of the squire, gentle breeding, and an aristocratic attitude toward things and persons was maintained and frequently revealed in one way or another; but they already had to some extent been toned down by association with the *raznochintsy*, the influence of philosophical training, the breadth and diversity of intellectual influences, and finally the leveling influences of student life. These noblemen's sons no longer passed from the university into military service; rarely and only by chance did they appear in the fashionable world and in official circles, living aloof, in small circles of friends where intellectual and moral influences predominated over all others.[18]

It is noticeable that this group was made up in the forties of

[17] For *Severnaya Pchela* see Skabichevskii, "Ocherki po istorii umstvennago razvitiya nashego obshchestva," *Otechestvennye Zapiski*, T. 193 (1870), 61–62; also see Nikitin, *Istochnikovedenie istorii S.S.S.R.*, 178–79. This paper in the last years of Nicholas cast aside all restraints in its extravagant praise of everything Russian and constantly lauded government policy.

[18] Ovsianiko-Kulikovskii, *Istoriya russkoi intelligentsia*, VII, Pt. I, III.

men who had been students in the thirties—Stankevich, Byelinskii, Konstantin Aksakov, G. Katkov, Klyushnikov, Nekrasov, and others—all drawn from the nontitled, nonserving nobility.[19]

Byelinskii's comments on this subject, made in 1845, are worth citing: "Our literature laid the basis for the internal *rapprochement* of the orders, educated a kind of public opinion, and produced something in the way of a special class in society which is distinguished from the ordinary middle class by the fact that it consists not only of merchants and tradesmen but persons of all ranks drawn together by education, which with us is consecrated to love of literature."[20]

The new constitution of the intelligentsia, which came in the middle of the nineteenth century, is a favorite theme of Plekhanov, who developed it at great length in his basic work *Istoriya russkoi obshchestvennoi mysli*. He stressed the fact that what constituted the middle class in Russia did not correspond to the *tiers état* in France and that, while there was a sprinkling of persons ordinarily supposed to make up the middle class, merchants and tradesmen, there was a large admixture of *raznochintsy* drawn from all strata. This lack of a true middle class gave a unique character to the history of Russian thought in the nineteenth century.[21]

The intellectual trends of the time are admirably mirrored in the mental development of Byelinskii. Born in 1811, he came to maturity in the period of reaction that followed the Decembrist rising of 1825. An unhappy home life and an unfinished university education gave him a poor start in life. He emerged from obscurity to become a contributor to *Teleskop*, whose suppression in 1836 ended this period of his activity. At this time Byelinskii's ideas were negative. He took an attitude hostile to the thought and life of eighteenth-century France, maintaining "that one ought to explain facts by ideas and not to deduce ideas from facts, and that in the eighteenth century, experiment led to nothing else but skepticism, materialism, infidelity, corruption, and complete blindness to truth in broad fields of knowledge."[22]

The specific influence at this time was unquestionably not the

[19] Skabichevskii, "Ocherki po istorii umstvennago razvitiya nashego obshchestva, 1825–1860," *Otechestvennye Zapiski*, T. 194 (1871), 99.

[20] Byelinskii, *Sochineniya*, IV, 284–85.

philosophy of Kant or Fichte, which made little appeal to Russians, but that of Schelling which had been introduced in the twenties and popularized by such persons as the Moscow professor M. G. Pavlov and V. F. Odoyevskii. According to one writer:

> In the low state of philosophical development, our society was still full of that empiricism for which an existence of things apart from ourselves seemed an unchallengeable axiom, instilled by simple external feelings, which believes without admitting the slightest chance of doubt that things in themselves are as they appear to us. In the meantime, the philosophy of Schelling more than any other corresponded to the concepts of thoughtful persons in the twenties and thirties. Based on the identity of soul and matter, recognizing that every existing thing is nothing else than the visible body of the unseen, deathless reason embodying in actual finite forms its infinite ideas, that philosophy took a great stride forward, by its pantheism freeing thought from the capricious, personal creation from the side, and, at the same time, completely satisfying persons accustomed to dualism and unable to renounce it, it reconciled philosophy with those traditions before which they continued to be a workshop. . . . At that time quite in harmony with the apotheosis of feeling and fancy in which the romantic movement found expression with us, the philosophy of Schelling, counting weak and fruitless the experimental method for determining the essences of every existing thing, placed above all else, intuition, something in the nature of Neo-Platonic ecstasy, an inner, immediate feeling by the help of which man would attain the absolute, infinite idea in relative forms of being; one of the products of such feeling, the philosophy of Schelling, considered poetic creation in which man himself becomes as it were an immortal soul, embodying his infinite ideas in forms of art identical with them . . . it was hard to think of any other philosophy which would have corresponded to their mental development and concepts.[23]

[21] G. Plekhanov, *Istoriya russkoi obshchestvennoi mysli*, I, 303.

[22] Skabichevskii, "Ocherki umstvennago razvitiya nashego obshchestva, 1825–1860," *Otechestvennye Zapiski*, T. 193, (1870), 2–4.

[23] Skabichevskii, "Ocherki umstvennago razvitiya nashego obshchestva, 1825–1860," *Otechestvennye Zapiski*, T. 193 (1870), 19.

The full significance of this philosophy for Russia raised tremendous problems for the writer.

The philosophy of Schelling first compelled the whole of our intellectual society to ponder on the fate of Russia among the other races of mankind. By presenting everything that exists as the form of this or that idea of absolute reason, the philosophy of Schelling subsumed under this formula the role of individual peoples in the course of human civilization. Each race is the embodiment of a particular idea which it works out in its life. . . . According to such a conception, every Schellingist could not help being forcibly struck by the utter irreconciliability with that idea of the whole development of our society from the time of Peter I. . . . There was no lack of all possible answers to them. . . . There appeared in literature so extreme an opinion as assigned the backwardness, ignorance of Russia, and her failure to take part in general civilization to the fact that Russia was not a member of that religio-moral union, represented by the Roman Catholic Church.[24]

These ideas were transmitted to Byelinskii by Stankevich in the thirties after Stankevich had attended a course on Schelling at the university and marked the period of his first activity, which came to an end in 1836. By 1838, however, both Stankevich and Byelinskii had gone over to Hegelianism and had adopted what one writer characterizes as "reconciliation with reality."[25] This was the period of Byelinskii's association with Bakunin and his contributions to *Moskovskii Nablyuditel'*, which ended in 1839. By 1843 Byelinskii had identified himself with left-wing Hegelianism. In this phase of his life he had become strongly influenced by French Utopian socialism. His associates were now Herzen and Granovskii.[26] Thus began Byelinskii's creative period, destined to be of short duration. The group mentioned above came to be known as *Zapadniki* (Westerners) and used *Otechestvennye Zapiski* as their mouthpiece. Byelinskii also became a contributor to *Sovremmenik*, which was now in the hands of Nekrasov and Panayev.

[24] *Ibid.*, 19 ff.

[25] Ovsianiko-Kulikovskii, *Istoriya russkoi intelligentsii*, VII, Pt. 1, 50.

[26] Skabichevskii, "Ocherki umstvennago razvitiya nashego obshchestva, 1825–1860," *Otechestvennye Zapiski*, T. 198 (1871), 460.

But changes were at hand. Herzen went abroad in 1847, and Byelinskii died in 1848. In 1848 came the February revolution in Paris. In April the Buturlin committee was named and inaugurated its harsh regime. A gray tone crept into journalism as it was forced into its new strait jacket. In 1849 came the arrest and trial of the Petrashevskii circle for the spread of Fourierist ideas.

Surveying developments in the field of journalism in the last years of Nicholas, the historian Lemke says:

In 1847 the Ministry of Public Instruction had under it fifty-five publications which could be regarded sometimes with some straining of the term as of more or less general interest, or, if they were specialized, published at least by private persons and societies. In 1848 only one private publication of general interest was added. This was *Severnoe Obozryenie*, and we thus went over into 1849 with fifty-six organs. This number remained constant for 1850, but to replace two that suspended publication, two new ones were established—*Arkhiv Istoriko-yuridich-eskikh svyedenii, otnosyashchikhsya do Rossii (Archive of historical-juristic news dealing with Russia)* of Kalachov, and *Zhurnal dlya Dyevits (Journal for young women)* and *Luchi (Beams)*. In 1851 came the publication of *Russkii Khudozhest-vennyi Listok (Russian leaf of Artists)*, in 1852 *Repertuar russ-koi Stseny (Repertoire of the Russian Stage)*; in 1853 and 1854 not one publication of more or less general interest was added. In general the number of political, social, and literary publications in the period 1848–55 oscillated between twenty and fifteen.[27]

Speaking of this period, the same author says:

This period is almost the darkest and the most oppressive period in the whole history of Russian journalism. Aside from the ordinary official and very severe censorship at that time, there hovered over the printed word still another censorship, secret and unofficial, in the hands of institutions endowed with the broadest powers and hampered in their operations in no way by the law. Such were the committee of April 2, 1848, famous

[27] Lemke, *Ocherki po istorii russkoi tsenzury i Zhurnalistiki*, 302.

in the history of our press, and its predecessor, the provisional unofficial committee of 1848 under the chairmanship of the Minister of Marine, Menshikov.[28]

But there came the twenty-seventh of August, 1855: the day of the fall of Sevastopol. The first and almost universal feeling was: "What a catastrophe for Russia. Poor humanity!" Nevertheless, this very event let in a flood of unprecedented intellectual and political currents.

[28] *Ibid.*, 185.

X

Historiography

PERHAPS the key to the understanding of the national mind of any people is furnished by the views which they hold of their history and of their place in the world. There can be little doubt that throughout its history, at least since the fifteenth century—perhaps earlier—the people of the Muscovite state and its heir—modern Russia—have entertained few doubts, at least as far as is revealed in their historical literature, of their world destiny. The causes of their confidence in Russia's world role are to be sought far back in the circumstances under which the grand principality first rose to pre-eminence among the other Russian states and seized the role of guardian and protector of the interests of "the whole of Russia" and of the national Orthodox church. The expansion of this task to include the whole Slavic world, which took place in the nineteenth century, and all the orthodox Christianity or even Marxist ideology as we have seen in our times, formed no great break with tradition. Indeed, it is surprising how easily the transition from an all-Russia to an all-Slav to an all-Orthodox and finally to a crusade against the whole West has been made. Part of the explanation is to be found in the facility with which competing ideas, owing to Russian isolation, could be excluded or repressed. In this the Soviet Union has fallen heir to a long and tenacious tradition.

Early Russ of the Dnieper Valley cannot be said to have had a history of its own; rather, perhaps, it had many histories. Literacy and some knowledge of Greek culture came in with Christianity, and within a hundred years monks were setting about, with the help of Greek models, recording events of their own day or the traditions that had been handed down. These accounts were

187

sometimes uncouth and rude, frequently uncritical, but they had a certain rough dignity and vigor of their own. The original chronicle of Kiev was begun in the tenth century and was continued by other hands in the eleventh and twelfth centuries. Moreover, it circulated widely; and when other monasteries or other cities wished to write a chronicle of their own, they simply built on the original. The result was a slightly bewildering array of differing versions. Sometimes the same events were recounted variously. The emphasis and the general effect of each individual chronicle might vary. Some were written to glorify this or that princely house. Still, in general, these early chronicles compare favorably with the chronicles of western Europe. In contrast with the latter they remain for the most part anonymous. They do, however, provide us with our main source of early Russian history.

With the Mongol period came a decline. The early principalities were divided and redivided. Civilization moved north or northwest or northeast, and Kiev became almost desolate. Gradually, partly with the support of the Khan of the Golden Horde and partly through their own efforts, the princes of Moscow raised themselves into a leading position in northern Russia; and by the end of the fourteenth century, with the annexation of Novgorod, their last rival, and with the emancipation from the yoke of the Golden Horde, the princes of Moscow were recognized as dominant in northern Russia.

The Muscovite princes now found a series of developments that played into their hands, and they took shrewd advantage of them. Having ravished and robbed other princes, having secured aggrandizement by duplicity and treachery as well as by naked force or by flattering the Khan of the Golden Horde, they now stood forth as the "princes of all Russia" and as "the gatherers of the Russian lands." These titles, which they assumed, show an astounding flair for the skillful manipulation of public opinion that drew the veil over their earlier rascality and surrounded them with a halo of national heroes which they hardly merited.[1]

When the Orthodox patriarch of Constantinople, in order to save the Byzantine Empire and his church from the Turks, was

[1] This wholesale distortion of early Muscovite history is elaborated in Milyukov's *Glavnye Techeniya russkoi istoricheskoi mysli*, Chap. I.

a party to the Union of Florence in 1439, which brought the Eastern church into submission to the papacy, the Russian grand prince and his people repudiated this move and drove the Metropolitan Isidore, who had acquiesced in it, from Moscow. The Muscovite prince and the Russian church assumed the position that Constantinople and her patriarch had shamefully betrayed the true church and henceforth could no longer command their allegiance. When in the absence of help from the West, Constantinople fell to the Turks in 1453 and the patriarch came under Turkish control, the Russians regarded the events as a righteous judgment; and their monarch put forward the claim that Moscow had now succeeded to the place of the old city on the Golden Horn, had become the Third Rome, and was entitled to the position of head of the ecumenical church.

A brief treatise of the great Duke of Moscovia, his genealogie, being taken out of the Muscovites' manuscript Chronicle written by Polacke. . . . Likewise the great duke of Moscovia, to make himselfe and his successours seeme the more sovereigne, deriveth the beginnings of his parentage from the Romane Emperours, yea even from Augustus Caesar. Albeit therefore no man is so fonde as to accept of this report for trueth. Yet will wee briefly set downe what the Moscovites have written in their Chronicles touching this matter.

Augustus (beleeve it who listeth) had certaine brethern or kinsfolkes which were appoynted governours over divers provinces. Among the rest, one Prussus (of whome Prussia was named) had his place of government assigned unto him upon the shore of the Eastern or Baltick Sea and upon the famous river of Wixel. This man's graundchildren or nephewes of the fourth generation were Rurek, Sinaus, and Truvar, who likewise inhabited the very same places.[2]

This interpretation of early Russian history, which the first English seafarers who reached Moscow encountered, was admirably calculated for the purpose "to make himself [the Duke of

[2] Richard Hakluyt, *The Principall Navigations, Voyages, Traffiques and Discovieries of the English Nation. . . .* The citation is taken from a reprint of the 2nd ed., 12 vols. (Glasgow, 1903–1905), II, 182–83. The ultimate source of this version is Macieia Stryikowskiego, *Kronika Polska.*

Moscow] and his successours seeme the more sovereigne." This story was enshrined with some embellishments in the version of Russian history known as the *Synopsis,* which first appeared in 1674 and quickly became the favorite textbook in Russian history for nearly 150 years. History also became the happy hunting ground of those in need of a noble genealogy in an age when genealogy was of supreme importance.[3]

But contacts with western Europe were already casting doubts on the authenticity of this version. Many noble houses already had fairly extensive libraries, and numbers of the boyars had traveled abroad in state service. Moreover, Western learning had already begun to trickle in through Kiev, and with it came the new history of the age of rationalism. The old history could not long stand up against the assaults of the new critical spirit.

With Peter a new age dawned, and it is not surprising to learn that Peter soon acquired a supreme contempt for the older hodge-podge of legend and tradition that passed in Russia for history.

We have spoken of the reckless perversion of history by the Russian princes of the fifteenth century. But history was already being perverted by other hands. The earlier chronicles had for the most part been local, and with the "gathering of the Russian lands" the need arose of consolidating the chronicles to correspond with the consolidation of the smaller principalities. Moreover, a new version of history was needed to emphasize the new position of Moscow among the Russian principalities. This need seems to have been provided by the Poles, who drew not only on the old Russian chronicles but on medieval legend as well. The new history that emerged was scarcely recognizable. Herberstein, who visited Moscow early in the sixteenth century as plenipotentiary of the Empire (he later served as an ambassador of Charles V), made inquiry regarding the early history of Russia. The reply he received indicates the new trend in historiography.

About the Varangians, however, I could learn nothing sure. But since they were wont to call the Baltic and the sea which

[3] Down to the end of the seventeenth century, rank in the government service was largely determined by family birth. This practice somewhat explains the craze for tracing ancestry back and, where possible, producing old and distinguished forebears. Hence the *Barkhatnaya Kniga* of the time of Sophia Tsarevna.

divides Prussia, Livonia, and a part of their own kingdom from
Sweden—the Varangian Sea—I thought forsooth that their chiefs
must have been Swedes or Danes or Prussians because of the
proximity of those peoples. But since Vuagria seems to have
been once a well-known city and province of the Vandals, not
far from Lübeck and the Duchy of Holstein, and the sea called
the Baltic to have received its name from this course, in the opinion of some; and since the sea which is the frontier which sepa-
rates Germany from Denmark, likewise Prussia, Maritime Livonia, and, finally, a part of the Muscovite Empire from Sweden,
still retains its name among the Russians (being called "Vuar-
etzkoe more", i.e., Varangian Sea) and since, in addition to this,
the Vandals at that time were more powerful and finally spoke
the language of the Russians and had the same customs and religion, it seems to me more likely that the Russians would have
sought their leaders among the "Vuagrii" or "vuae-regis," than
to have conferred sovereignty on foreigners of a different religion, of different customs, and speaking a different language.[4]

The old idea from the chronicles that the Varangians were of
Northern or Scandinavian origin has now disappeared. Further
changes in the accounts of the chronicles are seen in the sixteenth
century, when English travelers were regaled on the new version
of Russian history which came to be generally accepted and taught.
Nevertheless the native Russian chronicles had not quite passed into
oblivion. In the early sixteenth century the imperial envoy Sigismund von Herberstein drew on them for his account of the early
history of Russia.[5] But it was Peter, whose curiosity had made him
familiar with the existence of the chronicles, who issued directions
in 1703 that an effort should be made to bring them together.
Learning of the existence of the Radziwill manuscript in Königsberg, Peter gave orders in 1716 that a copy should be secured.[6]

[4] Freiherr Sigismund von Herberstein, *Rerum Moscovitarum Commentarii*
(Vienna, 1549), 5. (Author's translation.) Herberstein's work has been trans-
lated and published by the Hakluyt Society, Series 1, Vols. 10 and 12.
   The Varangians had now come to be identified with the Baltic Slavs. See
Lappo-Danilevskii, "Ocherk razvitiya russkoi istoriografii, Vvedenie," in
Russkii istoricheskii Zhurnal, Kn. 6 (1920), 24.
[5] Herberstein, *Rerum Moscovitarum Commentarii*.
[6] V. S. Ikonnikov, *Opyt Russkoi Istoriografii*, II, 1920.

Peter had already decided to make a fresh start with historical studies. In 1708 he instructed Musin-Pushkin to set someone to composing a history of Russia. Musin-Pushkin turned to the Archimandrite Polycarp for the accomplishment of this task. Polycarp was told to write an account of Russian history from the time of the Grand Prince Vasilii Ivanovich (Vasilii III) to the present; there were to be two accounts, one *in extenso* and another an abridged edition. In 1712 Musin-Pushkin had occasion to remind Polycarp of the task imposed on him. His letter to Polycarp on this occasion discloses how deeply the Emperor had been influenced by the rationalism of western Europe:

> His Imperial Majesty has enjoined this task on you with the utmost insistence. Since His Imperial Majesty wishes to know the history of the Russian state, it is necessary to work on this first and not from the creation of the world and about other states, since much has been written on these subjects [whence it is evident that Peter the Great had little use for the genealogy of the Slavs from Japhet and the parchment charter of Alexander of Macedon]. With this in view it is necessary for you to make a collection of Russian manuscripts and bring them into seemly order. Bestir yourself in this matter and you will win deep gratitude. From the Tsar's anger may God preserve you![7]

The task of composing a history of Russia was not abandoned and within a few years was passed over to another candidate. He was Vasilii Nikitin Tatishchev, one of Peter's "nestlings."

Tatishchev, born in 1686 of an old aristocratic family, had entered on a life of service at the court of Ivan, the brother of Peter the Great. Some time after the death of that monarch Tatishchev was enrolled in the school of artillery and engineering at Moscow under Yakob (James) Bruce, one of Peter's most trusted followers. After some years of service in the army (he was present at both the battles of Narva and Poltava), he went abroad for two years, visiting Germany. On his return he had entered the College of

---

[7] P. P. Pekarskii, *Nauka i literatura Rossii pri Petrye Velikom*, I, 318. Polycarp's manuscript apparently was later presented to Peter who found it unacceptable (1716).

Mines and Manufactures, again serving under Bruce. Bruce was much interested in Russian geography and, in 1719, Peter had asked him to prepare a detailed manual of geography. Pressure of work compelled Bruce to turn the project over to Tatishchev, who plunged into the task. He soon began to realize that such a work required a vast amount of historical knowledge which he lacked. He then turned to making good this lack, with the result that gradually more and more geography faded into the background, that field being taken over by others.[8]

The story of Tatishchev's historical studies reflects admirably the new forces that were at work in Europe and were slowly penetrating Russia. In composing his work Tatishchev practically started anew and took little notice of the chronographs or the *Synopsis*, the earlier versions of Russian history. He found one version of the chronicle among Peter's papers; and when ordered to Siberia in 1720, he found other versions there.[9]

The real work of assembling the chronicles was a necessary preamble to the task of rewriting Russian history and in particular in explaining who the Russians were. This work had first been undertaken by Bayer (one of the German scholars brought to Russia by Peter), who, without a knowledge of Russian or Slavonic, contributed two memorable studies in Latin to the *Commentarii* of the Academy of Sciences. These two studies were the *De Variagis* and *Origines Russicae*, published in 1735 and 1741 respectively. But the solution of the problem had to wait until the earlier chronicles were assembled and made accessible. In 1758, G. F. Müller made a start by inserting a translation (albeit an imperfect one) of the chronicle of Nestor in his *Sammlung Russischer Geschichte* (Vol. I). In a later volume (Vol. V) of this work, Müller stated: "Nestor and the continuators of his chronicle form a connected account of Russian history which is so complete that no nation can boast it possesses such a storehouse continuing through so long a period of time."

But the scholars of the Academy found no support among the clergy or the higher functionaries of the state. In 1734 the clergy

[8] K. Bestuzhev-Ryumin, "V. I. Tatishchev," in *Biografii i Kharakteristiki*, 5 ff. Joseph de l'Isle was brought from France for this purpose.
[9] Milyukov, *Glavnye Techeniya russkoi istoricheskoi mysli*, 18-20.

registered their opposition to these projects which threatened to destroy the version of Russian history now sanctified by time, and the Synod forbade their publication. Therewith this justification:

It has been learned that at the Academy they are planning to publish the chronicles, a project involving heavy expenditure and the use of a great deal of paper in vain, since in these books are found many clear distortions of truth . . . which may with their enticements lead the people astray.[10]

Yet the discovery of the Radziwill chronicle during the occupation of Königsberg by the Russian forces in 1758 led Müller to publish it with the co-operation of Schlözer, a scholar induced by Müller to come to Russia in 1762 to join the Academy, in a not very satisfactory edition.[11] Schlözer left Russia in 1769, but others interested themselves in the project—notably A. I. Musin-Pushkin, A. S. Stroganov, and Betskii. Despite the efforts, little came of the work since the cadres of scholars competent to undertake the task were still not to be found in Russia (or elsewhere) during the eighteenth century. Many manuscripts were lost in the burning of Moscow in 1812. Karamzin devoted much time to a search for chronicles and the utilization of those available in his writing of his Russian history.[12] He also projected a vast scheme for the publication of all the chronicles, but the project languished in the early nineteenth century for want of interest. Phillip Krug, one of the younger scholars, bewailed this complete indifference:

Until learning enjoys greater prestige, until literary fame is rated higher, Russia will not acquire that force which acts so powerfully in foreign countries. There, the scholar who has attained fame enjoys general esteem. It never occurs to any to ask his rank; they are familiar with his name and his attainments. A young man sees in this a model and tries to emulate it. To achieve such fame becomes the chief end of his efforts. Here, on the other hand, the young man ordinarily is concerned how to attain rank and distinction as quickly as possible and remains indifferent to everything which does not lead to that

10 Ikonnikov, *Opyt Russkoi Istoriografii*, II, 1,923.
11 *Ibid.*
12 *Ibid.*, II, 1,931.

end; consciousness of his own deserts in the field of science, the approval of eminent scholars, etc., or else, finds no persons sympathetic with such things, or they have slight attraction for them.[13]

Despite this indifference, some progress was made. At least two scholars did not flag in their efforts—Karamzin and Schlözer. On the initiative of Schlözer the "Obshchestvo istorii i drevnostei rossiiskikh" (Society of History and Russian Antiquities) was organized in 1804 to complete the work of assembling and publishing the chronicles. But by 1811 only a beginning had been made. In 1768 Schlözer had published his *Probe Russischer Annalen* (Bremen and Göttingen) and after an interval of almost forty years finally brought out his *Nestor*—a German translation in 1802 and a Russian edition in 1809. On the death of Schlözer the task was assumed by Timovskii, Count N. P. Rumyantsev (the well-known and wealthy patron of learning under Alexander I), and P. M. Stroyev. Owing to Stroyev's tireless efforts and ardor, there came into existence in 1834 the *Arkheograficheskaya Kommissiya*, from the persistent co-operative work of whose scholars the labor conceived 150 years earlier by Peter was finally brought to fruition. Between 1841 and 1914 the publication of the chronicles was completed in twenty-four volumes.[14]

The slow recovery of Russia's past literary and historical treasures eventually led to the complete rewriting of Russian history, but the new versions were not greeted with universal acclaim. From the first there was resentment against German scholars, first for their nationality and secondly for their ruthless exploding of the myths of the older Russian historical traditions, enshrined in such works as the *Synopsis* on which the Russian elite had been brought up. Although Bayer had been unable to use the chronicles, he had by his careful assembling and critical treatment of reliable sources in other languages begun the task, but it is questionable whether his publication, written in Latin, had made much impression. V. I. Tatishchev had also given the current perversion of

[13] *Ibid.*, II, 1,931–32.
[14] *Ibid.*, II, 1,936–46. Later revisions and editions have come out, the most recent being one issued by Soviet scholars.

Russian history cavalier treatment, but his work had not been completed until 1739 when the first volume was submitted to the Academy of Sciences. By that time Tatishchev was no longer in favor and had already come under suspicion of being a free-thinker.[15] Publication was apparently refused; and in 1743 Tatishchev availed himself of the presence in Astrakhan of Jonas Hanway, the English merchant, to seek to have his work translated and published by the Royal Society. Hanway's account of this event is of some interest:

He [Tatishchev] mentioned that he had been about twenty years writing the history of Russia. Upon his recall from Astrakhan two years afterward, he sent me part of the history in manuscript, requesting me to procure a translation; but this by no means suited my convenience. The letter he wrote to my partner on this occasion runs as follows:

Gentlemen:
Since I left Astrachan, I have had no opportunity of writing to you, altho I retain a constant remembrance of the affection and regard which you have always shown me.
You know I have been engaged for near thirty years in writing a history of Russia, which I am about finishing, and I hope it will soon appear in print, to the satisfaction of the learned world. The history is the more to be esteemed by the curious part of mankind, as none of the ancient GREEK AND ROMAN historians, nor any geographical accounts of this empire, have gone so far as to inform us of the original dialect, &c., of the principal nations, viz., the SCLAVONIANS, SCYTHIANS, and SARMATIANS: nor of the AMAZONS, VANDALS, GOTHS, CIMMERIANS, who descended from them; neither have we any perfect account remaining of the HUNS and AVARI. The great distance of places and ignorance of the languages, have made it difficult to obtain a right information of them; add to this, the GREEKS, have so great a taste for fables, rather than a diligent search for truth, that they have rendered facts very obscure, of which the foolish talk of the AMAZONS is a proof. Of all these accounts I have endeavored as much as possible to give a clear and par-

[15] Milyukov, *Glavnye Techeniya russkoi istoricheskoi mysli,* 18–20.

M. V. Lomonosov

ticular account, which composes the first part of my history of Russia.

The second begins with RURIK, *prince of the* FINNS, *who invaded this country and founded the* RUSSIAN *empire which continued from the year 860 to the incursions of the* TARTARS *in 1238. This part contains many things relating to the histories of other countries; as affinities by marriages, alliances, wars, and treaties between the* RUSSIAN *monarchs, and other nations, particularly the* NORWEGIANS, SWEDES, HUNGARIANS *and both the western and eastern monarchies; which in the histories of those countries are either entirely lost or transmitted down in a very dark manner. I take no notice of natural history.*

Induced by the particular affection I have for the ENGLISH *nation, and my veneration for your royal society, on account of the great advantages the world receives from their several learned works, and their encouragement of useful knowledge, I have thought proper, as a mark of respect, to dedicate my history to them; but I am at a loss for want of translators, and dare not venture to send it to England in the original, lest the mistaking of facts, through want of a perfect knowledge of the* RUSSIAN *language should render the translation defective. I have, therefore, thought it the best way, and desire that you will please to recommend to me two good translators in the* GERMAN *for, as I understand, I can myself correct any mistake that shall happen and, when this is done, it will not be a difficult matter to have it translated into other languages.*[16]

This project did not materialize and Tatishchev's work did not see publication at the time. The original was lost by fire, but a copy was salvaged by G. F. Müller, and its publication was begun in 1768 (although not completed until 1848). The letter quoted above is an admirable illustration of the careful way in which Tatishchev worked.[17]

[16] Jonas Hanway, *An Historical Account of the British Trade with the Caspian with a Journal of Travels from London through Russia into Persia and back through Russia, Germany and Holland.* The citation is from the 2nd ed., I, 78.

[17] Although Tatishchev does not mention it, he was much indebted to Müller for archival material supplied by the latter for the second part of his work.

Hanway further comments:

The governor [i.e., Tatishchev] made no secret of his work, and having brought it down no lower than PETER THE GREAT, he could hardly have given offence; however, the envy of his parts among the *literati,* the resentment of the pious for his infidelity, which I fear was great; and the clamours of merchants for his rapaciousness, occasioned him being sent to banishment to his own estate near Mosco, where he ended his life. His works seem to have died with him, at least they have not found a favorable reception at the academy of ST. PETERSBURG. It is, however, probable that the great pains he took in collecting several choice materials, may be a means of some other person's building a reputation upon his labors.[18]

Tatishchev divided his work into the following parts: (1) from the beginning to the foundation of the Russian state (A.D. 862); (2) from A.D. 862 to 1238 (the date of the Mongol invasion); (3) from A.D. 1238 to 1462 (the date of the accession of Ivan III); (4) from A.D. 1462 to 1613 (the election of Mikhail Romanov). He refused to continue his history beyond the last date for various reasons "but especially because at present many noble families have blots on their escutcheons; if you write about them, you arouse their resentment; if you pass them over in silence, you would pervert the truth and the clarity of history."[19] Tatishchev made the center of his thinking natural law, with natural morality and natural religion. His ideas were drawn from Samuel Pufendorf. He seems to have made free use of the *Philosophisches Lexicon* of Johann Georg Walch published at Leipzig in 1726. To him natural law meant the law of self-preservation.[20]

The bitter resentment against the short shrift given by the German scholars to the hitherto accepted canon of Russian history finally burst out in the Academy in 1749. The occasion was a public meeting of the Academy on the name day of the Empress Elizabeth, when Müller was called upon to give an address. The topic of his

---

[18] Hanway, *An Historical Account of the British Trade,* I, 78.

[19] Bestuzhev-Ryumin, "V. I. Tatishchev," in *Biografii i Kharakteristiki,* 166.

[20] Milyukov, *Glavnye Techeniya russkoi istoricheskoi mysli,* 17–18.

lecture was *"Origines gentis et nominis Russorum."* For the first time the issue was brought out into the open by Müller's unqualified statement that the founders of the Russian state had been a group of Scandinavian adventurers—referred to in the chronicles as *Variagi* (English, "Varangian")—thus implying that Russia was indebted to a foreign people of Teutonic origin for its earliest political organization. The champion who rushed into the lists against Müller was none other than the Russian savant Lomonosov, afterward justly famous for his attainments in almost every field of scholarly and scientific endeavor of the time. But the grounds of Lomonosov's attack were less scholarly than they might have been because of his outraged patriotism.

I noticed that Herr Müller lost an admirable opportunity to extol the Slavic people. For it is known that the Scythians had no fear of the Persian king Darius, nor of Philip or Alexander, kings of Macedon, nor even of the Romans, but actually attacked them boldly and won victories over them. It is easy to conclude from this that the Slavic people were a mighty and brave people who defeated the valiant Scythians and repelled them from their extensive settlements, which would have been impossible without terrible battles and extraordinary victories. It is true that Herr Müller says (p. 13): Your forefathers from their famous deeds were called Slavs.

But throughout his dissertation he continually tries to prove the opposite of this, for on almost every page the Scandinavians beat the Russians, harry them with impunity, and defeat and waste them with fire and sword; the Huns take Kii with them to war against his will. This is so strange that if, perchance, Herr Müller had a lively style with which to draw a picture, he would have made the Russian people a poor folk, as no other, not even the most craven people in the world, have been depicted by any writer.[21]

The opinion of other members of the Academy was by no means unanimous, since Müller was generally supported by Trediakovskii. But the chief chancellery ruled against him:

[21] M. V. Lomonosov, *Sochineniya M. V. Lomonosova, Prilozhenie* (appendix), 897–907.

The Varangians-Rus—Rurik, Sineus, and Trevor—uncertain of their origin, are sitting in the prisoners' box and are awaiting sentence. One of the judges: After long and aimless wandering on the Varangian Sea, we, having failed to discover your real origin, most humbly beg you and the public to return to this hall in exactly one thousand years to hear the final verdict. (Occasioned by a famous debate between Pogodin and Kostomarov on the subject, "Who were the Varangians?")

Of all the unacceptable and improper statements that are scattered throughout his dissertation, the worst cannot be amended, but must be completely eliminated; viz., that the author intended (and in this had the approval of the president) to give the reader a shameful distortion of the great and glorious achievements of the Russian people, and considering their great number, at the beginning of the speech, one might not know where to start; in fact in the whole speech he did not take one opportunity to praise them, but he mentioned only what might be discreditable; how on numerous occasions, they destroyed in battle, they devastated by pillage or sword, and stole the treasures of the tsars.[22]

The speech was thereupon suppressed.

But Lomonosov persisted in his strong opposition to Müller. In 1761 Müller began to publish *Sammlung Russischer Geschichte*, announcing that he proposed to take up the task of describing Russian history where Tatishchev left off, that is, in 1613. Immediately he was attacked by Lomonosov in the preface to his own work, *Kratkaya Lyetopisets:*

> Not only in the *Yezhemesyachnye Primyecheniya* (a monthly publication edited by Müller), but also in his other works, Müller, according to his custom, inserts some supercilious comments; for instance, in describing the Chuvash, he cannot refrain from rating their domestic cleanliness higher than that of the Russian population. He prefers to look at the blots on the garments of his Russians, shutting his eyes to their good qualities. A very clear and mortifying proof of this statement of mine is that Müller writes and prints in German an account of the Time of Troubles of Godunov and of the desecrated nun— the darkest period of Russian history, from which foreigners will form unfavorable opinions of our national reputation. Are there not tales of other Russian deeds in which it would be at least possible to see good and evil in equal degree?[23]

Skabichevskii, who quoted Lomonosov's statement given above, comments that at this time:

> the authorities agreed that Russian history ought not to end with the death of Fedor Ivanovich; that in the period since that

---

[22] *Ibid.*, V, 10–11. Complete objectivity in the writing of history was quite incomprehensible to the Russian savant. Far from being anti-Russian, Müller endeavored to write according to the formula of Tacitus: "sine ira atque studio." In Müller's own words: "the historian should seem to be a man without a country, without belief, and without [loyalty to] a monarch . . . all that a historian says ought to be true and should never give any occasion for suspicion of flattery." Pekarskii, *Istoriya Akademii Nauk*, I, 381, cited by Milyukov, *Glavnye Techeniya russkoi istoricheskoi mysli*, 96–97.

[23] Skabichevskii, *Ocherki po istorii russkoi tsenzury*, 25. For the full title of Lomonosov's work, see Bibliography under "Historiography."

time our country's history contains such scandals, which it would be better to pass over in silence. In particular the era of the pretenders was represented by contemporaries of Lomonosov as so dark a blot on Russian history that it should be passed over and consigned to oblivion instead of holding it up to the scorn and laughter of the West.[24]

Lomonosov's animus against the Germans in the Academy of Sciences was not yet appeased. By 1759 Schlözer had completed the time for which he had contracted with the Academy and decided to leave Russia. Lomonosov reported to the Senate that Schlözer intended, after going abroad, to write a history which would not redound to Russia's praise.[25] He managed to clear himself, however, despite the fact that his language had already offended Russian sensibilities.[26]

It seems incredible that one of the leading figures in the scholarly world should have regarded Russian history solely from the point of view of whether it redounded to the glory or the shame of Russia. Great man that he was, Lomonosov showed none of his greatness in the field of history, which was foreign to him (he had interested himself in it late in life and only upon instructions from the government). That he did not view history impartially is due partly to the terrible heritage of the "Bironovshchina" under Anne, when German favorites had lorded it over the native Russians; partly to the excessive sensitiveness of a people going through the stage of adolescence. They were ready to take offense when anything derogatory to Russia appeared on the printed page.

Thus began the endless controversy over the relationship of Russian history to that of the West. The dispute whether the Varangians were of Norse origin or of some other race (preferably Slav) was for long the focal point of this battle. The lines were soon drawn between Normanists and anti-Normanists and the fight was to last on into the nineteenth century; in fact, it had hardly ceased at the time of the October Revolution, when it became obscured by other issues dearer to the Marxian heart. During the

[24] *Ibid.*, 25–26.

[25] Starchevskii, *Ocherk literatury russkoi istorii do Karamzina*, 282.

[26] See passage cited from Schlözer's work by Zabyelin, *Istoriya russkoi zhizni*, I, 57. "The Germans on this side of the Rhine . . . had been destined to sow the first seeds of enlightenment in the vast northwestern world, etc."

eighteenth century, however, the question was involved with other things that touched Russian pride to the quick. In 1761 Abbé Chappe d'Auteroche had with the permission of the government made a trip to Siberia to view the transit of Venus across the sun and on his return to France had written *Voyage en Sibérie*,[27] in which he had said some unflattering things about Russia and her people. The book was so critical of Russian habits and institutions that Catherine felt called upon to reply.[28] About the same time a French physician, Le Clerc, visited Russia at the invitation of Elizabeth and later wrote a history of the country.[29] Champions, however, were found among historical scholars. The fullest reply was given by General Boltin in his *Primecheniya na istoriyu Rossii gospodina Leklerka (Notes on the history of Russia, by M. Le Clerc)*.[30] Boltin tried to make out a good case for Russia. His claim was that in reality native Russian culture had some claims to preeminence even over the culture of the West that had been introduced by Peter and sedulously cultivated by Catherine.[31] Boltin's contemporary, Prince Shcherbatov, was not quite so sure of this and in his *The Corruption of Morals in Russia* had much to say that was highly derogatory to Russian society.[32]

Russian historiography took an immense step forward with Karamzin (1766–1826). Karamzin early came under the quickening influences of the Enlightenment at the University of Moscow, where Novikov and Schwartz and the Masonic circle were in the ascendant. These progressive and cosmopolitan tendencies, however, were not enduring. He soon discarded them for strong nationalistic and romantic leanings, and his increasing interest in Russian history recommended him to the Emperor Alexander, who named him historiographer to write a history of Russia. His *History of the Russian State* was a landmark in Russian literature. But Karamzin's strong nationalism was tempered by the experience gained

[27] 2 vols. (Paris, 1768).

[28] See V. F. Gnucheva, *Materialy dlya istorii ekspedtsii Akademii Nauk v XVIII–XIX vyekakh*, 89.

[29] Nicolas Gabriel Le Clerc, *Histoire physique, morale, civile, et politique de la Russie ancienne et moderne*.

[30] 2 vols. (St. Petersburg, 1788).

[31] See Anatole G. Mazour, *An Outline of Modern Russian Historiography*, 13–15.

[32] *Ibid.*, 11, 13.

from European travel and by the maturer judgment which he had thus acquired. In style he was immensely superior to his predecessors. On the Varangian question, despite his strong patriotism, he took a moderate view:

> The chronicles of the Middle Ages loved to give peoples old names slightly different from their real ones; thus Luka David in his chronicle calls the Russian, Roxolani. Müller in his speech on the antiquities of our fatherland, along with Bayer, called the Varangians, Scandinavians, and correctly proved the error of those who only because of the similarity of name called the Varyagi-Rus' the ancient Roxolani; for the first lived in the North, while the others lived in the neighborhood of the Sea of Azov. Now it is hard to understand the persecution undergone by the author for his dissertation in 1749. Popov, Struve, and Fischer made attacks upon every page. The story ended by Müller being overwhelmed with confusion, and they suppressed the dissertation which had already been printed. Finally Müller admitted that the Varyagi-Rus' might be the Roxolani in the sense of the Geographer of Ravenna, but not the *ancient ones*.[33]

Yet, while Karamzin succeeded in weaving Russia's story into a romantic tale, told in fresh and colorful language, for most persons of the mature period of Russian scholarship his history was marred by his excessive glorification of autocracy and the military character of the Russian state, while completely ignoring the backwardness of the country and the terrible problems this condition created. The most trenchant criticism was that of A. N. Pypin, who wrote: "But the learned scholar brought from history only one ideal, that of the repressed, stupified life of the seventeenth century which was only a mournful stage for the new Russia."[34]

Karamzin's history was one of the great literary achievements of the reign of Alexander I. This book may be said to close one literary epoch, for Karamzin had taken all that Russia with the aid of eighteenth-century Europe had to offer and embodied it in a great encomium of the Russian state.

The historians who followed Karamzin drew their inspiration from nineteenth-century Europe. Polevoi derived his ideas from

[33] Quoted in Lomonosov, *Sochineniya*, V, *Prilozhenie* (appendix), 105.
[34] A. S. Pypin, *Obshchestvennoe Dvizhenie pri Aleksandrye I*, 253 ff.

Thierry, Guizot, and particularly Niebuhr. He regarded history as "a practical revaluation of philosophical conceptions concerning the universe and mankind, an analysis of a philosophical synthesis." Pogodin, inspired rather by Karamzin and Schlözer, devoted himself to the early period of Russian history, seeking to find the roots of the forces that had created Russia. He distrusted systems of writing history that pretended to a universal philosophy of history. He believed that history should glorify the country's past, particularly its great contributions of orthodoxy and autocracy. Pogodin, in spite of his academic vocation, was an indefatigable journalist, editing the *Moskovskii Vestnik* and *Moskvityanin*, the latter a fanatically nationalist periodical.[35]

But the great historical issue that began to overshadow all others in the second quarter of the nineteenth century was the controversy between the Slavophiles and the Westerners. The prelude to this controversy was the publication in 1836 in Nadyezhdin's *Teleskop* of Chaadayev's *Philosophical Letters*. These letters roundly charged that Russia was a barbaric country whose civilization was not worthy of the name, that western Europe owed its superior civilization in great part to the Roman Catholic church, which Chaadayev extolled as the great pillar of Christianity.[36] This view set off a great battle of the books between those who glorified old Muscovite Russia and those who extolled Peter for introducing reforms and learning from the West, with all the consequences which this act involved for Russia. The new battle involved a far more profound discordance of view. While the Varangian issue touched on racial or national pride, the new controversy was one of the fundamental nature of civilization.

It must be emphasized that Slavophilism was more than a blind reaction against Western civilization. There had been signs of gathering xenophobia as early as the first years of Alexander I's reign, and this xenophobia had received its most decisive expres-

---

[35] His frequently quoted saying is typical: "History is above all the people's crown, for in it the people recognize itself." *Moskovskii Vyestnik*, Chap. VI, cited in Milyukov, *Glavnye Techeniya russkoi istoriocheskoi mysli*, 3.

[36] The events in connection with the publication of the *Philosophical Letters* and its consequences to the author and the periodical are given in Chap. VII above.

sion in Karamzin's *On the Old and New Russia*, presented to Alexander in 1811. The main thesis of his book was that the foundations of Russia were to be discovered in her characteristic institutions, among the chief of which was autocracy, and that to tinker with these institutions as proposed by Alexander's adviser Speranskii was to pull out the props from under the state.[37] Karamzin had also seen fit to protest in 1817 in a similar way against the grant of constitutional rights to the Poles, whom Karamzin labeled as the inveterate and irreconcilable foes of the Russians.[38] The current which had set in against foreign influences doomed the Russian Bible Society, which was finally suppressed by Nicholas in 1826. The strongest proponent of this antiforeign trend was Admiral Shishkov, who became minister of public instruction in 1824. Shishkov had already become famous for his fanatical patriotism, which had found expression during the French invasion of 1812 and which attracted Alexander to him. His ardor had taken fantastic forms, and he had been propagating his bizarre ideas of Slavic antiquities and pure Slavicism in language in his publication *Democritus*. After Shishkov's departure from the official scene in 1826, these trends became even stronger and eventually took form in the well-known threefold principle of Uvarov, the minister of public instruction, which laid the foundation for official nationalism—Autocracy, Orthodoxy, and Nationalism. While this principle was purely an official proclamation, it found an echo among many of the intellectuals, and there came into existence, in addition to the official patriotic school (Grech and Bulgarin), other schools, such as the one of Pogodin, who without completely agreeing with the government's line, nonetheless put forward similar views and gave them a philosophical basis either in university lectures or in the press. Such were Pogodin and Shevyrev, whose work has already been discussed.

But perhaps the most characteristic figures in this period were the Slavophiles, a group of young writers who came to maturity in the generation after the Decembrist Revolt and whose life and activity was associated with Moscow and that city's intense intel-

37 N. M. Karamzin, *Zapiska o drevnei i novoi Rossii.*

38 N. M. Karamzin, *Zapiska predstavlennaya Gosudaryu 18 Oktyabrya 1819 goda.* This work appeared later in print, but without place or date of publication.

lectual life.[39] The core of the movement consisted of young aristocrats who possessed landed estates, who had acquired an extremely
broad, although perhaps not profound, education, and who, after
finishing their education and having traveled, in some cases tried
out a few years of government service before settling down to the
leisured life of a landlord, interrupted only by occasional visits to
Moscow or to foreign countries or varied by the writing of poetry,
philosophical treatises, or polemical pamphlets. The most famous
of this circle were the Kireyevskii brothers, Ivan and Peter, the
Aksakovs, Konstantin and Ivan, Aleksei Khomiakov (perhaps the
most influential), and Yurii Samarin. In general, they shared the
distrust and criticism of the West which was common in their day,
but with them the distrust was not blind and irrational, but was
formulated with clarity and given a plausible philosophical basis.

Since most of the Slavophiles either were Hegelians or had
passed through a Hegelian phase, it was natural that their phrase-
ology should be Hegelian. They were constantly seeking for opposed principles of life, like Heraclitus of old. Khomiakov made
his contribution to Slavophile history by composing a history of
the world, printed in three volumes, which was published after
his death. Khomiakov set two great principles in opposition to each
other in world history—the Iranian and the Kushite. The Iranians
were creative and freedom loving; the Kushites believed in necessity, their creation being limited to enormous constructions, such
as the pyramids, completed by forced labor. The Iranians, of
course, included the Slavs; all the races and peoples who have been
admired for their virtues manage to get into the first class; all those
who for any reason have earned mankind's odium were relegated
to the second. In the words of Yurii Samarin, history involves "the
struggle of the religion of moral freedom with the religion of necessity, material and logical."[40] While Khomiakov intended his work
to be a universal world history based on careful research and
scholarship, the manner in which he twisted and distorted his evidence in order to make his points repels the modern reader, and it

[39] The writer is greatly indebted to Mr. Nicholas Riasanovsky for allowing him to read his manuscript, at this time unpublished, on Slavophilism.
In the main the author has followed Mr. Riasanovsky in his interpretation of
the historical side of Slavophilism.
[40] From the Riasanovsky MS, 89.

is questionable whether he had much influence on his contemporaries. It was Konstantin Aksakov who really made the Slavophile contribution to historical thought. At the outset of his book he remarks:

> The history of the Russian people is the only history in the world of a people Christian, not only in the profession of faith, but also in its life, or at least in the aspiration of its life.[41]

> The Russian state was founded not by conquest, but by a voluntary invitation of the government. Thus, in the foundation of the Western states, violence, slavery, and history; in the foundation of the Russian state, free will, liberty, and peace.[42]

But it was against Peter the Great that the Slavophiles directed their most venomous shafts. Peter had by his reforms, imported from the West and violently imposed, shattered the natural development of the Russian people. In thus singling out Peter for attack, the Slavophiles placed themselves in direct opposition to the Western culture that had come in with Peter and a fortiori became the champions of the older Muscovite civilization. What, then, were the characteristics of this civilization held up for the Russians to admire? First, the Slavophiles' chief emphasis was on the Orthodox church, which was almost the center of their whole scheme of things. Their criticism of the West was largely an attack on the churches of the West, both Roman Catholicism and Protestantism coming in for condemnation for their rationalism and materialism. In addition to their exaltation of the Orthodox church and faith, the Slavophiles strongly idealized the old patriarchal life of the Russian countryside with which they were familiar and which was being threatened by the assaults of the modern industrialism. They believed that the landlord should be a father to his peasants, and they picked out the peasant commune as one of the admirable institutions of Slavdom that held out great hopes for the future of mankind. But the Slavophiles' chief grounds of attack on the West were that the West was decadent and based on wrong

[41] *Ibid.,* 95.

[42] *Ibid.,* 96. It is to be observed that with the Slavophiles the year 1613 takes on a special significance. This was the year when, after the long civil wars, the people met together and chose a new monarch and voluntarily placed their destiny in his hands.

principles, while Slavdom was strong and vigorous and endowed with the Messianic destiny of redeeming the world.

The Slavophiles could scarcely be called historians in the strict sense of the word, nor did they actually produce a real philosophy of history. They were essentially polemicists, using history merely to support their unique views on Russia and on the relation of Russia to the West. The actual carrying on of the serious work of history was in other, perhaps more ordinary, hands. Karamzin's task of writing Russian history was taken up by the historians of the skeptical school, whose chief members were Kachenovskii and Polevoi. The former professor of Russian history at the University of Moscow distrusted the veracity of the early Russian chronicles and preferred to base his work on the documents. He was compelled in 1835 to leave the university for his unpatriotic views. Polevoi (1796–1846), who has already been mentioned a number of times, composed a six-volume history of Russia in an attempt to combine Russian history with that of western Europe in a great synthesis. His principal theory was that Norman feudalism in early Russ, based on family seniority, had led to the splitting up of the principality and to the weakening of the Kievan state so that it fell easily before the Mongol hordes.[43] Polevoi also emphasized the fact that Russia took civilization from Byzantium during the period of her decadence and thus lacked the true classical element which was the heritage of the West.

The first great figure in Russian historiography who shows evidence of complete mastery of his subject and of maturity of mind was Sergei Mikhailovich Solov'ev (1820–79). Solov'ev was profoundly influenced by Hegelian philosophy and was personally acquainted with both the Slavophiles and their opponents, the *Zapadniki* (the Westerners). He held that human historical movements were movements of the absolute spirit and that the historian must study ideas and their reflection in law and government. Only great figures and heroes count, he said; the masses have no historical significance.[44] Solov'ev assimilated Russian historical development to that of the West from the point of view of organic growth. He insisted that, as in the West, society in Russia had progressed from

[43] V. I. Picheta, *Vvyedenie v russkuyu istoriyu*, 111.
[44] *Ibid.*, 119–25.

a primitive patriarchal stage and that the patriarchal system tends to disappear with the increase of population and urban culture. In its early development, a people is much influenced, he said, by external nature. In this early period its reactions are emotional. A primitive society eventually escapes from these influences when it meets another people and enters the second period of the formation of the state.

In this second period, when the breakdown of kin relationship occurs, two principles assert themselves—what Solov'ev calls the governmental principle and the antigovernmental principle. The conflict of these two principles caused the time of troubles in Russia. The third stage of Russian history began with Peter the Great, when Russia came under the influence of other countries.[45] The patriarchal argument was a great blow to the Slavophiles (who wished to insist on the diversity between Russia and western Europe) and led Konstantin Aksakov to reverse himself and to deny the existence of patriarchal institutions in Russia.

Solov'ev amplified this principle into a comprehensive theory that there are three determining forces in history: (1) the character of the country in which the people live (this determines their history only in their youth); (2) the character of the race—when their racial character begins to assert itself, the people escape from the determination of their environment; and (3) the course of external events (coming from the people around them). According to Solov'ev, Russian feudalism differed from Western feudalism in that the Russian warrior class or *comitatus* (*druzhina* in Russian) was never assigned grants of land as were the Western vassals, but remained with the prince and moved from one *volost'* to another somewhat capriciously, owing to the vast extent of the country.[46] Solov'ev's comparative treatment of early Russian history and his attempt to bring it into the same scheme of things as Western feudalism did not, as we have seen, recommend it to the Slavophiles, or to some later scholars, for example, Pavlov-Silvanskii and Kareyev; but, nonetheless, it was very fruitful.

Solov'ev's original views on early Russian history are given in the opening pages of the first volume of his history, but by the

45 N. P. Pavlov-Silvanskii, *Feodalizm v drevnei Rusi*, 9ff.
46 *Ibid.*, 13.

time he wrote the eighth volume he had somewhat modified his views. He had come under the influence of Buckle and had begun to develop the sociological theory, emphasizing the general laws of the organic development of all peoples.

If vast erudition, sound scholarship, and ability to draw broad generalizations are the mark of the historian, Solov'ev can be said to have raised history to a level none of his predecessors had attained. Not only did he free himself from national prejudices and faulty conceptions of early Russian historiography, but he also assimilated the teaching of western European historians and was able to treat Russian history with the scrupulous regard for truth and the bold originality of conception that mark the great historian. One can say that, despite the national characteristics that his work displays, we feel in Solov'ev—at least in the field of history—that the Russian mind has at last attained some measure of maturity. Russian scholars have now a European point of view.

XI

The Peasants

WHILE Russia's greatest historian to date was maintaining that only great figures and heroes count, that the masses have no historical significance, a view directly contrary to this attitude was already gaining ground in the literary world. Whereas at the opening of the eighteenth century there was almost complete unconcern among the upper classes about the lot of the peasants, within a hundred years the peasant and the wrongs done to him were the subject of impassioned appeals to a public slowly becoming aware of social and political problems. Where are the explanations of this startling change of attitude to be sought?

It is obvious that this new attitude toward the peasants was not merely a new idea conceived by the watcher in his ivory tower. It strikes the observer as something in the nature of a ground swell, whose first stirrings are discernible at the end of the eighteenth century in the works of Radishchev and Novikov. The first expressions of dissatisfaction were readily silenced by the state, but discontent again found utterance under Alexander I, in whose reign the Decembrists took up arms on the peasants' behalf. To put these events into their right setting, it is necessary to gain some idea of the problem of the peasant at the beginning of the nineteenth century.

In spite of the generous hopes that she encouraged at the outset of her reign, the Empress Catherine II did little to better the peasants' lot. She confiscated church lands and brought the church peasants under state control, ultimately assimilating their lot to that of the so-called "state peasants." But Catherine reduced the peasants in the Ukraine to the status of landlords' peasants in the rest of Russia; she, also, by the bestowal of crown lands on her favorites, fastened on the peasants living on these lands the yoke of a private landlord. The Pugachev Revolt had apparently convinced her that her interests and those of the landlords were bound up together. But what probably was the most significant was the emancipation of the gentry from compulsory state service, which at a stroke singled them out for an especial privilege, a unique phenomenon in a country where hitherto all citizens, without discrimination, had been yoked to the state juggernaut.[1]

It will be instructive to review briefly developments in the field of public opinion and public policy in order to trace the rise of the aforementioned ground swell. In the general low level of culture at the beginning of the eighteenth century, it is difficult to find evidences of any broad understanding of the peasant problem. The only views expressed were official views or those of individuals who looked at the problem from the official standpoint. Pososhkov, who touched on this issue in his book *On Poverty and Wealth*, although of peasant origin himself, contented himself with regarding the peasant solely as a producer and with suggesting such measures as would raise the peasant's productivity—measures largely restricted to overcoming by punishment the peasant's sloth and negligence. The only improvement advocated by Pososhkov that can be regarded as a plea on the peasant's behalf, and this actually had an ulterior motive, was that Pososhkov argued that the peasant's obligations to his lord should in some manner be fixed. Thus, said Pososhkov, the peasant would have an incentive to greater exertions to produce. The other prolific writer of the period of Peter, V. N. Tatishchev, was the first to note the advantages that other countries—notably Sweden—had derived from the abolition of serfdom, but he believed that Russia could hardly afford to emulate the example of the Scandinavian country "since such an innovation did not agree with our monarchical government, and it would be dangerous to remove the habit of servitude which is deeply rooted."[2] For theoretical defense, Tatishchev fell back on the then

[1] Kluchevsky in his *Istoriya Soslovii v Rossii* emphasizes the fact that originally classes had been distinguished merely by difference in obligations. Distinction in the matter of privileges was a modern development.

[2] V. V. Semevskii, *Krest'yanskii Vopros v XVIII i pervoi polovinye XIX*

current belief in "natural law."[3] He did, however, urge that the peasant's obligation to his landlord be fixed.

During the generation that followed, the peasant had no chance to express his views, even had he been class conscious; and no voice from the other classes was raised in his behalf. Meanwhile, his lot was growing steadily worse. What might be taken as a ray of hope were the words of Catherine written shortly after the court revolution that brought her to the throne in 1762: "Freedom is the soul of everything in the world. . . . I want obedience to the laws, but I do not want slaves."[4] Was the new Empress to be taken at her word? And if this were the case, was this new "freedom" to be extended to the peasants?

There is some evidence that Catherine not only had embraced the views of the Enlightenment in regard to the advantages of freedom and of free enterprise in human affairs, but was prepared when the opportunity arose to put at least some of these views to the test of experience.[5] In 1865 she founded the Imperial Free Economic Society for the study of Russia's agriculture and the needs of country life. Cynics sneered that the "Free" in the society's title was mere window dressing and that the last person to benefit from its work would be the peasant. Nevertheless, for over a century the society was to make no little contribution to the peasant's welfare. One of the first acts of the Economic Society was to hold a competition for a prize consisting of a considerable sum of money. The contestants were to submit essays on the following topics:

1. What constitutes the property of the peasant, the land he works or his movable property?
2. What claim, consistent with the welfare of the state, can be advanced by him to the one or the other?

---

vyeka, I, Vvedenie, vii. It is to be noted that this "habit of servitude" was broken by the reform of 1762.

[3] Georgii Plekhanov, *History of Russian Social Thought*, 103–109.

[4] See footnote 35 under Chapter III.

[5] It was at this time, also, that Catherine relaxed the government monopoly of the fur trade in Siberia, allowing private traders to participate in the trade across the Chinese frontier. She also consistently turned a deaf ear to appeals of private individuals for grant of a monopoly of trade in the Aleutian Islands. Raymond H. Fisher, *The Russian Fur Trade, 1550–1700*, 227; William Coxe, *An Account of Russian Discoveries*, 201–10.

The competition evoked a vast amount of erudition, but it is significant that of the total number received, 129 essays were in German, 21 in French, 3 in Latin, 1 in Dutch, and 1 in Swedish. Only 7 essays written in Russian were received.

The winning essay, by a Frenchman, emphasized the value of freedom for the peasant, citing England as an example of what could be achieved by a free peasantry. In one of the native Russian compositions we find, however, a significant departure from the prevailing views. The author of this essay voiced a protest against slavishly following the West and suggested that the peasant should receive both his freedom and the land; the author, Polyenov, said: "It is not necessary to take examples from others, but our [system] ought to be based solely on sound judgment and on principles of humanity, without losing sight of the public good.[6]

This competition was held in preparation for the meetings of the Commission for the Codification for the Laws already announced for 1767. This body was to some degree representative, yet it hardly met modern requirements in that regard since many of the towns were represented by nobles, while the landlords' peasants had no representatives at all. What strikes one, however, is that almost no attention was directed to the grievances of the peasant. It is true that in deference to the humanitarian ideas of the time, protests were raised against the current practice of selling peasants without land and breaking up families in order to dispose of their members individually. In general, the meeting of this body degenerated into a squabble between the nobility and the middle class (merchants and *myeshchane*) over the right to own landed estates with peasants, a right which the gentry wished to deny to the middle class. There was also feeling between the two classes of the nobility—the old "highborn" nobility and the new official nobility who had acquired that rank through service—over the right of the latter to possess peasants, which the old families had never conceded.[7]

[6] Semevskii, *Krest'yanskii Vopros v XVIII i pervoi polovinye XIX vyeka*, I, 1-9.

[7] *Ibid.*, II, 540. Here is given a summary of this whole discussion. See also *Velikaya Reforma*, I, 209-10. For a discussion of the new official nobility, see V. I. Lebedev, *Reformy Petra I*, Chapter: "Sotsial'naya Politika," under the Table of Ranks.

The First Turkish War, 1768–74, put an abrupt end to these forensic exercises which the English ambassador Shirley had characterized as a "farce." Catherine's energies and attentions were absorbed with the war and with the first partition of Poland in 1772. Perhaps these events and the demands they made on her were in themselves sufficient to account for the abandonment of her other projects. Yet possibly more significant is the revolt of Pugachev, the Cossack leader, which flared up in 1773 in the frontier regions of the Southeast—the Don, the lower Volga, and the Urals—and which carried peasant risings almost to the doors of the capital. The frightful *jacquerie* and savage vengeance taken on state officials and landlords appalled the government and made the Empress reconsider her plans for freedom. At any rate, nothing further was heard of easing the lot of the peasant, and ten years later the Empress even reversed the trend by restoring to serfdom the peasants of the Ukraine, most of whom had already acquired their freedom. The peasant question was to slumber thus for another forty years.

The first overt challenge to the prevailing oppression of the peasant was Radishchev's *Journey from St. Petersburg to Moscow*, whose publication in 1790 at once involved the author in official displeasure and exile to Siberia. Likewise, the arbitrary imprisonment of Novikov in 1792 was inspired by the Empress' suspicion that he was in league with the forces that were working on the peasants' behalf. Catherine had traveled a long way from her first apostrophe to freedom, uttered in 1762, when in 1773 she assured Diderot: "I do not know of a land where the cultivator of the soil has a greater love for his land and for his hearth than in Russia. [Moreover] our free provinces have no greater production of grain than our unfree."[8]

The first parting of the clouds for the peasants came in 1797 when the Emperor Paul issued an edict limiting the demands for labor which the landlords could make on their peasants to three days of the week. We are not informed of the exact motives that prompted this act. On the other hand, it seems that public opinion was at last stirring; not much longer could the prevailing abuses continue to be ignored.

[8] V. A. Bil'basov, *Istoricheskie Monografii*, IV, 334.

The Peasants

The death of Paul and the accession of his young son Alexander were hailed as the dawn of a new era. The Emperor in his adolescence had had the loftiest ideals of freedom and humanitarianism instilled into him by his tutor Laharpe, and his reign was looked forward to with the highest hopes. With regard to the peasants, what little discussion had been allowed had centered on the personal wrongs to which they had been subjected at the hands of their lords—the exaction of excessive services, the traffic in peasants without relation to land, and the separation of families in the process of sale. Such practices could be readily cured by simply releasing peasants from the control of their landlords, an act that would be following the experience of the most advanced countries of western Europe, where civil liberty was the first boon to be attained by the peasants. Generally, England was held up as a shining example of what might be done to stimulate agriculture by the bestowal of liberty; the Anglophiles, like the Princess Dashkova, made much of this example, as Speranskii and Mordvinov did later. Yet even here caution was the watchword. The Princess Dashkova believed that the peasants should first be educated before emancipation could be won by their own efforts. There was little thought that the state had any further responsibility.

Alexander's efforts were along these latter lines. In Livonia and the other Baltic provinces, legislative acts passed between 1804 and 1809 permitted the liberation of serfs, in the great majority of cases without land—an operation that later was held up as the example of the way not to free the peasants. Further legislation of the Emperor, adopted on the recommendation of his "non-official" committee, permitted the landlords to liberate their peasants, allowing the peasants to pay a yearly rental for the usufruct of their land or to redeem it by payment of a somewhat larger annual sum, which would cease at the death of their master. It was hoped that large numbers of the proprietors would use this method to obtain some considerable compensation for the meritorious act of emancipation and that thus would be established a substantial body of "free husbandmen." But the results were disappointing. The total number of peasants to profit from this act never exceeded 100,000 persons—only 33,000 during the reign of Alexander himself.

The relative freedom in the first years of Alexander's reign, however, did allow considerable discussion of the peasant problem. The most important steps taken to bring the situation to a head were the two competitions held by the Free Economic Society in 1812 and 1819. The contest of 1812 posed the problem of the relative merits of serf and free labor. Professor Yakob of the University of Kharkov carried off the prize with an essay that proved, to at least his own satisfaction, that free labor was more efficient than slave labor. While his essay was to have enormous influence in the future, it is extremely significant that the second prize was won by a Russian with an essay that advocated the grant of land along with personal freedom; otherwise, he maintained, the position of Russian peasants would be as bad as that of the landless proletariat of western Europe.

The competition of 1819 was concerned solely with the question of redistribution of land. It called for a practical demonstration, by way of an experiment, to be carried out to a successful conclusion. And since the one person who was prepared to carry through such a scheme had his request turned down by the state council, the competition was a farce.[9]

The Decembrists were somewhat disposed to be more generous with the peasant. The sharp contrast between their native land and western Europe was a shock to returning officers after 1815. The absence of personal freedom stifled them individually, but inspired as they were by the humanitarian ideals of the Enlightenment, they could not fail to be even more appalled by the deep wretchedness of the peasantry, and they yearned to raise the peasants at least to the level of their counterparts in the West. Yet many Decembrists were landowners with peasants of their own and were inclined to share the feelings of landed proprietors, fortified by the views on the sanctity of property rights which were one of the heritages of the French Revolution. This conflict on basic principles was reflected in the great divergence of opinion among the Decembrists.

Among the foremost representatives of the group which stood for a scheme of peasant emancipation that safeguarded fundamental property rights was the leader of the Southern Society and the most outstanding figure of the movement: Paul Pestel. He favored the division and redistribution of the land in each township

[9] Semevskii, *Krest'yanskii Vopros*, I, Intro. xvii and 410.

(*volost'*); and, if each peasant was provided with land, he felt that the original owners had to be compensated. In his plan the land assigned to peasants was not to be owned exclusively by individuals; half of it was to belong to the village community. Bestuzhev-Ryumin held somewhat similar views. However, he also believed that all peasants (including state peasants) should purchase their freedom by money or labor before entering the community as free citizens. It is significant that in the above cases, peasant reform yielded first place to constitutional reform.

Other reformers took an even more radical stand. The boldest was N. I. Turgenev, the most ardent advocate of peasant reform. He defined his position at this time in his work *La Russie et les Russes*, published many years later.

In regard to the controversies on political freedom and constitutions,

> I was so completely preoccupied with the question of serfdom that I could give them no attention. I was not indifferent [to them]. I had definite views, naturally, on the chief issues of political organization, on representation, on freedom of the press, on equality before the law, and on the organization of the legislative, executive, and judicial powers; I did not refuse to participate [in these discussions] or to secure institutions that guaranteed all these rights, but only after serfdom had first been abolished; while serfdom persisted, all my thoughts were concentrated on what I considered the greatest evil that called for the most rapid reform. In my opinion, all questions were secondary to serfdom.[10]

Turgenev believed that emancipation must be accompanied by bestowal upon each peasant of the land which he was in possession of at the time of his liberation, thus anticipating the solution finally arrived at in 1861.

Typical of the more extreme views on serfdom were poems by another Decembrist, Zavalashin, which were read into the record of the examining commission in 1826. The first of these poems was a general call to freedom:

[10] N. I. Turgenev, *La Russie et les Russes*, I, 77–78, 81–83.

For the first time, I have taken my lyre in hand.
O, Slavonic race, rouse ye,
Spring from thy bed, take courage,
Show thyself great to the world.

Flow as the swollen rivers flow
When they have gone out over their banks,
Freeing thyself for all time,
Free also the slaves.

Our ancestors were free,
Free they descended to the grave.
They did not yield up their freedom,
But slaves introduced Tsars among us.

Ah! Will our patience soon be exhausted,
Or will we long abide in slavery?
Ah! How long will we endure
The theft of our freedom?

The second poem was related particularly to the peasant question:

Nobles—so I call you all—
I prophesy destruction to you—
How dare ye take pride in the fact
That ye own slaves?
Ye ought rather to be ashamed,
Possessing slaves, that ye are in bondage yourselves.
And do ye dream of freedom
While ye oppress others?
When ye go among the people, they hate you.
Slaves yourselves, will ye escape at their hands?
And so ye strive to
Silence the yearning for unrestrained freedom,
Ye strive to avert the fierce rising of the people,
Till ye provide a better lot,
For the slaves themselves,
That ye may be inviolate,
In this holy struggle.[11]

The Peasants

In summing up the views of the Decembrists, the historian of the peasant question, V. I. Semevskii, cites an anonymous article:

All the Decembrists, as far as I am aware, recognized the necessity of emancipating the peasants . . . as for the measures by which this was to be obtained, opinions differed. Some voiced the most sweeping views on the right of the peasants to possession of the land [Pestel and some members of the Southern group], which to others seemed Utopian. The liberation of the peasant without land was in their eyes unthinkable. Others were for personal emancipation . . . and believed emancipation with the land impossible of attainment. A third group, among them N. M. Murav'ev, thought that the peasants should receive as their property only their houses and their kitchen gardens, while the balance of the land should remain with the landlord or the state (in the form of "economic" or "*udyel*" estates).[12]

Nicholas I on his accession to the throne in 1825 is said to have found in his brother's desk a list of Alexander's projected reforms. In any event, in most matters Nicholas regarded himself as the heir and continuator of his brother's work. As such, he must also have shared Alexander's views on the peasant question, influenced as these views were by the Anglophile and Francophile members of his entourage. Nicholas is said, probably with justification, to have first been in favor of emancipation without land (a scheme that fitted in well with eighteenth-century trends). Later he was converted to a plan for emancipation with land by P. D. Kisel'ev, recalled in 1834 from his post as administrator of the Danubian principalities and named by Nicholas in language that was half jocular, half serious, "Chief of the [Tsar's] general staff" on the peasant question. Under Alexander, Kisel'ev had long given proof of good will toward the peasant, and his administration in the principalities had added to this reputation.

[11] Under date of May 22 and 23, 1826. They were at first ascribed to Ryleyev who later denied their authorship. Tsentrarkhiv, *Vosstanie Dekabristov*, III, 389 (the author's translation).

[12] Semevskii, *Krest'yanskii Vopros*, I, 508. It is ascribed to E. Ya., without further identifying him. The "economic" peasants were those on church lands secularized by the state; "*udyel*" peasants were those on estates belonging to the imperial family.

During the age of Nicholas, discussions on public matters were at a minimum. In gauging public opinion, especially for the early period, one is forced back to official statements or chance references in literature. With the failure of the Decembrist Revolt, the clamor for reform was silenced. That the peasant continued to be a live issue and some amelioration of his lot was attempted privately are more than suggested by passages in Pushkin's *Evgenii Onyegin:*

Alone among his new possessions,
At first Eugene began to dream
Of making certain grand concessions
And setting up a new regime;
For the corvee he substituted
Light quit-rent, and the slave, well-suited
Because there was not much to pay,
Blessed his new master every day.
And so his calculating neighbor
Who thought our Eugene was a gull;
Another neighbor touched his skull:
Why thus dispense with lawful labor?
The youth was called on every hand,
A faddist and a firebrand.

              *   *   *

Another landowner come newly
To his estate about this time
Was also picked to pieces duly,
For gossip is not held a crime.
Vladimir Lenskii, handsome, youthful,
A Kantian, unspoiled and truthful,
Whose soul was shaped at Göttingen,
And who could wield a poet's pen,
From misty Germany, Vladimir
Had brought the fruits of learning's tree:
An ardent faith in liberty,
The spirit of an oddish dreamer,
Rapt eloquence in speech and song,
And curls as black as they were long.[13]

[13] Alexander Pushkin, *Evgenii Onyegin*, II, IV, and VI. By permission of Random House, Inc. Translation by Babette Deutsch.

Yet the climate of public opinion was changing. English and French models were ceasing to charm, and sober second thought was suggesting that after all the Russian peasant was not so badly off. In 1832, years before the Slavophiles had begun to sound the praises of the old bucolic life of the countryside, Pushkin had written:

If you read the complaints of the English factory worker, they will make your hair stand on end with horror. What fearful torture! What cold-blooded cruelty on the one hand, what frightful misery on the other! It is not a question here of the building of the pyramids of the Pharaohs. . . . We are talking of Mr. Smith's cloth, of Mr. Jackson's needles. One gets the impression that there is no more wretched worker in the world than the Englishman. Just see for yourself what the invention of a machine means there, by which fifty to sixty thousand workers are displaced and lose their only source of livelihood. Now look at the Russian peasant. Is there a trace of slavish debasement in his behavior or his speech? We need not mention his keen glance, his alertness. His ability to learn is well known; his intelligence and cleverness are extraordinary. . . . In Russia, there is no man who does not own his own home. The pauper, with his beggar's staff in hand, owns his own cottage. That is not the case in foreign lands. The lot of the Russian peasant improves from day to day.[14]

It seems incredible that Pushkin should have written such nonsense; but it is fairly good evidence that the enthusiasm for mere liberty was on the wane and that it was to be replaced by the idea of attaining economic security.

In the absence of intimate papers, we have nothing to guide us in attempts to trace the policies of Nicholas on the peasant question. His brother had left to him a number of papers embodying suggestions. But Alexander had also left him an unfortunate heritage of unsolved problems. The military colonies founded after the Napoleonic Wars, although brought under control by measures of savage repression and subjected to stern discipline, were known

[14] Alexander Pushkin, *Sochineniya* (Anskii Edition), V, 222–23. Cited from Valentin Gitermann, *Geschichte Russlands*, III, 122.

to be seething with sullen resentment.[15] The peasants could not but be disturbed by the events of December 14, 1825. The Emperor himself was just beginning to forget these things and was plunging into other pressing matters. Nicholas did find time, however, to name a secret committee to go over the late emperor's papers on the peasant question and to submit suggestions. With the exception of Speranskii, the committee was undistinguished. Perhaps it was for this reason that its somewhat innocuous recommendations were ignored.

The long wars, the Polish revolt, and stirring events in foreign affairs drove all others matters from the Emperor's mind until 1835. Whether Nicholas's mind reverted spontaneously to the peasant problem, or whether the return of Kisel'ev from the principalities occasioned a revival of interest, we do not know. Russia entered now into a period of intense activity, of which Kisel'ev was the center. By this time, the categories of peasants had been reduced to comparatively few: the landed peasants of private landlords (forming the largest class); the landless household peasants (a relatively small number); the state peasants with which the church peasants had been merged in the eighteenth century; the one-household peasants (*odnodvortsy*); the "free husbandmen" created by Alexander; and the peasants of the Imperial families. A few special categories still persisted, such as possessional peasants assigned to mines and factories. But the peasants we hear most about were those of the first three classifications.

The committee was named to attack the problem of the peasants of the first of these groups. It finally drew up a scheme providing for the passing of the peasants through three successive stages from their present condition, under which they were dependent on their lords and subject to the three days' obligatory work provided by the *ukaz* of 1797; through a stage in which they were "bound to the land," but with the claims of the landlords reduced to a moderate amount of work; and finally to a third stage in which they were to have the full right of removal from landlord

[15] These settlements were a combination of peasant commune and military cantonment where the soldiers, although under military discipline, lived at home with their families. But they were artificial creations, had no traditional roots, and were bitterly detested. For an account of them, see N. K. Shilder, *Imperator Aleksandr Pervyi*, IV, 23–39.

to landlord and to engage for labor on a purely contractural basis. This scheme also provided that the "state peasants" might be embraced in the scheme by being included in the second or transitional phase. For some obscure reason, this committee's work was not satisfactory, and a second committee was named in 1839 to take up the task. The work of this second committee was approved by the Emperor in 1840, and a *ukaz* was issued in 1842, which provided for the transition of the peasants as indicated above. Yet only a mere handful of the gentry (the initiative of the landlord was necessary) took advantage of the *ukaz*, and its results were quite insignificant.[16]

Perhaps one reason why the committee was reorganized was that Kisel'ev had already received a more important assignment. The manner of administering the state peasants was quite inadequate, especially since the enormous accession of territory of the late eighteenth and early nineteenth centuries and the vast increase in the area of crown lands. A so-called Provisional Fifth Section of the Imperial Chancery was formed in 1836 to take charge of all crown lands and peasants; and to head this agency Kisel'ev was named. A nationwide survey and census of these lands was made, and in 1837 there was organized on the model of the ministries created by Alexander I the new Ministry of Imperial Domains for the purpose of administering this property, and a total of 8,148,728 state peasants settled on these lands.

The landless household servants had long been a scandal to public opinion in Russia. They swarmed in the country homes and town residences and accompanied the family like an army of retainers on its migrations from town to country and country to town. Some few of these servants were trusted personal attendants, on terms of intimacy and affection with the family. The great majority, however, were without special skills and training, and in the disordered conditions of many households, were without adequate supervision. As a class they were idle, unreliable, quarrelsome, and given to petty thievery, and were inveterate scandal mongers who spoiled or corrupted the children. In general they gave a poor return for their maintenance, but most families took

[16] Semevskii, *Krest'yanskii Vopros v XVIII i pervoi polovinye XIX vyeka*, II, 63.

pride in the number of such servants attached to their households. At the best, these servants were without incentive to industry or thrift, subject to the whims and caprices of each member of the family, without personal responsibility, experiencing by turns the indulgence or wrath of the master or mistress, their only protection being the traditional cunning and deceit of the peasant. The plight of the young women was even worse than that of the men, for in the close intimacy of the household they were exposed to constant solicitation by the male members of the family, whose legitimate prey society was prone to regard them.

Again in 1840 Kisel'ev, despite his other preoccupations, was named to a secret committee to report on the household peasants. This committee's deliberations over a period of three years finally issued in a report accepted by the Emperor. The *ukaz* based on this report, which was decreed in 1844, provided a scheme of redemption under which the *dvorovye* (household peasants) would purchase their freedom under a contractual scheme which set the amount to be paid and the term required to work it out. If entered as household servants on the last revision, the peasants were to continue in that category until the debt was discharged.

These measures, coming in rapid succession, had seriously alarmed the gentry, for they seemed to endanger property rights. And this repeated alarming of the gentry, by raising the issue of emancipation—however ineffective the successive steps might be—had in addition an unsettling influence upon the peasants. Echoes of this unrest finally reached the Emperor's ears by way of a memorandum of Perovskii, minister of the interior. This memorandum sounded alarm and urged that the whole question be subjected to far-reaching investigation. Perovskii's greatest fear was the creation, through the measures already in effect, of a landless proletariat. Perovskii got a committee (as he had requested), but this committee with true bureaucratic evasion confined itself to remedying the abuses in the present system rather than attempting any fundamental changes. These abuses were to be referred to the Second Section of the Imperial Chancery.

The agitation of the gentry over their threatened property rights finally came to a head in 1847–48 in the matter of sale of private estates. The first issue concerned the right of peasants to protection of their property when the estate of which they were a part was put up for sale. The rights of the peasants in this case were not secure. Resort was again had to a secret committee, which included Kisel'ev. A decree of Nicholas, issued on March 3, 1848, put the rights of the peasants beyond doubt. The second case was the right of the peasants to redeem themselves and thus obtain their freedom if the estate on which they lived was put up for sale. Against some silent opposition, the Emperor gave them this right, provided they could produce the money within thirty days. Complaints and protests were heard, which Nicholas referred to a special committee. He tried to reassure the gentry in a speech of March 21, 1848, at the same time that he stubbornly stood his ground. His speech is worth recording:

Special attention must be paid to their [the peasants'] welfare. Some persons have ascribed to me on this point the most absurd and the rashest opinions and aims. I reject these with indignation. When I issued the *ukaz* about the "bound peasants" [see above], I declared that without any exception all the land belonged to the noble-landlord. That word is sacred, and no one can gainsay it. But I am bound to say that we have among us a mere handful of conscientious and considerate landlords, but a great many of the ordinary run, while we have a still larger number of bad ones; and in the spirit of the times, apart from the dictates of conscience and of law, we are bound in our own interest to look after the welfare of those entrusted to us and to try by every means to win their love and respect. If there is among us a landlord who is immoral or cruel, we are bound to turn him over to the severity of the law. Some Russian periodicals have allowed themselves to print articles which incite the peasants against the landlords and which, in general, were improper; but I have taken the appropriate steps, and there will be no more of this.[17]

Nicholas' efforts to talk down the opposition were of no avail. Fresh complaints and reports of fresh peasant disorders kept coming in. Once more the favorite device of a special committee was

[17] *Ibid.*, II, 189. The "appropriate steps" referred to obviously refer to tightening of the censorship. See Chap. VII above.

tried. The events in Paris in February aggravated the situation, making the application of the law more difficult in the agitated state of the public mind. The committee finally came to a division: four members (including Kisel'ev) believed that repeal would only make the situation more critical and were against any action; five members (including the heir apparent, the future Emperor Alexander II) voted solidly for the repeal of the law of 1847 on these grounds:

> However just and beneficial were the intentions of the government in issuing the law of November 8, 1847, nevertheless, experience has demonstrated, on the one hand, that the landlords' peasants are, in very few cases, able to produce the money to take advantage of the right to purchase their freedom.[18]

On the other hand, these five members urged, the decree had tended to unsettle the minds of the more ignorant, and the country was now threatened with the direct consequences, rising from this uncertainty, which would call for the sternest measures of repression. They therefore strongly recommended the repeal of the offending act. Finally, according to Semevskii, the monarch hesitated and procrastinated. Going off to Moscow, Nicholas took further counsel there with those members of the State Council then in that city, and on his return he directed the Grand Duke Alexander to announce that it was the Emperor's pleasure, having read the outline proposed by the four members of the special committee (the minority), to direct Count Bludov to proceed with the drafting of a manifesto dealing with the disposal of estates by public sale.[19]

The manifesto was finally prepared and issued on July 19, 1849. While nominally confirming the decree of November 8, 1847, it actually reduced the 1847 decree to a nullity by requiring the landlord's consent as an indispensable prerequisite to the peasant's purchase of freedom.

The efforts of Nicholas on behalf of the peasant therefore produced insignificant results. Perhaps the time for half-measures had gone, and any efforts to correct the abuses without abolishing the

[18] *Ibid.*, II, 189.
[19] *Ibid.*

Tsar Nicholas I

A. I. Herzen

N. V. Gogol

V. G. Byelinskii

evil were doomed to failure. It is more likely the bureaucracy simply reflected the growing alarm in higher circles at tampering with Russia's traditional institutions. Perhaps the views of the committee, which was named on the recommendation of Perovskii and which frustrated his attempts at reform, were typical of these bureaucratic circles. The committee had proclaimed that:

Until Russia loses her unity and greatness, other countries cannot serve as an example to her. This colossus requires a different foundation and different concepts of freedom, not only for the peasants, but for all classes of society as well. The foundation of Russia has been and ought to remain autocracy; without it she cannot continue to exist in her present might. Freedom in her territories ought to consist in protecting each individual in his person and property from oppression by others and in obedience to the laws that issue from a single source.[20]

Such was the prevailing view of the bureaucracy and of the landed proprietors whom they, in part at least, represented. Property rights were to be prized more highly than the benefits that could be conferred on the peasants by a reasonable program of redemption. Disasters on a national scale were required to give the needed shock to set the process in motion again; when these occurred, more drastic solutions would be the natural result. The Crimean War—1854–55—was later to liberate the forces needed to compel these changes.

[20] *Ibid.*, II, 144.

XII

The Russian Mind

❦❦❦❦❦❦❦❦❦❦❦❦❦❦❦❦❦❦❦❦❦❦❦❦

B Y the time of the conclusion of the Crimean War, influences
from western Europe had been flooding Russia for a century and a half and outwardly had wrought great changes
in Muscovite life. Many age-old habits had been discarded;
established institutions had been superseded by others more suited
to the times and to Russia's new place in the world. But to what
extent had basic native traits been modified? How far had Russia
assimilated her culture to the culture of the models of the West?
Were the observable changes merely on the surface? These are
some of the questions that call for an answer.

One thing is certain: not all institutions transplanted into Russian soil necessarily took root; and even when they did, the fruits
were not always those the institutions produced in the West. As
Diderot had remarked to the Empress Catherine, "Ideas transplanted from Paris to St. Petersburg take on a different shade."[1]
Indeed, the first contacts of Russia with Europe could transmit
nothing of importance since Russians were not sufficiently advanced to absorb these ideas. The impressive architectural monu-
ments of western Europe, which today astound and delight the
modern tourist, were wasted on early Russian travelers, who saw
only masses of stone and mortar of such and such dimensions. An
unknown who accompanied Peter the Great on his travels describes
the great bronze statue of Erasmus in Rotterdam (since destroyed
by the Nazis) in some detail without concerning to inform himself on the name of the person it commemorated or his achievements.[2] Even Karamzin, the historian who was in Paris during the

[1] Bil'basov, *Istoricheskie Monografii*, IV, 366.
[2] Plekhanov, *Istoriya russkoi obshchestvennoi mysli*. An English translation of Book II, Chaps. 1, 2, and part of 3 was prepared under the Board of

sessions of the National Assembly in 1789 when events of supreme importance were being enacted, was preoccupied with his sightseeing to the entire neglect of politics.[3] Russians simply had few points of intellectual contact with eighteenth-century France.

By the beginning of the nineteenth century, one can say that Russia had gone to school to Europe for well over half a century. Whatever else he might know of European culture, the young Russian gentleman could in most cases speak French and discuss French literature. He was certain to be a connoisseur of French wines, and he mixed French expletives with his conversation.[4] The fashionable jargon of the day—natural law and the rights of man—was often on his lips. Even during Catherine's day, among the upper classes this talk had developed into a frenzy of Gallomania.[5] The Revolution also brought swarms of French Royalist refugees to Russia in search of an asylum in the case of the noble *émigrés* and to eke out a livelihood in the case of the more humble.

Nor were German influences much less potent. Since the annexation of the Baltic states, German Balts had been making themselves indispensable in the state service, and their numbers were swelled by scores of others from Germany itself. The Imperial family had shown a preference for German wives, and the parents and relatives of these wives had found a promising career for sons and nephews in the Russian Army and state service. Indeed, the roster of higher officers in the Russian Army was dominated by German names. German influences were perhaps somewhat less in cultural than in the field of military and administrative affairs. Nevertheless, these influences were impressive in the universities where German personnel predominated and German learning had taken root.

In attempting to summarize the changes wrought by this Germanic sway, we must be aware that the circle of those who were

Education of the City of New York and the Department of Social Sciences of Columbia University, New York, in 1938. The reference is to the English translation, 2 ff.

[3] Karamzin, *Pis'ma russkogo puteshestvennika* (*Letters of a Russian Traveler*).

[4] See Dmitrii von Mohrenschildt, *Russia in the Life of Eighteenth-Century France*.

[5] Griboyedov, *Gore ot Uma*, Act I, sc. 4, and passim.

thus affected was of necessity relatively small in the eighteenth century. Illiteracy among the upper classes had largely disappeared, but there was no immediate prospect of education's shortly becoming the property of all people. The intellectual class was confined to the gentry and, indeed, to a minority of that class. Few native Russians attained distinction in letters or science until fifty years after Peter's death.[6]

But it must be conceded that the system of education so brilliantly inaugurated by Catherine and actually put into effect by her grandson, Alexander I, had begun to show results by the end of the Napoleonic wars. Of this generation the Decembrists were perhaps the elite, not in birth (few among them belonged to the "highborn" gentry) but in sheer ability and character. But new elements—more particularly, the sons of priests—began to appear among the intellectuals; Speranskii and Nadezhdin are the best examples.[7] Under Nicholas we find members of the nonserving nobility, of the merchant class, and even peasants making their way in the literary world. The intelligentsia had ceased to be aristocratic.

This new social make-up of the intellectual classes requires more than a passing attention to discover its impact on modern Russian thought and the extent to which it set Russia off from the rest of Europe. Plekhanov's comments are especially pertinent:

> . . . the intelligentsia among us has never formed a well-defined class and it never can. It has only been a refined social stratum; but this refined social stratum has played an important role in the history of Russian Enlightenment. Byelinskii was right when he said that to this group belonged persons drawn together through Enlightenment. . . . However in the seventeenth century we quite miss, among the progenitors of the Russian intelligentsia, persons of mercantile or trading origin. In the course of the following two centuries the merchants and tradesmen contribute their own quota to the ranks of the in-

[6] This movement is described in some detail in K. Miller, *Frantsuskaya Emigratsuya i Rossiya.*

[7] M. M. Speranskii had served Alexander I as Imperial secretary but fell from grace in 1812. He was later recalled and filled other posts. Under Nicholas I, he headed the commission that assembled the two great collections of laws, *Polnoe Sobranie Zakonov* and *Svod Zakonov.* Nadezhdin was a journalist and for a time edited *Teleskop.*

telligentsia, but right up to the sixties of the nineteenth century, when the *raznochintsy* came forward, they constituted a minority. It was this that marked the difference between the Russian and the French intelligentsia, that, in the latter, for long, predominance was exercised by persons of that class which Byelinskii refers to as the middle class, but in France bore the title *tiers état*. And that is understandable. We know that in France the monarchial power in its struggle with the feudality relied for the most part on the third estate. It is this relative difference in the two historical processes that explains the difference just pointed out by me, in the constitution of the intelligentsia in Russia on the one hand, and in France on the other. Below we shall see how this relative uniqueness in the constitution of the Russian intelligentsia, caused by the relative uniqueness of the historical process in Russia, was reflected in the further course of the development of Russian social thought.[8]

The want of a middle class in the western European sense is a cardinal fact not only in the history of Russian thought but in the whole development of Russia. In the West circumstances had brought the townsmen to the fore and made them the bearers of culture. The Russians, however, are accustomed to regard the superior culture of the Westerner as due solely to the protection afforded him during the Middle Ages by the East against the swarms of nomads from Asia; and in no sense to his own merits. The Russians set no great store by the virtues developed by the town life of medieval Europe, the discipline exercised by the guilds, or the building up of a system of habits of thrift. They looked on the West as profiting by the security thus enjoyed to perfect the arts it had inherited from Rome—arts which the West (once it had attained a superiority) was in duty bound to share with Russia. The West regarded this sharing from their point of view as an act of extreme generosity for which there was little justification. Their arts were their own possessions. While the West were willing to impart them for a price to the Russians, the latter saw themselves as the victims of exploitation. Nor did they see any occasion

[8] Plekhanov, *Istoriya russkoi obshchestvennoi mysli*, I, 303.

to emulate the thrift and industry of the Germans, virtues which they despised and which had nothing to do with technical superiority. In other words, for the most part, industrial skill, military proficiency, and success in business are in the West regarded as inseparable from the standards of the business world. It is to integrity, industry, and thrift that Western moralists like to ascribe their superior civilizations, while the Russian regards these virtues as extraneous. The skill can be acquired for a price, and once it is acquired, the West's whole scheme of moral values can be dispensed with—with all the dull and pedestrian virtues of which they are made up.[9]

The change in social make-up was attended by an equally sharp break in thought. Signs of this break were already to be discerned. Chaadayev had already in 1829 challenged the idea of the infinite perfectibility of man, the favorite theme of the Enlightenment; he had also called attention to the dreadful emptiness (by European standards) of Russian life, by this criticism outraging national pride both in and out of official circles.[10] Actually, the French thought of the Enlightenment was already losing ground to the new German philosophy in western Europe. But there was perhaps an additional reason why it found the ground prepared in Russia; here French rationalism had set tasks that were unattainable without a somewhat belated progress, by way of imitation and borrowing, over the course already traversed by the West. But German writers from Herder on had emphasized the organic nature of the development of distinct national cultures and did not envisage the necessity of a universal pattern to which all peoples had to conform. Each people could make its own unique contribution. Moreover, the new philosophy of Hegel and Schelling was more congenial to the Russians with their peculiar theological background. It made no great demands by way of objectivity or painful accumulation of facts. The mind could by intuition leap to all—embracing theories which would light up the universe. These ideas were finding their way into Russia and being discussed during the thirties in the Stankevich circle. They inspired the Slavophile doctrine of the

[9] D. Tsvetayev, *Protestantstvo i Protestanty*, 698–99.
[10] Chaadayev, "Philosophical Letters," *Sochineniya*, I. The above is a condensation of several passages in his letters.

uniqueness and worthwhileness of Russian national culture, and the susceptible mind of Byelinskii at once took fire from them. In the words of one writer:

> In the first period of his activity, Byelinskii took a hostile attitude toward the trend of literature and thought in France, especially in the eighteenth century, maintaining that one ought to explain facts by ideas and not deduce ideas from facts; that in the eighteenth century, experiment led to nothing but skepticism, materialism, corruption, and blindness to truth in broad fields of knowledge . . . experiment leads nowhere, except in religion to godlessness; in learning to endless wandering amid a mass of detached bits of knowledge . . . the only salvation for mankind lay in abstract concepts, in the explanation of all existence drawn from an abstract idea which proceeds to self-consciousness in human reason.[11]

If we are in search of the roots of some of the basic concepts which up to the present have colored Russian life and thought, we will find at least two of them here: a firm belief in the uniqueness of Russian national culture which is true to its own standard and does not need to conform to any world pattern, and an equally fanatical devotion to "an abstract idea which proceeds to self-consciousness in human reason."

A passion for facts is the soul of modern science and indeed inspires most of our modern life, even though we must needs, from time to time, frame hypotheses to enable us to explain our facts. Yet these hypotheses have only a provisional character, and the Western world does not often allow them to usurp the role of dogma. The West never assumes that they have a universal validity for all times and all people. Yet at a time when they were taking over this heritage of thought, which from the time of the Greeks has painfully insisted on the factual basis of knowledge, the Russians, like Xenophanes of old, rejected this whole empirical approach as leading nowhere and decided in favor of an a priori one. Philosophical discussion turned less on the facts adduced by the participants than on the concepts from which they started. As

[11] Skabichevskii, "Ocherki umstvennago razvitiya nashego obshchestva 1825–1860," in *Otechestvennye Zapiski*, T. 194 (1871), No. 1, 116–17.

Lev Tikhomirov, writing in the late nineteenth century, said: "In Russia little attention is paid to facts as they are."[12]

A hundred years ago, the Marquis de Custine, who visited Russia in 1839, wrote:

... Up to now I believed that man could no more do without truth for the spirit than air and sun for the body; my journey to Russia disabuses me. Here to lie is to protect the social order; to speak the truth is to destroy the state.[13]

Even Herzen excuses the peasant who lies to a stranger with the explanation that the latter hears only what he wishes to hear. But even more penetrating is the comment of Mr. Dillon, for many years St. Petersburg correspondent of the London *Daily Telegraph*. Mr. Dillon drew on his long experience in Russia for a series of articles, under the pseudonym "Lanin," on "Russian Characteristics," which appeared in the *Fortnightly Review* in 1890. He says:

They [the Russians] lack that reverence for facts that lies at the root of the Anglo-Saxon character. A Russian can no more bow to a fact, acknowledging it as final and decisive, than he can to a personal appreciation or to a mere opinion founded upon insufficient or no grounds; he is ever ready to act in open defiance of it.

Moreover, the result of raising intuitively-arrived-at so-called "truth" to the level of dogma is that it must be pushed to its extreme limits:

... in knowledge and practice, where powerful forces come on the scene, the truth is never in the "golden mean" between them; neither is the warfare of paganism with Christianity, of Catholicism with Protestantism, nor in any other struggle between inertia and progress. A real force is true to itself and pursues its own end, rigid consistency in knowledge and life and firm consistency in practice—these are manifestations of one and the same principle.

Eclecticism is a peculiar kind of professional disease of the intelligentsia. The group that occupies a middle position midst

[12] This citation from Custine is taken from *Journey for Our Time*, by permission of Pellegrini and Cudahy.

[13] Lev. Tikhomirov, *Russia, Social and Political*, II, 23.

powerful classes, that is always wavering in its relations with them, the intelligentsia reflects these features in its thought.[14]

There seems to be no need to enlarge on the implication of these two predominating characteristics of Russian thought: (1) a preoccupation with theory to the exclusion of facts; and (2) the acceptance as a fixed point in thought of some concept arrived at (usually in someone else's mind) intuitively. Thus is laid a philosophical basis of intolerance which refuses to accept a factual basis of agreement and rejects all compromise.

This tendency may or may not be a national trait. It certainly became axiomatic with most Russian revolutionary writers that the "compromiser" was a coward or a villain. Writing at a somewhat later period, Tikhomirov has this to say:

> A man of energy, of animation, devoted unreservedly to the public interest will in Russia scarcely ever become a liberal; he becomes a socialist and a revolutionist. A man more circumspect, more moderate, not in conviction but in character, adheres to the liberals.[15]

By the middle of the century, the term "liberal" had become discredited. It was a term of opprobrium applied to the economist who was a doctrinaire adherent of the Manchester school or to the individual who from excessive caution was perpetually a "trimmer." This fact is admirably illustrated by a cartoon reproduced from the files of *Iskra* which shows the "liberal" engaged in the precarious task of balancing himself on a tightrope. Trotsky in his *History of the Russian Revolution* uses the term "Compromisers" as the most scornful he could draw from his vocabulary. Lenin, everywhere, applies the term "Liberal" (which to him means a compromiser) to all who believe in moderation in politics. But already by 1850 the term had acquired a distasteful connotation in Russia.

As a matter of fact, compromise as a working rule of life has a long and honorable history. The Greeks distilled it into the adage "nothing in excess"; the "golden mean" was proclaimed in Aris-

---

[14] "Dorovatskii i Chernuzhnikov," *Ocherki realistrcheskago mirozryeniya*, Intro., v–vi.

[15] Tikhomirov, *Russia, Social and Political*.

"A liberal is a tight-rope walker who skillfully sways this way and that to maintain his balance in the middle" (*A caricature of P. A. Baluev, minister of the interior under Alexander II. Representing a widespread Russian prejudice against all moderate reformers, it appeared in No. 21 of* Iskra *in 1862.*)

totle's *Ethics;* today it is the basis of most business and political deals. As in ancient Greece, modern Europe with its multitude of conflicting forces has preferred an equilibrium of these forces to the complete ascendancy of any one. But in Russia power was concentrated; there was no church to dispute the secular arm; no aristocracy to curb the monarch; no towns to bring the monarch to terms by withholding taxes. This is the readiest explanation of the phenomenon to which it is fashionable to apply the term "maximalism"—the resolve to press measures, ameliorative in themselves, to their extreme limit. Such a passion for extremes was abhorrent to the Greeks; nor does it recommend itself to life in a free state where politics is a matter of compromise. Compromise is accepted as so much a part of our way of life that it passes all but unnoticed in our literature.[16] For instance, how many have given even passing thought to George Eliot's mischievous jibe at English compromise in *Silas Marner:*

"Come, come," said the landlord, "a joke's a joke. We are good friends here, I hope. We must give and take. You're both right, and you're both wrong, as I say. I agree with Mr. Macey here, as there's two opinions; and if mine is asked I should say they're both right. Tookey's right and Winthrop's right, and they've only to split the difference and make themselves even."

Whence comes the Russian's passion for extremes? One is forced to have recourse to Chaadayev, who so long ago saw into the Russian soul:

So long as societies are in a state of uncertainty, without convictions and rules even for everyday affairs, and so long as life is not regulated, what chance have the seeds of good to ripen? It is the chaotic ferment in the moral sphere, corresponding to the whirling of the globe that preceded the present state of our planet. We are still at that stage. In the West, the child in its cradle, at play, and in its mother's arms has already absorbed certain ideas. What are these ideas; [they are those of] duty, justice, law, and order. These are born amid the very events that fashion society; they are integral parts of the social life of those countries. . . . Foreigners who admire our national audacity forget that the same characteristics which make us so bold and reckless also rob us of depth and tenacity; they fail to observe that what makes us indifferent to the dangers of life also makes us insensible to [distinctions of] good and evil, truth and falsehood, that robs us of those sustaining motives that impel other nations along the road of progress.[17]

[16] This problem was not overlooked by the English liberals. See John Morley, "On Compromise," *Works*, III.

[17] Chaadayev, *Sochineniya.* I, 79–81.

Chaadayev implies that it was this complete lack of a sustaining tradition that impelled Russians to the greatest extremes. It ran all through the revolution and the post-revolutionary period. "Never allow your left flank to be turned."

This passion to seek virtues in the extreme has made violence and terror the chief arbiter of our times. Mass deportations, wholesale liquidations and purges, and the dreaded concentration camps are the logical outcome of a system that fixes its eye on the distant Utopia. As medieval man regarded the inquisition and *auto-da-fé* as the necessary means to save the soul of the victim otherwise lost, so the modern believer in absolutes shrinks from no human cost in attaining his goal. For the first time in the modern world, we have the revival of such practices as the deportation of whole peoples, banned for the last two thousand years. International relations are no longer exclusively between equal and sovereign people and members of a civilized family; and war is no longer a mere pause in an otherwise uninterrupted state of harmony. We are to be in a state of continuous war between two irreconcilable systems, waged by means long abandoned by civilized man, by which it is hoped to usher in the glorious year of jubilee—a new world order.

A third feature stands out clearly from the literature of the time: the new acceptance of national culture as preferable to an imported one. Chaadayev's picturesque jeremiads had assigned Russia a place on the merest fringe of the civilized world:

Look around. Is not everything in a state of agitation? One would say we were on the road [for somewhere]. We have no fixed abode; no settled habits, no rules for anything; we have not even our own fireside, nothing that anchors us or evokes our attachments, our sympathies, our affections; nothing that endures, nothing that abides; everything is on the move, is passing away without leaving a trace on us or our environment. We seem to camp in our homes; we seem strangers in our own families; we pause for the night like nomads in our cities, more so than the nomads who graze [their flocks] over our steppes, for they are more firmly rooted to their deserts than we to our cities . . . There is no natural progress, no integral development . . . We grow but do not mature; we advance but in an oblique line that leads nowhere . . . We live in a restricted present, without past and without future, in the midst of a dead calm.[18]

Yet even Chaadayev had foretold the day when Russia would instruct the West. This dawning pride in the old way of life the Slavophiles made their own creed, but Slavophiles and Westerners were at one in proclaiming the cultural self-sufficiency of Russia. In the time of Alexander I, Russia had not questioned the necessity of the slow and painful progress along the well-worn path long since trodden by the West as the price of attaining civilization. But now suddenly the swift rise of a new national literature filled Russians with pride in their achievement and with an immense self-confidence. Yet this natural and praiseworthy reaction quickly took on a different tone. Herzen's letters written from his sanctuary abroad echoed a human homesickness for the scenes of his homeland, but quickly became a diatribe against the defects of Western civilization. At their worst his letters degenerate into a shrill xenophobia.

In this respect, Herzen seems to have given a turn to Russian thought that was to be decisive. After settling in Paris, he dashed off his impressions of European civilization in a work entitled *Letter from the Avenue Marigny.* This piece is more than sheer xenophobia. In addition to the Russian's natural feeling of being out of place in Paris, it reflects the aristocrat's distaste for everything connected with the workaday world of business. It is a complete and utter repudiation of everything for which Europe stands. However, it is true that Herzen visited France at a time when public life had sunk to its lowest ebb.

The aristocracy and the common people were adolescents, children, poets; the revolutionaries were idealists. The bourgeoisie seemed to represent the prose of life, the practical side of the proprietor who built factories instead of temples, who substituted the colossal structures of the engineer for the colossal structures of the architect; this was his own way of consecrating his life, of giving respectability to his occupation, his labors. They argued about self-sacrifice and despised (at least in words) material advantage—the bourgeoisie openly seeks profit and smiles at self-sacrifice: they have sacrificed people to ideas—the

[18] Chaadayev, *Sochineniya,* I, 78.

bourgeoise has sacrificed ideas to itself. . . . What can never be forgiven the bourgeoisie is its full consciousness that it knows full well that it has dishonored France in the eyes of Europe, in the eyes of the people, that there is no security for it in selling its votes, its ballots. . . . The most thoroughgoing conservatives of the Chamber of Deputies, some Mornet, and two hundred men, who in the face of the whole of Paris were not ashamed to vote for the acquittal of the persons accused by Girardin at the very moment when they were being convicted by Girardin. All of these gentlemen are such sticklers for legality and correctness that they cannot involuntarily allow themselves to make such a crass mistake—they only want peace and order and ministerial protection for their commercial operations; hence comes this possibility quite foreign to the French character; . . . this is the only class that has political rights, the class from which the lawmakers are chosen, the class that controls all the wealth, that relies, in its role as protector of a party, on government funds, on the national guard, on the army, on the police, and on human inertia, which furnishes a negative support which is mighty important.[19]

In a later passage, Herzen is even more caustic in his characterization:

They [the bourgeoisie] are cautious in their judgments, never departing from the facts; they are even more cautious in their conduct, never stepping from the beaten track. . . . All they say is true, but they could not do anything else. . . . Everything about these fine gentlemen is correct, decorous, timely; they show the proper respect for virtue and shun vice; everything about them is not devoid of a certain charm of a gray summer day, without rain or sun, but lacking what they do, all else is worthless.

Or again, in another passage:

. . . he personifies delight in moderation and mediocrity, when he is in a position to throw mud at everything that is his superior.[20]

[19] Herzen, *Polnoe Sobranie Sochinenii i pisem*, V, 167–68.
[20] Ivanov Razumnik, *Istoriya russkoi obshchestvennoi mysli*, I, 342.

It is somewhat anomalous that at a time when Russia was making belated efforts to emulate the industrial and commercial achievements of western Europe, one of its greatest writers should have used the French as a horrible example of what these efforts would lead to. Moreover, it became the basis of Herzen's whole attitude toward Russian life. By 1862, Herzen's views on France had somewhat altered, and he had come to regard not the great French bankers and entrepreneurs as the ruin of France, but the lower middle class—the *"petite bourgeoisie."* Starting from this premise, Herzen quickly transferred the vices of this class to their Russian equivalent, the *myeshchanin*—a class thus described by Semevskii:

> The *myeshchane*, a respected and honorable class in other countries, is here insignificant, poor, encumbered with obligations, without means to eke out a livelihood. In other countries they live in the cities, but here cities exist only on the map, and the craft guilds oppress freedom in them; and so, the *myeshchane* are migrants, like gypsies, engaged in peddling and tinkering. The decline of trade affects them the more in proportion to their poverty, for they are dependent on the merchants in their capacity as traders or as workmen in the factories.[21]

It seems incredible that Herzen should have seized on this wretched class (which he cannot have known anything about from personal experience) to use as his whipping-boy and to hold them up to scorn for the vices of the despised middle class he saw in Russia. He further saw them as typical of all that hard, material, modern world in which we live and against which we sometimes protest inwardly. Much as the term "Philistine" was used by Matthew Arnold in England, *myeshchanin* and *myeshchanstvo* are applied to all nineteenth-century civilization and its vices, even when these had nothing to do with the middle class. It became, thus, a term with ethical connotation. In a famous passage, Herzen characterizes it:

> "The *myeshchanstvo* is the last word in civilization founded on the absolute power of property, the democratization of aristocracy—the aristocratization of democracy; in this environ-

[21] Semevskii, *Politicheskie Idei Dekabristov*, 99.

ment, Al'mavina is equal to Figaro—everything rises from below to *myeshchanstvo;* everything from above falls into it. The
American states represent only a "middle class" in which there
is neither an upper stratum nor a lower stratum, but the mores
remain those of a *myeshchanin.* . . . Art that finds in the home
of the *myeshchanin* only vulgarity can only regard *myeshchanstvo* with loathing; the thinker who longs to see personality
in man can only condemn it—but attempts to stop the triumphal
progress of *myeshchanstvo* are inevitably doomed to failure. . . .
With *myeshchanstvo* personalities are polished smooth; but the
persons so polished are more well to do, wear cheap clothing,
not custom-made, not fitted—but their numbers are greater.
Everything is mass produced, wholesale, common, accessible to
everyone, but allowing no esthetic finish, no personal taste.
Nearby around the corner everywhere waits the hundred-
headed hydra ready to listen to everything without discrimination, to gaze at everything, to eat anything, wear anything;
this is the all-powerful mob of conglomerated mediocrity."[22]

If the gentry of Russia was slowly becoming bankrupt and the
middle classes were becoming corrupted by the false standards
which were everywhere supplanting aristocratic virtues, on what
was the future of the country to depend? Herzen had no hesita-
tion in replying "on the peasant." We have already seen how
Russian public opinion on the peasant question had slowly altered
during the course of the eighteenth century. In earlier times the
peasant had been regarded as a means of production for the landlord and indirectly for the state, and even Peter had done nothing
for the peasant except to regularize his state payments and his discharge of military service. Pososhkov's chief concern, as we have
seen, was not in the peasant as an individual, but as a class capable
of producing wealth for the state. While the eighteenth century
had sacrificed the peasant's interests to that of the gentry, the impact of Western humanitarian ideas, especially through the Masons,
had slowly wrought a change. In 1790 we find, apparently for the
first time, a realization of the disadvantages of the peasant's position
as compared with that of a member of the privileged classes in

[22] Ivanov Razumnik, *Op. Cit.,* I, 343-44.

Radishchev's book, *Journey from St. Petersburg to Moscow*. For the first time the peasant appears in literature as a human being. Although the book was suppressed, its vogue was enormous and its impact powerful. On the return of peace in 1815, the peasant's case was taken up again by the Decembrists, and peasant reform was involved with the question of constitutional reform. While peasant reform was secondary to the latter in the minds of most of the Decembrists, there was among them a minority, the chief representative of whom was N. I. Turgenev, who pleaded their cause to the neglect even of a constitution.

> As far as the controversies on political freedom and constitutions, I was entirely preoccupied with the question of serfdom, so that I could give them no attention.[23]

This "preoccupation" of Turgenev became a passion. It was not necessarily based on intimate knowledge of the peasant's problems. There are no references in his book to the rural commune. Indeed, few of the young men of Turgenev's generation had contacts with the peasants, and since most of these gentlemen habitually spoke French, their familiarity with their native language was somewhat restricted; hence, they could scarcely meet the peasants on their own level. The desire on the part of some aristocrats for peasant reform was an emotional attitude that astonished many of their own contemporaries by its extravagance. This amazement has been recorded by at least one author:

> "In your eyes, then," Mordvinov used to say to Turgenev, "all serfs are saints and all landlords tyrants." "That is about right," Turgenev is said to have replied.[24]

While Turgenev may have been ahead of his time, by the middle of the century he had a large following committed to his idealization of the peasant, not the least of whom was Herzen himself. By this time the celebrated work of Haxthausen had appeared and drawn the attention of Russian intellectuals to the vigor of village life. This ideal of village life Herzen made the center of much of

[23] Turgenev, *La Russie et les Russes*, I, 77–78.
[24] Given in several sources. See V. S. Ikonnikov, *Graf N. S. Mordvinov*, 235. Turgenev, we are told, meant his words to be taken in earnest in however jocular a tone they may have been spoken.

his political writing, and it provided the later theoretical basis for the *narodniki*.[25] It is almost impossible to exaggerate the impact of Herzen on Russian thought on social problems. But his direct influence was greatly assisted by other writers. Down to the end of the eighteenth century, indeed, one may say to the end of the first quarter of the nineteenth, the projects for emancipation were based largely on western European models (English and French?) of emancipation without land. This scheme was what the Princess Dashkova had advocated; it was to some extent what both of the Anglophiles, Speranskii and Mordvinov, had (with some reserves, it is true) accepted. And we are told that it was the idea held by the Emperor Nicholas until 1826, when he was persuaded otherwise by Kiselev. But there was already a growing conviction that society had a heavier responsibility toward the peasant than merely turning him loose and expecting him to shift for himself. By the middle of the century, public opinion had pretty well swung around to the view that the peasant must also be given some measure of economic security.

By this time solicitude for the peasant, at first partaking somewhat of the nature of remorse for wrongs committed by the gentry (hence the repeated references to the "remorseful noblemen"), had become transformed into a passionate conviction that the peasant represented what was best in Russian society. Of course, sober historians, such as Solov'ev, did not go along with this idea. (Solov'ev was emphatic that the moving forces of history were the great figures).[26]

In fact, the Russian historical process, according to Solov'ev, is strongly influenced in its development by the clash between the state principle (reason) and the anti-state principle which is a brake on development.[27] The Slavophiles were not slow to reply that in Solov'ev's *History of Russia* the people were absent. In this attack they found common cause with Herzen, who based his whole scheme for Russia's future on the peasant and the peasant commune. In this plan, of course, Herzen found support among the Socialist

[25] The immediate impression on Herzen of Haxthausen's book appears in his review (in French) published in 1847. See Herzen, *Sochineniya*, v, 308.

[26] See M. V. Dovnar–Zapol'skii "Istoricheskii Protsess Russkago Naroda v russkoi istoriografii," *Russkaya Mysl'* (March, 1902), 177–78.

[27] *Ibid.*, 178.

writers in western Europe who were already laying the foundation for that cult of the common man which was to sweep all before it in Russian literature of the nineteenth century. Russian literature was born in this movement, and no writer could fail to be swayed by it.

"I have from time to time been and still am," said Goncharev in his preface to *Menservants of Other Days*, "subject to something in the nature of a reproach or at least a question as to why, though I introduce into my works characters from all walks of life, I never deal with peasants. . . . It is possible to draw from this the conclusion, and perhaps they [i.e., his critics] do, that I purposely avoid the people, that I do not love them, that is, that I do not feel sorry for them, that I do not commiserate with their lot, their toil, their misery, their sorrows, in a word that I do not suffer with them. This is due, they say, to fastidiousness, to gentility, epicureanism, and love of comfort."

Goncharev's reply was simple: ". . . I do not know the peasant's way of life, his mores. I have no acquaintance with country life, farming, the details of the conditions of the peasant's existence. . . . I have not owned peasants, I have never even lived in the country."[28]

Dostoyevsky did not often treat the peasant's life specifically. Indeed, many of his characters are of middle class or aristocratic origin. He is more interested in people as individuals, not as members of a class-conscious group. Even Tolstoi, who did so much for the peasants of Yasnaya Polyana and who had a general tendency to idealize the peasant, did not feel that it was necessary to treat the common man exclusively. Yet it became a powerful trend which no writer could ignore in the late nineteenth century. Even Kluchevsky in his *History of the Classes in Russia* deplores this trend, which, inasmuch as it was directed against the privileged members of society, he calls *aristophobia*—the singling out for denunciation of one or more classes—as responsible for Russia's ill. Yet Kluchevsky in his monumental *History of Russia* goes along with the stream in exalting the lower classes and heaping contempt on the privileged.

In general, all the educated classes in Russia by the middle of

[28] It might be noted that Goncharev was of mercantile, not noble, origin.

the nineteenth century were inclined to accept without question this one-sided view of their own society. The latter half of the century was merely to accentuate this trend.

Another marked tendency that became conspicuous at this time was a belief in the ameliorative power of the state in promoting reform and a complete distrust of the individual's ability to achieve anything worthwhile in lifting the world's burden of suffering. "The majority of social phenomena," wrote Dobrolyubov at this time, "cannot be changed simply by the will of private individuals; environment must be altered, new principles of social activity must be introduced; we will then discover those not able to take advantage of the new set up."[29]

Spontaneous private philanthropy had played a slight role in the social life of Russia. During the eighteenth century when humanitarian ideals were in the ascendant, the English poet Blake had written: "He who would do good to another must do it in minute particulars. General good is the plea of the scoundrel, hypocrite, and flatterer."[30]

Eighteenth-century England was the sprouting bed of scores of experiments in the field of private charity, education, prison reform, and missionary activity.[31] This sort of thing roused Russian Masons to emulation. Similarly, during the vogue of the Russian Bible Society, English agents of that organization on tour under Imperial patronage insisted on visiting the prisons and houses of correction to the extreme annoyance of the local authorities. But such activities were frowned upon by the state and without some degree of official tolerance could achieve little. Perhaps there were good grounds for widespread distrust. But this prejudice against such activities in part simply mirrored a belief in the all-embracing powers of government to mend society. Herzen and Byelinskii made a great play for individualism in their protest against the official *myeshchanstvo*, but this *myeshchanstvo* was what we would call "Philistinism" rather than the interference of an all-powerful government in the life of the people. In the words of Chaadayev:

[29] N. A. Dobrolyubov, *Sochineniya*, I, 110.

[30] William Blake, *Works*, Plate 55.

[31] See *The Character of England* (Ed. by Ernest Barker), Chap.: "Religion," by A. T. P. Williams, for examples.

The most profound trait of our historical physiognomy is the absence of any spontaneity in our social development. Every important trait in our history is imposed on us from above, every new idea is imported. Peter the Great found at home in Russia only a blank sheet of paper. With his powerful hand, he wrote on it "Europe and the West"; since then we have belonged there.[32]

This supreme confidence in governments' ability to usher in a Utopia was a by-product of the development of strongly centralized governments of the modern nation-states. In the case of Russia, it was the stronger that the Russian state had gathered into its hands the weapons of persuasion and coercion to a greater degree than the somewhat less absolute states of the West. It went hand-in-hand with a complete absence of a strong and enterprising middle class on which western Europe had largely been able to count for not only its enormous expansion of trade, industry, and banking, but the thousand and one activities that have made the modern business world what it is; this same class had made unique contributions in the fields of art, science, and philosophy. But the Russians, hating their autocracy, grudging the aristocracy their privileges (of which they had failed to take advantage to make their contribution to civilization), had fallen back on the Russian *muzhik* as the hope of the future. The *muzhik* and his institutions were to be the center of the new life; but this Utopia was to be achieved (at least at this time before Marx had anticipated the state's "withering away" as a useless organ) through the exercise of the government's power.

To some extent Russia shared these vagaries of revolutionary thought with the more radical writers of western Europe. But in the West experience had bred caution, and in any event traditions had become too deeply rooted in men's minds to be shaken by the breath of doubt and skepticism. As Chaadayev had said: "We have no enchanting memories, no satisfying pictures drawn from our past, nothing in our tradition to guide us by example. We are involuntary outcasts of history. . . ."[33]

[32] Chaadayev, "Apologie d'un fou," *Sochineniya*, I, 223. Quoted from Hare, *Pioneers of Russian Social Thought*, 9-10, by permission of Oxford University Press.
[33] Chaadayev, *Sochineniya*, I.

Bibliography

These references on the intellectual life of modern Russia are given to supplement the footnotes and to provide the reader with the means of pursuing the subject further. In at least two subjects, however, no attempt has been made at full bibliographies, the reader being directed to other sources.

Some effort has been made to arrange the titles in groups that will parallel the chapters in the text, but a number of departures have been made. The first four divisions are intended to be general, but with the fifth division the classifications begin to fit into the arrangement of the text, although not too closely since some subjects in the text have had to be treated chronologically in chapters. It is hoped that the reader will not be at a loss to find references to suit his purpose.

In general, the Library of Congress system of transliteration has been used, but some modifications have been introduced.

General Treatments of Intellectual Development:

Bienstock, J. W. *Histoire du mouvement révolutionnaire en Russie.* Paris, 1920.
Brückner, Aleksandr Gustavovich. *Beiträge zur Kulturgeschichte Russlands im XVII Jahrhundert.* Leipzig, 1887.
Brückner, Alexander. *Die Europäisierung Russlands, Land und Volk.* Gotha, 1888.
———. *Russlands geistige Entwickelung im Spiegel seiner schönen Literatur.* Tübingen, 1908.
Dovnar-Zapol'skii, M. V. *Iz Istorii Obshchestvennykh Techenii v Rossii.* Kiev, 1905.
Florovsky, Georgii P. *Puti russkago bogosloviya.* Paris, 1937.

Herberstein, Baron Sigismund von. *Notes Upon Russia* Trans. by R. H. Major. 2 vols. London, 1851–52.

Herzen, A. (Iskander). *Du développement des idées révolutionnaires en Russie.* London, 1853.

Intelligentsiya v Rossii. *Sbornik Statei.* St. Petersburg, 1910.

Ivanov-Razumnik, Razumnik Vasilevich. *Istoriya russkoi obshchestvennoi mysli.* St. Petersburg, 1907.

———. *Chto takoe intelligentsiya.* Berlin, 1920.

Likhachev, D. S. *Kultura Rusi: epokhi obrazovaniya russkogo natsional'nogo gosudarstva, (konets XIV–nachalo XVI v.).* Moscow, 1946.

Masaryk, Thomas. *Zur Russischen Geschichte und Religionsphilosophie: Soziologische Skizzen.* 2 vols. Jena, 1913.

———. *The Spirit of Russia.* 2 vols. London and New York, 1919.

Mel'gunov, Sergiei Petrovich. *Religiozno-obshchestvennye dvizheniya XVII–XVIII v v. v Rossii.* Moscow, 1922.

Milyukov, Pavel. *Ocherki po istorii russkoi kul'tury.* 3 vols. Jubilee Edition. Paris, 1930.

———. *Outlines of Russian Culture.* 3 pts. Ed. by Michael Karpovich. Trans. by Valentine Ughet and Eleanor David. Philadelphia, 1942.

———. *Le mouvement intellectuel russe.* Trans. by J. W. Bienstock. Paris, 1918.

———. *Iz istorii russkoi intelligentsii, Sbornik statei i etyudov.* 2nd Ed. St. Petersburg, 1902.

Mohrenschildt, Dmitri von. *Russia in the Intellectual Life of 18th Century France.* New York, 1936.

Nötzel, Karl. *Die Grundlage des geistigen Russlands.* Jena, 1917.

———. *Die slawische Volksseele: zwei Aufsätze von Karl Nötzel und Aleksandr Berwinskyi.* Jena, 1916.

Obshchestvennye Dvizheniya v Rossii v pervuyu polovinu XIX vyeka. Compiled by V. Semevskii and P. E. Shchegolov. 4 vols. 2d Ed. St. Petersburg, 1905.

Ovsyaniko-Kulikovskii, D. N. *Sobranie Sochinenii.* Vols. 7 to 9: *Istoriya russkoi intelligentsii, Izd. 5-oe.* St. Petersburg, 1914.

Pazhitnov, K. A. *Razvitie sotsialisticheskikh idei v Rossii.* 2d Ed. Petrograd, 1924.

Bibliography

Pekarskii, P. P. *Nauka i Literatura v Rossii pri Petrye Velikom.* 2 vols. St. Petersburg, 1862.

Plechanow, G. W. *Geschichte der sozialen Ideen in Russland.* Moscow and Leningrad, 1925.

Plekhanov, G. V. *Istoriya russkoi obshchestvennoi mysli.* 4 vols. Moscow and Leningrad, 1925.

———. *History of Russian Social Thought.* New York, 1938.

Pokrovskii, M. I. *Ocherk Istorii Russkoi Kul'tury.* 2 vols. Petrograd, 1923.

Pyatkovskii, A. P. *Iz Istorii nashego literatur'nago i obshchestvennago razvitiya.* 2d Ed. 2 pts. St. Petersburg, 1876.

Riasanovsky, V. A. *Obzor Russkoi Kul'tury.* 3 vols. Eugene, Oregon, 1947.

———. *Razvitie russkoi nauchnoi mysli v XVIII–XIX st. st.* Eugene, Oregon, 1949.

Shchapov, Afanasii Prokof'evich. *Sotsialno-pedagogicheskiya usloviya umstvennago razvitiya russkago naroda.* St. Petersburg, 1869.

———. "Istoricheskie Usloviya Intellektual'nago Razvitiya v Rossii," *Dyelo* (St. Petersburg, 1868), No. 1, 179–215; No. 3, 1–33; No. 4, 1–35.

Skabichevskii, A. M. "Ocherki umstvennago razvitiya nashego obshchestva, 1825–1860," *Otechestvennye Zapiski* (St. Petersburg), 1870: T. 192, No. 10, 255–321; T. 193, No. 11, 1–62; 1871: T. 194, No. 6, 85–123; No. 2, 331–64; T. 195, No. 3, 73–110; T. 198, No. 10, 442–84; T. 199, No. 11, 207–42; 1872: T. 201, No. 4, 373–410; T. 202, No. 5, 55–88; No. 6, 395–430.

Stählin, Karl. *Geschichte Russlands von den Anfängen bis zur Gegenwart.* 4 vols. Berlin and Königsberg, 1923–35.

Tarasov, E. I. *K istorii russkago obshchestva vtoroi poloviny XVIII stoletiya.* St. Petersburg, 1914.

Velikaya Reforma. 6 vols. Moscow, 1911.

Vernadskii, George. *Ocherk istorii prava Russkago Gosudarstva XVIII–XIX v. v.* Prague, 1924.

Williams, A. T. P. "Religion," *The Character of England.* Ed. by Ernest Barker. Oxford, 1947.

Zen'kovskii, V. V. *Russkie Mysliteli i Evropa; kritika evropeiskoi kul'tury u russkikh myslitelei.* Paris, 1926.

Special Figures and Movements

Bestuzhev-Ryumin, K. *Biografii i Kharakteristiki*. St. Petersburg, 1822.

Bogoslovskii, M. M. *Petr I. Materialy Dlya Biografii*. 5 vols. Published in Soviet Union, 1940–48.

Brückner, Alexander. "Ivan Pososhkov," *Zhurnal Ministerstva Narodnago Prosvyeshcheniya* (October, 1875), 181 ff.

Brückner, Alexander G. *Possoschkow: Ideen und Zustände in Russland zur Zeit Peters des Grossen*. Leipzig, 1878.

Byelinskii, V. G. *Sochineniya V. G. Byelinskago*. 4 vols. 3rd Ed. St. Petersburg, 1906.

Chaadayev, Petr Yakovlevich. *Sochineniya i Pis'ma P. Ya. Chaadayeva*. Ed. by M. Gershenzon. 2 vols. Moscow, 1913.

Chappe d'Auteroche. *Voyage en Sibérie*. 2 vols. in 3 pts. Paris, 1768.

Daschkaw, Princess. *Memoirs of the Princess Daschkaw, Lady of Honour to Catherine II, Empress of all the Russias, Written by herself*. London, 1840.

Domostroi. Po Spisku Imperatorskago Obshchestva Istorii i Drevnostei Rossiiskikh. 2 vols. Moscow, 1882.

———. *Domostroi po Konshinskomy spisku i podobnym k izdaniyu privgotovil A. Orlov*. Obshchestvo istorii i drevnostei Rossiiskikh: Chteniya. Moscow, 1908.

Dovnar-Zapolskii, M. V. *Politichiskie Idealy M. M. Speranskago*. Moscow, 1905.

Evgen'ev, Boris Sergeevich. *Aleksandr Nikolaevich Radishchev*. Moscow, 1943.

Fedotov, G. P. *A Treasury of Russian Spirituality*. New York, 1948.

Fisher, Raymond H. *The Russian Fur Trade, 1550–1700*. Berkeley and Los Angeles, 1943.

Gershenzon, M. O. *P. Y. Chaadayev: Zhizn'i myshlenie*. St. Petersburg, 1908.

———. *Istoricheskie Zapiski*. Berlin, 1923.

Golovine, Ivan. *La Russie sous Nicholas I*. Paris, 1845.

Goncharov, I. A. *Oblomov*. New York, 1915.

——. *Slugi Starago Vyeka.* Oxford, 1918.

Hakluyt, Richard. *The Principall Navigations, Voyages, Traffiques and Discoveries of the English Nation* ... 3 vols. 2d Ed. London, 1598–1600.

Herzen, Alexander. *Errinerungen von Alexander Hertzen.* 2 vols. Berlin, 1907.

——. *Sochineniya A. I. Gertsena.* T. 16. Geneva, Bâle, Lyon, 1876.

——. *My Past and Thoughts.* London, 1924–27.

——. *Polnoe Sobranie Sochinenii i Pisem* Ed. by M. K. Lemke. 21 vols. Petrograd, 1919–23.

Ikonnikov, Vladimir Stepanovich. *Graf N. S. Mordvinov. Istoricheskaya Monografiya.* Moscow, 1873.

Khodnev, A. I. *Istoriya Imperatorskago Vol'nago Ekonomicheskago Obshchestva S 1765 do 1865 goda.* St. Petersburg, 1865.

Kireyevski, I. V. *Polnoe Sobranie Sochinenii Ivana Vasil'evicha Kireyevskago.* 2 vols. Moscow, 1861.

Kitchin, George. *Prisoner of the Ogpu.* London, 1935.

Kohler, Phyllis Penn. *Journey for Our Time.* Trans. from de Custine. New York, 1951.

Korf, M. A. *Zhizn' Grafa Speranskago.* 2 vols. St. Petersburg, 1861.

Lebedev, V. I. *Reformy Petra I.* Moscow, 1937.

Leont'ev, K. *Vostok, Rossiya i Slavyanstvo.* 2 vols. Moscow, 1885–86.

Lomonosov, M. V. *Sochineniya M. V. Lomonosova.* 7 vols. St. Petersburg, 1891–1934.

——. *Drevnaya Rossiiskaya Istoriya* ... St. Petersburg, 1766.

Longinov, M. N. "Graf Speranskii," *Russkii Vestnik* (Moscow, October, 1859), 337–78, 527–76.

Lyubimov, N. "Lomonosov i Peterburgskaya Akademiya Nauk," *Russkii Vestnik,* Vol. XXVI (Moscow, March, 1865), 401–22.

Menshutkin, B. N. *Zhizneopisanie Mikhaila Vasil'evicha Lomonosova.* 3rd Ed. Moscow and Leningrad, 1947.

——. "A Russian physical chemist of the eighteenth century," *Journal of Chemical Education,* Vol. 4, No. 9 (September, 1927), 1,079–87.

Miller, K. *Frantsuskaya Emigratsiya i Rossiya.* Paris, 1931.

Milyukov, Pavel Nikolayevich. *Gosudarstvennoe Khozyaistvo*

Rossii v pervoi chetverti XVIII stoletiya i reforma Petra veli-kago. St. Petersburg, 1892.

———. *Razlozhenie Slavyanofilstva.* Moscow, 1893.

Myakotin, V. A. *Iz istorii russkago obshchestva.* St. Petersburg, 1902.

———. "Na zarye russkoi obshchestvennosti," *Iz istorii russkago obshchestva.* St. Petersburg, 1902. (On Radishchev).

Pavlov-Silvanskii, N. "Pestel Pered Verkhovnym Ugolovnym Sudom," *Byloe* (May, 1906), 23.

Platonov, S. F. *Moskva i Zapad v XVI–XVII Vekakh.* Leningrad, 1925.

Popov, Nil. *V. N. Tatishchev i ego Vremya.* Moscow, 1861.

Pypin, Aleksandr Nikolayevich. *Sochineniya imperatritsy Eka-teriny II na osnovanii podlinnykh rukopisei i s obyasnitel' nymi primechaniyami akademika A. N. Pypina.* 8 vols. St. Petersburg, 1901.

———. *Istoricheskie ocherki: Kharakteristiki literaturnykh mnyenii ot dvadsatykh do pyatdesyatykh godov:* Izd. 2. St. Petersburg, 1890.

———. *Panslavizm v ego Proshlom i Nastoyashchem.* St. Petersburg, 1913.

Quénet, Charles. *Tchaadaev, et les lettres philosophes: contribution a l'étude du mouvement des idées en Russie.* Paris, 1931.

Radishchev, A. N. *Sochineniya A. N. Radishcheva.* 3 toms. Leningrad, 1938.

———. *Reise von Petersburg nach Moskau 1790.* London, 1858; Leipzig, 1876; St. Petersburg, 1868.

Radishchev, Pavel. "Aleksandr Nikolayevich Radishchev," *Russkii Vestnik,* Vol. XVIII (St. Petersburg, 1858), 394–432.

Riasanovsky, Nicholas V. *Slavophilism* (MS of a doctoral dissertation submitted in partial fulfillment of requirements of Oxford University for a degree.) 293 pp.

Schilder, N. K. *Imperator Aleksandr Pervyi.* 4 vols. St. Petersburg, 1897–98.

Sakhulin, Pavel Nikitich. *Sotsializm Byelinskogo: Stat'i i pis'ma.* Moscow, 1925.

———. *Russkaya Literatura i Sotsializm.* 2d Ed. Moscow, 1924.

Bibliography

Singer, Eugenie. "Alexander Nikolaevich Radishchev," *Jahrbücher für Kultur und Geschichte der Slawen* (Breslau, 1931), 113–62.

Shchegolev, P. (Ed.) "Pavel Ivanovich Pestel," *Russkaya Pravda* (St. Petersburg, 1906).

Skabichevskii, A. M. *Istoriya noveishei russkoi literatury* (1848–92 g.g.). 3rd Ed. St. Petersburg, 1897.

Sochineniya Imperatritsy Ekateriny II. Ed. by G. W. Miram. 3 vols. St. Petersburg, 1849.

Speranskii, M. M. *Plan Gosudarstvennago Preobrazovaniia, grafa M. M. Speranskago.* (Vvedenie k ulozheniyu gosudarstvennykh zakonov 1809 g.). Moskva, 1905.

Tikhomirov, L. *Russia, Political and Social.* 2 vols. London, 1892.

Troyat, Henri. *Pushkin.* New York, 1950.

Ustryalov, N. G. *Istoriya tsarstvovaniya Petra Velikago.* 7 vols. St. Petersburg, 1858.

Valdenberg, V. (Waldenberg). *Gosudarstvennye idei Krizhanicha.* St. Petersburg, 1912.

Veselovskii, Aleksei Nikolaevich. *Zapadnoe vliyanie v novoi russkoi literatury.* Moscow, 1916.

Winkler, Martin. *Peter Jakovlevic Caadaev: ein Beitrag zur russischen Geistesgeschichte des XIX Jahrhunderts.* Berlin, 1927.

Wischnitzer, Marcus. *Die Universität Göttingen und die Entwickelung der liberalen Ideen in Russland im ersten Viertel des 19 Jahrhunderts. Historische Studien.* Heft LVIII. Berlin, 1907.

Zabyelin, Ivan. *Istorii russkoi zhizni s drevnieshikh vremen.* 2 vols. Moscow, 1876.

Literature

Blagoi, D. D. *Istoriya russkoi literatury XVIII vyeka.* Moscow, 1945.

Brückner, A. *A Literary History of Russia.* London, 1908.

Griboyedov, A. S. *Gore ot Uma (The Mischief of Being Clever).* Trans. by B. Pares. St. Petersburg and London, 1925.

Gudzii, Nikolai Kallenkovich. *Istoriya drevnei russkoi literatury; uchebnik dlya vysshykh uchebnikh zavedenii,* 2nd Ed. Moscow, 1945.

———. *History of Early Russian Literature.* New York, 1949.

Gukovskii, G. A. *Russkaya Literatura XVIII vyeka. Filologicheskii Fakultet Leningradskogo gosudarstvennogo universiteta.* Moscow, 1939.

Kropotkin, Petr Alekseievich. *Ideals and Realities in Russian Literature.* New York, 1915.

Lourie, Ossip. *La psychologie des Romanciers Russes du 19me siècle.* Paris, 1905.

Luther, Arthur. *Geschichte der russischen literatur.* Leipzig, 1924.

Mirsky, Prince D. S. *History of Russian Literature.* New York and London, 1927. (New edition, New York, 1949.)

Nezelenov, Aleksandr Il'ich. *Literaturniya Napravleniya v Ekaterinskuyu. Epokhu. Sochineniya A. Nezelenova.* St. Petersburg, 1889.

Osvyaniko-Kulikovskii, D. N. (Ed.). *Istoriya russkoi literatury XIX vyeka.* 5 v. Moscow, 1909.

Pushkin, A. S. *Sochineniya A. S. Pushkina.* 7 vols. 2nd Ed. St. Petersburg, 1822.

Reinholdt, Alexander von. *Geschichte der russischen Literatur.* Leipzig, 1886.

Tikhonravov, N. S. *Lyetopisi russkoi literatury i drevnosti.* Moscow, 1859–63.

Waliszewski, K. *Littérature Russe.* Paris, 1900.

———. *A History of Russian Literature.* New York, 1900.

Wesselovsky, A. *Die Russische Literatur.* Berlin and Leipzig, 1908.

Philosophy

Bakewell, Charles. *Source Book in Ancient Philosophy.* New York, 1907.

Berdyaev, Nicolas. *The Russian Idea.* New York, 1948.

———. *Russkaya Ideya (Osnovnye problemy russkoi mysli XIX vyeka i nachala XX vyeka).* Paris, 1946.

———. *De L'esclavage et de la Liberté de l'Homme.* Paris, 1946.

Bobrov, E. *Filosofiya v Rossii.* 6 vols. n.p., 1889–1902.

———. *Literatura i Prosvyeshchenie v Rossii v XIX-om Vyekye.* 3 vols.

Chyzhevs'kyi, Dmytro (Chizhevskii). *Filosofia G. S. Skovorodi.* Warsaw, 1934.

Bibliography

——. "Hegel bei den Slawen, im Auftrage der Deutschen Gesell-schaft für Slavistische Forschung in Prag," *Deutsche Univer-sität, Prag. Slavistische Arbeitsgemeinschaft Veröffentlichun-gen, Reihe 1.* Reichenberg, 1934.

——. *Gegel v Rossii.* Paris, 1939.

Fedotov, George P. *The Russian Religious Mind.* 2 vols. Cambridge (Mass.), 1946–47.

Gavril, Arkhim. *Istoriya russkoi filosofii.* Kazan, 1839.

Kolubovskii. "Materialy dlya istorii filosofii v Rossii," *Voprosy filosofii i psikhologii.* Moscow, 1898.

Kropotkin, Petr Aleksieevich. *Ideals and Realities in Russian Lit-erature.* New York, 1915.

Lannes. "Coup d'oeil sur l'histoire de la philosophie en Russie," *Revue de Philosophie* (Paris, 1891–92).

Lossky, N. *History of Russian Philosophy.* New York, 1951.

Lourie, Ossip. *La Philosophie russe contemporaine.* Paris, 1902.

Morley, John. "On Compromise," *WORKS*, Vol. III. London, 1921.

Pyatkovskii, A. P. "Opyt filosofskoi razrabotki russkoi istorii," *Iz istorii nashego literatur'nago i obshchestvennago razvitiya.* 2nd Ed., (St. Petersburg, 1888), 196–220.

Radlov, *Ocherk istorii russkoi filosofii.* Moscow, 1920.

Shpet, T. *Ocherk razvitiya russkoi filosofii.* Petrograd, 1922.

Hare, Richard. *Pioneers of Russian Social Thought.* New York, 1951.

Tsvetayev, Dmitrii Vladimirovich. *Protestantstvo i protestanty v Rossii do epokhi preobrazovaniya.* Moscow, 1890.

Tukalevskii, V. "Iz istorii filosofskikh napravlenii v russkom obsh-chestvye XVIII–go vyeka," *Zhurnal Ministerstva Narodnago Prosvyeshcheniya* (St. Petersburg, 1911).

Yershov, M. *Puti razvitiya filosofii v. Rossii.* Vladivostok, 1922.

Zen'kovskii, V. V. *Istoriya russkoi filosofii.* 2 vols. Paris, 1948.

Miscellaneous

Bil'basov, V. A. *Istoricheskiia Monografii.* 5 vols. St. Petersburg, 1901.

Fletcher, Dr. Giles. *Of the Russe Commonwealth* and *The Travels of Sir Jerome Horsey*. Hakluyt Society Publications, Ser. I, No. 20. London, 1856.

Gnucheva, V. F. *Geograficheskii Department Akademii Nauk XVIII vyeka*. Moscow and Leningrad, 1946.

———. *Materialy dlya istorii ekspedtsii Akademii Nauk v XVIII–XIX vyekakh*. Moscow and Leningrad, 1940.

Hanway, Jonas. *An Historical Account of the British Trade with the Caspian*. 4 vols. London, 1753.

Haumant, E. *La culture française en Russie*. Paris, 1910.

Kucharzewski, Jan. *The Origins of Modern Russia*. New York, 1948.

Lanin, E. B. (pseudonym of Emile Joseph Dillon). *Russian Characteristics*. London, 1892.

Lenin, V. I. *Sobranie Sochinenii*.

Olearius, Adam. *The Voyages and Travells of the Ambassadors sent by Frederick, Duke of Holstein to the Great Duke of Muscovy and the King of Persia begun in the year MDCXXXIII and finished in MDCXXXIX*. 2nd Ed. (corrected). London, 1669.

"Journey for Our Time," *Time* (March 5, 1951), 146, 158.

Tompkins, Stuart Ramsay. *Alaska: Promyshlennik and Sourdough*. Norman, 1945.

Tompkins, Stuart R. and Moorehead, Max. "Russia's Approach to America," *British Columbia Historical Quarterly* (April, June, October, 1949).

Wisin, D. J. (Fonvizin, Denis Ivanovich). *Pervoe Polnoe Sobranie Sochinenii*, 2 vols. in 1. St. Petersburg, 1830.

Barker, Ernest (Ed.). *The Character of England*. Oxford, 1947.

Classes

Un Diplomat. *Organization sociale de la russie, la noblesse, la bourgeoisie, le peuple*. Paris, 1864.

Golikov, Ivan. *Dopolnenie k Dyeyaniyam Petra Velikago*. T. III (18 v.). Moscow, 1790.

Gradovskii, A. D. *Sochineniya*. 9 vols. St. Petersburg, 1841–89.

———. *Istoriya myestnago upravleniya v Rossii*. Vol. II of *Sochineniya*. St. Petersburg, 1868.

Bibliography

Haxthausen, Baron von. *The Russian Empire; its people, institutions and resources*. 2 vols. London, 1856.

Klyuchevskii, Vasilii Osipovich. *Boyarskaya duma drevnei Rusi*. St. Petersburg, 1919.

——. *Istoriya Soslovii v Rossii*. Moscow, 1914.

Korf, S. A. *Dvoryanstvo i ego soslovnoe upravlenie za stoletie 1762–1855 godov*. St. Petersburg, 1906.

Pavlov-Silvanskii, N. P. *Feodalizm v Drevnei Rusi*. St. Petersburg, 1907.

——. *Feodalnyia Otnosheniia v udyel'noi Rusi*. St. Petersburg, 1901.

——. *Gosudarevye Sluzhilye Lyudi. Proiskhozhdenie Russkago Dvoryanstva*. St. Petersburg, 1898.

Porai-Koshits, I. A. *Ocherk istorii russkago dvoryanstva ot poloviny 9 do kontsa 18 vyeka, 862–1796*. St. Petersburg, 1874.

Romanovich-Slavatinskii, A. *Dvoryanstvo v Rossii ot nachala XVIII vyeka do otmyeny kryepostnago prava*. St. Petersburg, 1870.

Yablochkov, Mikhail. *Istoriya dvoryanskago sosloviya v Rossii*. St. Petersburg, 1876.

Zagoskin, Nikolai. *Ocherki organizatsii i proiskhozhdeniya Sluzhilago sosloviya v do-Petrovskoi Rusi*. Kazan, 1875.

Znamenskii, D. V. *Prikhodskoe dukhovenstvo v Rossii so vremeni reformy Petra*. N.p., n.d.

Education

Aleshintsev, I. *Istoriya gimnasicheskago obrazovaniya v Rossii (XVIII i XIX vyek)*. St. Petersburg, 1912.

Andreyev, A. I. "Osnovanie Akademii Nauk v Peterburgye," *Petr Velikii-Sbornik Statei*. (Moscow and Leningrad, 1947), 284–333.

Andriyashev. *Materialy dlya istorii uchebnykh zavedenii Chernigovskoi direktsii (1789–1832)*. Kiev, 1865.

Arkhangel'skii, A. S. *Imperatritsa Ekaterina II v istorii russkoi literatury i obrazovaniya*. Kazan, 1897.

Arsen'ev, K. "Istoriko-statisticheskii ocherk narodnoi obrazovanosti v Rossii do kontsa XVIII vyeka," *Ucheniye Zapiski. Akademiya Nauk,* Kn. 1 (St. Petersburg, 1848).

Brückner, Alexander. *Die Europäisierung Russlands, Land und Volk.* Gotha, 1888.

Chernyavskii, I. M. *Materialy po istorii narodnago obrazovaniya v Ekaterinoslavskom nam, pri Ekaterinye II i Pavlye (1784–1805).* Ekaterinoslav, 1895.

Chistovich, Ilarion Alekseyevich. *Rukovodyashchie Deyateli dukhovnago prosvyeshcheniya v Rossii v pervoi polovinye tekushchago stoletiya.* St. Petersburg, 1894.

Demkov, M. I. *Istoriya russkoi pedagogii.* 2 vols. Reval, 1895.

Feoktistov, E. M. *Magnitskii: materialy dlya istorii prosvyeshcheniya v Rossii.* St. Petersburg, 1865.

——. "Magnitskii: materialy dlya istorii prosvyeshcheniya v Rossii," *Russkii Vestnik,* T. 52, Vols. 7 and 8 (July, 1864), 5–55; (August, 1864), 361–449.

Ferlyudin, P. *Istoricheskii Obzor myer po vysshemy obrazovaniyu v Rossii.* Saratov, 1894.

Golovin, N. V. "Nauchno-obrazovatel'nyya snosheniya Rossii s Zapadom v nachalye XVII vyeka," *Chteniya Obshchestva Istorii i Drevnostei.* Vol. II (1898).

Golos. *Pedagogicheskaya deyatelnost' iezuitov.* 1809.

Gorzhalchinski, A. *Iezuitakiya Shkoly v yugo-zapadnoi Rossii.* Kiev, 1869.

Grigoriev, V. V. *Imperatorskii S. Peterburgskii universitet v techenie pervykh pyatdesyati lyet ego sushchestvovaniya . . . Istoricheskie Zapiski.* St. Petersburg, 1870.

Hans, Nicholas A. *History of Russian Educational Policy (1701–1917).* Westminster (England), 1931.

Ikonnikov, V. *Opyt izsledovaniya o Kultur'nom Znachenii Vizantii v Russkoi Istorii.* Kiev, 1869.

Johnson, William H. E. *Russia's Educational Heritage.* Pittsburgh, 1950.

Kaidanova, Ol'ga Vladimirovna. *Ocherki po istorii narodnogo obrazoveniya v Rossii i SSSR na osnove lichnogo opyta i nablyudeniya.* 2 vols. Berlin, 1938.

Kharlampovich, K. *Zapadnorusskie pravoslavyniya shkoly XVI i nachala XVII vv.* Kazan, 1898.

Bibliography

Knyazkov, S. A. and Serbov, N. I. *Ocherk istorii narodnogo obrazovaniya v Rossii do epokhi reform Aleksandra II.* Moscow, 1910.

Krusenstern, A. *Précis du système des progrès et de l'état de l'instruction publique en Russie, (d'après des documents officiels).* Warsaw, 1837.

Lappo-Danilevskii, A. S. "Science and Learning in Russia," *Russian Realities and Problems.* Cambridge, 1917.

Lavrovskii, N. *O pedagogicheskom znachenii sochinenii Ekateriny Velikoi.* Kharkov, 1856.

————. *Pamyatniki starinnago russkago vospitaniya. Chteniya Obshchestva Istorii i Drevnostei.* Moscow, 1861.

Leary, D. S. *Education and Autocracy in Russia.* Buffalo, 1919.

Likhacheva, E. *Materialy dlya istorii zhenskago obrazovaniya v Rossii.* 3 vols. St. Petersburg, 1890–95.

Longinov, Michael. "Materialy dlya istorii russkago prosvyeshcheniya i literatury v kontsye XVIII vyeka," *Russkii Vestnik,* T. 25 (Moscow, 1860), 631–50.

Pavlovich, A. "Iezuity kak vospitateli Pol'shi i zapadnoi Rossii," *Vestnik Zapadnoi Rossii* (Kiev, 1860).

Pekarskii, Petr. *Istoriya Imperatorskoi Akademii Nauk v Peterburgye.* 2 vols. St. Petersburg, 1873.

Petrov. "Ocherki po istorii gramotnosti v Rossii," *Novoe Slovo* (October–November, 1896).

Pinkevich, A. P. *Kratkii ocherk istorii pedagogiki.* Kharkov, 1930.

Rozhdestvenskii, S. V. *Ocherki po istorii sistem narodnago prosvyeshcheniya v Rossii v XVIII i XIX vyekakh.* Vol. I. St. Petersburg, 1912.

Sbornik materialov dlya istorii prosvyeshcheniya v Rossii. 3 vols. St. Petersburg, 1893–98.

Schmid, E. *Istoriya srednykh uchebnykh zavedenii v Rossii.* St. Petersburg, 1876.

Shevirov, Stepan. *Istoriya Moskovskogo Universiteta.* Moscow, 1885.

Sipovskii, V. D. "Znachenie Petra Velikago v istorii russkoi shkoly," *Izbrannye pedagogiicheskiya sochineniya V. D. Sipovskago* (St. Petersburg, 1911), 251–313.

Simkovich, Vladimir G. "The History of the School in Russia," *Educational Review*, Vol. XXXIII (May, 1907), 486–522.

Sukhomlinov, M. I. *Istoriya russkoi akademii.* 8 vols. in 7. St. Petersburg, 1874–87.

———. *Materialy dlya istorii obrazovaniya v Rossii v tsarstvovanie Imperatora Aleksandra I-go. Izslyedovaniya i Stat'i.* Vol. II. St. Petersburg, 1889.

———. "Materialy dlya istorii prosvyeshcheniya v tsarstvovanie Imperatora Aleksandra I," *Zhurnal Ministerstva Narodnago Prosvyeshcheniya.* (St. Petersburg, 1865–66).

Tolstoi, D. A. *Das Akademische Gymnasium und die Akademische Universität im XVIII Jahrhundert.* St. Petersburg, 1886.

———. "Gorodskie uchilishcha v tsarstvovanie Ekateriny II," *Zapiski Imperatorskoi Akademii Nauk*, Tom LIV.

Veselii, F. *Ocherk istorii morskago kadetskago korpusa.* St. Petersburg, 1852.

Vladimirov. *Istoricheskie Zapiski o Kazanskoi gimnazii XVIII stolyetiya.* Kazan, 1867.

Vladimirskii-Budanov, Mikhail Flegontovich. *Gosudarstvo i narodnoe obrazovanie v Rossii XVIII vyeka.* Yaroslav, 1874.

Voronov, A. *Istoriko-statisticheskoe obozryenie uchebnykh zavedenii S. Peterburgskago uchebnago okruga s 1715 po 1828 g. vklyuchitel'no.* St. Petersburg, 1849.

Woldemar, C. *Zur Geschichte und Statistik der Gelehrten und Schulanstalten des K. russ. Min. der Volkaufklaerung nach officiellen Quellen bearbeitet.* St. Petersburg, 1865.

Zhelvakov, N. A. *Khrestomatiya po istorii pedagogiki.* Moscow, 1936.

Press

Afanas'ev, A. *Russkie satirecheskie Zhurnaly, 1769–1774 godov.* Moscow, 1859.

———. "Satiricheskie izdaniya devyanostykh godov," *Moskovskie Vyedomosti*, Nos. 80, 83 and 84 (Moscow, 1856 g.).

Borodin, S. "Russkaya Zhurnalistika v kontsye XVIII st.," *Nablyuditel'*, Vol. III (1891 g.).

Bibliography

Dobrolyubov, N. A. "Russkaya Satira Ekaterinskago vremeni," *Sochineniya N. A. Dobrolyubova.* 6 vols. St. Petersburg, 1876.

Dubrovin, P. N. F. "Nashi mistik-sektanty; A. O. Labzin i ego Zhurnal, "Sionskii Vestnik," *Russkaya Starina,* Vol. LXXXII (September, 1894), 145–203.

Gershenzon, M. O. "Epoka Nikolaya I," *Russkaya Byl',* Vol. 7 (Moscow, 1910).

Nikitin, S. "Zhurnalistika. Pamyatniki obshchestvenno-politicheskoi mysli," *Istochnikovedenie Istorii SSSR XIX v (do nachala 90-kh godov),* Tom II (Moscow, 1940).

Ostroglazov, I. M. "Knizhnye Ryedkosti," *Russkii Arkhiv,* II (1891), 441–63; III, 83–104, 275–306, 521–63; 1892: I, 233–58, 391–416; II, 202–21; III, 305–49, 393–433.

Pekarskii, P. P. *Materialy dlya istorii zhurnal'noi i literatur'noi deyatel'nosti Ekateriny II. Prilozhenie k III^{mu} Tomu Zapisok Imperatorskoi Akademii Nauk.* Vol. XXV, No. 6. St. Petersburg, 1863.

———. *Redaktor, Sotrudniki i Tsenzura v Russkom Zhurnalye, 1755–1764. Prilozhenie k XII^{mu} Tomu Zapisok Akademii Nauk.* No. 5. St. Petersburg, 1867.

Pyatkovskii, Aleksandr Petrovich. "Russkaya Zhurnalistika pri Aleksandrye I," *Sovremennik,* No. 1 (1866), 17–68; No. 4, 545–63.

———. "Russkaya Zhurnalistika pri Aleksandrye I," *Dyelo,* No. 1 (1868), 162–76; No. 2, 197–212; No. 3, 203–19; No. 6, 149–86; No. 1 (1869), 41–65.

Pokrovskii, V. I. *Stoletie satiricheskago Zhurnala Chto nibud ot bezdyel'ya na dosugye, (1800–1900 gg.).* Moscow, 1901.

Vesin, S. *Ocherki istorii russkoi zhurnalistiki dvadtsatykh i tridtsatykh godov.* St. Petersburg, 1881.

Censorship

Engelhardt, Nikolai Aleksandrovich. *Ocherki istorii Russkoi Tsenzury v Sviazi s Razvitiemy Pechati, 1703–1903.* St. Petersburg, 1904.

Istoricheskya Svyedeniya o Tsenzure v Rossii. St. Petersburg, 1862.

THE RUSSIAN MIND

(Ostroglazov, in *Knizhnyye Ryedkosti,* ascribes this to P. K. Shchebal'skii.)

Lemke, M. *Ocherki po istorii russkoi Tsensury i Zhurnalistiki XIX Stolyetiya.* St. Petersburg, 1904.

Nagradov, W. J. *Moderne russische Zensur und Presse vor und hinter den Coulissen.* Berlin, 1894.

Notovich, Aleksyei N. *Dukhovnaya Tsensura v Rossii.* St. Petersburg, 1909.

Pyatkovskii, A. "Tsenzurnyi Proekt Magnitskago. Iz Istorii Tsenzury v Rossii," *Otechestvennyye Zapiski,* T. CLXXXVI, No. 10, 455–82.

Sbornik Postanovlyenii i Razporyazhenii po Tsenzurye s 1720-po 1862 god. St. Petersburg, 1862.

Semevskii, M. I. *Slovo i Dyelo, 1700–1725.* St. Petersburg, 1884.

Shchebal'skii, Petr Karlovich. "Materialy dlya istorii russkoi tsenzury," *Besyedy v Obshchestvye Lyubitelei Rossiiskoi Slovestnosti.* Vyp. 3–1 (1871), 6–46.

Shishkov, A. S. *Zapiski, Mnyeniya i Perepiska Admirala A. S. Shishkova.* 2 vols. Berlin, 1870.

———. *Memoiren des Admirals A. Schischkow während des Krieges mit den Französen in den Jahren 1812– bis1814.* Leipzig, 1832.

Skabichevskii, A. "Ocherki iz istorii russkoi tsensury (1700–1863)," *Otechestvennye Zapiski.*

———. *Ocherki Istorii Russkoi Tsensury (1700–1863).* St. Petersburg, 1892.

Smirnov, S. "Tsenzurnaya vyedomost 1786–1788 godov," *Osmnadtsatyi Vyek,* Vol. I (Moscow, 1869), 490–502.

Sukhomlinov, M. I. "Materialy dlya istorii russkoi tsenzury," *Besyedy v Obshchestvye Lyubitelei rossiiskoi Slovestnosti,* T. III, Nos. 8–9.

"Tsenzura v Tsarstvovanie Imperatora Nikolaia I," *Russkaya Starina:* 1901 (1st instalment)—July, 151–70; Aug., 395–409; Sept., 643–68; 1903 (2nd instalment)—Feb., 305–28; Mar., 571–91; April, 163–82; May, 379–96; June, 643–71; July, 137–59; Aug., 405–37; Sept., 641–66; Oct., 165–83; Dec., 683–98; 1904 (3rd instalment)—Jan., 207–22; Feb., 433–43.

Freemasonry

Anderson, James. *The Constitutions of Free-Masons*. London, 1723.

Apologiya, ili zashchishchenie ordena vol'nyk kamen'shchikov, Per. s nyem. I. Turgeneva. St. Petersburg, 1784.

Backvis, Claud. *Nicolas Novikov et la franc-maçonnerie russe au XVIII siècle*. Bruxelles, 1936.

Barskov, I. *Perepiska moskovskikh masonov XVIII-go vyeka*. Petrograd, 1915.

Bogolyubov, V. A. *Nikolai Ivanovich Novikov i ego vremya*. Moscow, 1916.

Bratskiya uvyeshchaniya k nyekotorym bratyam svbdnm. kmnshchkm. Pisany bratom Seddagom (Eli). Moscow, 1784.

Engel, Leopold. *Geschichte des Illuminaten-Ordens*. Berlin, 1906.

Fallou, Fr. Albert. *Mysterien der Freimaurerei, oder die verschleierte Gebrüderung, Verfassung und Symbolik der teutschen Baugewerke . . .* Leipzig, 1848.

Francesco, Grete de. *The Power of the Charlatan*. New Haven, 1939.

Friedrichs, E. *Geschichte der einstigen Maurerei in Russland*. Berlin, 1904.

Kiesewetter, Karl. *Geschichte des neuren Occultismus*, Vol. I. *Die Geheimwissenschaften*, Vol. II. Leipzig, 1895.

Kushelev, E. A. "Zapiska o masonskikh lozhakh," *Russkaya Starina*, T. XVIII (1877), 455–79; 641–50.

Les plus secrets mystères des hauts grades de la Maçonnerie dévoilés, ou le parfait Rose-croix. Jerusalem (Orléans), 1768.

Longinov, M. *Novikov i Schwarz*. Moscow, 1857.

———. *Novikov i Moskovskie Martinisti*. Moscow, 1867.

Matter, Jacques. *S.-Martin, le philosophe inconnu, sa vie et ses éscrits, son maître Martinez et leurs groupes*. 2nd Ed. Paris, 1862.

Mel'gunov, Sergiei Petrovich and Sidorov, N. P. (Eds.). *Masonstvo v ego, proshlom i nastoyashchem*. 3 vols. Moscow, 1914–22.

Neselenow, A. I. *Novikow und seine Jünger*. St. Petersburg, 1875.

Nezelenov, A. I. *Nikolai Ivanovich Novikov, izdatel'zhurnalov, 1769–85*. St. Petersburg, 1875.

——. "Novikov v Shlissel'burgskoi Kryeposti (po novymi doku-mentam)," *Istoricheskii Vyestnik*, Vol. X (St. Petersburg, 1882), 481–500.

Pekarskii, Petr P. *Dopolinenie k istorii masonstva v Rossii v XVIII Stolyetie*. St. Petersburg, 1869.

Pypin, A. N. *Russkoe masonstvo XVIII v pervoi chetverti XIX v.* Petrograd, 1916.

——. "Russkoe Masonstvo Novikova," *Vestnik Evropy*, T. 3, No. 6 (1868), 546–89; T. 4, No. 7 (1868), 167–222.

——. "Russkoe masonstvo v XVIII v," *Vestnik Evropy*, T. 2 (1867), 51–106; T. 3 (1867), 1–59; T. 4 (1867), 1–70.

Savva, V. I. "Iz dnevnika masona (A. Ya. Il'ina)," *Chteniya Ob-shchestva Istorii i drevnostei Rossiiskikh*. 1908, IV, i otd. Mos-cow, 1909.

Schwartz, I. G. "Zapiska I. G. Shvartsa," *Lyetopisi russkoi litera-tury i drevnosti*. Vol. V (1863).

Semeka, A. V. "Russkie rozenkreitsery i otnoshenie k nim Ekateriny II," *Zhurnal Ministerstva Narodnago Prosvyeshcheniya*, No. 2 (St. Petersburg, 1902).

Semenikov, V. P. *Knigoizdatel'skaya deyatel'nost N. I. Novikova i tipograficheskaya kompaniya*. St. Petersburg, 1921.

Semevskii, V. I. "Dekabristy-Masony," *Minuvshie Gody*, Vol. II (1908), 1–51.

Sidorov, A. P. "Masonstvo i Krepostnoe Pravo," *Velikaya Re-forma, 1861–1911*. 6 vols. Moscow, 1911. Vol. II, 157–75.

Sipovsky, V. "Novikov, Shvarts i moskovskoe masonstvo," supple-ment to his book, *N. M. Karamzin*. St. Petersburg, 1899.

Sokolovskaya, T. *Russkoe Masonstvo i ego Znachenie v Istorii Obshchestvennago Dvizheniya*. St. Petersburg, 1908.

——. "Kapitul Feniksa. Vysshe Tainoe masonskoe pravlenie v Rossii (1778-1822)," *Vyest. Obshch. Ist. i Drevn*, T. II, i otd. (Petrograd, 1916).

——. "Spisok g. g. voennykh koi prinadlyezhali k masonkim loz-ham," *Russkaya Starina*, Nos. 6–9 (1909).

——. "V masonskikh lozhakh (Dnevnik L. A. Simanskago), *Vyestnik Obshchestva Istorii i Drevnosti*, T. I, i otd. (St. Petersburg, 1914).

——. "Brat'ya zlatorozovago kresta," *Russkii Arkhiv*, god. 44, Kn. 3, (Moscow, 1907), 89–93.

Tarasov, E. I. "Novye Danniya k istorii Novikovskago Kruzhka (Iz neizdannykh dokumentov)," *Isvyestiya otdyeleniya russkago yazyka i Slovestnosti*. St. Petersburg, 1908.

——. "K istorii masonstva v Rossii. Zabytyi Rosenkreitser A. M. Kutuzov," *Sbornik statei v chest' S. F. Platonova*. St. Petersburg, 1911.

Tikhonravov, Nikolai. "Zapiska I. G. Shvartsa ob otnosheniyakh k nemu I. I. Melissino," *Lyetopisi Russkoi Literatury i Drevnosti*, T. V. (Moscow, 1863), 96–110, *Prilozheniya*.

——. "Novyya Svedeniya o N. I. Novikovye i chlenakh kompanii Tipograficheskoi," *Lyetopisi Russkoi Literatury i Drevnosti*, T. V. (Moscow, 1863), 3–96, *Prilozheniya*.

Tukalevskii, V. N. "Iskaniya russkikh masonov," *Zhurnal Ministerstva Narodnago Prosvyeshcheniya* (St. Petersburg, 1911).

Vernadskii, G. V. *Russkoe Masonstvo v Tsarstvovanie Ekateriny II*. Petrograd, 1917.

Yeshevskii, S. V. "Moskovskie Masony vos'midesyatykh godov proshedshago stolyetiya, 1780–1789," *Russkii Vyestnik*. T. 52, No. 8 (1864), 361–406; T. 56, No. 3 (1865), 1–52.

Zaleski, ks. Stanislaw. *O masonyi w Polsce od roku 1738-do 1822*. 2 pts. in 1 vol. Krakow, 1908.

Mysticism

Bonch-Bruevich, Vladimir (Ed.). *Sobranie Sochinenii G. S. Skovorody*. T. I., Vol. 5 of *Materialy k istorii i izuchenii sektantstva i staroobryadchestva*. 6 Vols. St. Petersburg, 1912.

Ern, Vladimir. *Grigorii Savvich Skovoroda; Zhizn' i obuchenie (Prepodavanie)*. Moscow, 1912.

Ewald, J. L. *Briefe über die alte Mystik und den neuen Mysticismus*. Leipzig, 1822.

Galakhov, A. D. "Obzor misticheskoi literatury v tsarstvovanie Imperatora Aleksandra I," *Zhurnal Ministerstva Narodnago Prosvyeshcheniya*, No. 11 (Noyabr', 1875), 87–175. Pyatoe dyesyatelyetie. Chast' CLXXXII. (St. Petersburg, 1875).

Grass, K. "Mysticism (Christian, Russian)," *Encyclopaedia of Religion and Ethics*, Vol. IX (Edinburgh, 1917), 103–69.

Haase, Felix. "Die Kulturgeschichtliche Bedeutung des ukrainischen Philosophen Gregory Skovoroda," *Jahrbücher für Kultur und Geschichte der Slawen*, Bd. IV, Heft 1 (Breslau, 1928), 21–173.

Heinroth, J.C.A. *Geschichte und Kritik des Mysticismus, aller Bekannten Voelker und Zeiten*. Leipzig, 1830.

Inge, William Ralph. *The Philosophy of Plotinus*. 2 vols. London, New York, and Toronto, 1929.

James, William. *The Varieties of Religious Experience*. New York, 1917.

Luchet, Jean Pierre. *Essai sur la secte des illuminés*. Paris, 1789.

Nadler, V. K. *Imperator Aleksandr I i Ideya Svyashchennago Soyuza*. 5 vols. in 3. Riga, 1886–92.

Noack, Ludwig. *Die christliche Mystik*. Königsberg, 1853.

Otto, Rudolf. *Mysticism East and West: A Comparative Analysis of the Nature of Mysticism*. New York, 1932.

Schmid, Heinrich. *Der Mysticismus des Mittelalters, in seiner Entstehungsperiode dargestellt von H. Schmid*. Jena, 1824.

Vertelovskii, Aleksiei Fedorovich. *Zapadnaya Sredenvyekovaya Mistika i otnoshenie eya k katolichestvu*. 2 vols. Kharkov, 1888.

Decembrists

For a full bibliography of the Decembrists see Mazour, *The First Russian Revolution*, Berkeley, 1937. I have listed below only a few of the most important titles.

Dovnar-Zapol'skii, M. V. *Idealy Dekabristov*. Moscow, 1907.

———. *Tainnoe Obshchestvo Dekabristov*. Moscow, 1906.

———. *Memuary Dekabristov*. Kiev, 1906.

Gershenzon, M. O. *Dekabrist Krivtsov i ego brat'ya*. 1st Ed. Moscow, 1914.

Gessen, Sergiei. *Dekabristy pered sudom istorii (1825–1925)*, Leningrad, 1925.

———. *Dekabrist Lunin i ego vremya*. Leningrad, 1926.

Kulczycki, Ludwig. *Geschichte der russischen Revolution: Einzig autorisierte Übersetzung aus dem polnischen von Anna Schapire-Neurath.* 3 vols. Gotha, 1910–11.

Lincoln, Gilbert H. *The Russian Constitutional Crisis of 1730.* Unpublished manuscript of dissertation submitted in partial fulfillment of the requirements for the degree of Master of Arts, University of Oklahoma, 1951.

Mazour, Anatole G. *The First Russian Revolution, 1825. The Decembrist Movement.* Berkeley, 1937.

Paradizov, P. *Dekabristy,* Kharkov, 1930.

Pokrovskii, M. N. *Dekabristy: Sbornik Statei.* Moscow and Leningrad, 1927.

Pypin, A. N. *Obshchestvennoe Dvizhenie pri Aleksandrye I.* 2nd Ed. St. Petersburg, 1885.

Rusanov, N. S. "Vliyanie Evropeiskago Sotsializma na Dekabristov i Molodogo Gertsena," *Minuvshie Gody,* Vol. III (1908).

Russia: Kommissiya dlya izyskanii o zloumyshlennykh obshchestvakh (Donosenie slyedtsvennoi kommissii ego imperatorskomy velichestvu). St. Petersburg, 1826.

Russia (1917 R.S.F.S.R.). Tsentral'noe Arkhivnoe upravlenie. *Vosstanie Dekabristov, Materialy po istorii vosstaniya Dekabristov.* Ed. M. N. Pokrovskii. 8 vols. Moscow, 1925.

Salkind, Eugenie. "Die Dekabristen in ihrer Beziehung zu Westeuropa," *Jahrbücher für Kultur und Geschichte der Slawen.* Breslau, 1928.

Semevskii, V. I. and Shchegolev, P. E. (Eds.). "Dekabristy," *Obshchestvennyia Dvizheniya v Rossii v Pervuyu Polovinu XIX Veka,* Vol. I (1905).

——. "Volnenie v Semenovskom Polkye v 1820 Goda," *Byloe,* Vol. II (1907).

——. *Politicheskie i Obshchestvennye Idei Dekabristov.* St. Petersburg, 1909.

——. "Baron V. I. Steingel," *Obshchestvennyia Dvizheniya v Rossii v Pervuyu Polovinu XIX Veka,* Vol. I (1905).

——. "Dekabristy i Krestyanskii Vopros," *Velikaya Reforma, 1861–1911,* Vol. II. 6 vols. Moscow, 1911.

——. *Krestyane v Tsarstvovanie Imperatritsy Ekateriny* II. 2 vols. St. Petersburg, 1903.

Shil'der, N. K. *Imperator Nikolai Pervyi: ego Zhizn' i tsarstvo-vanie.* v. 2. St. Petersburg, 1903.

Syroechkovski, B. E. "K Kharakteristike Religioznago Volno-dumstva Dekabristov," *Katorga i Ssylka,* Vol. 61 (1929).

Tainoe Obshchestvo i 14 Dekabria v Rossii. Leipzig, 187-.

Tarasov, E. I. *Dekabrist N. I. Turgenev.* Samara, 1923.

———. "Dnevniki i Pis'ma Nikolaya Ivanovicha Turgeneva," *Arkhiv Brat'ev Turgenevykh,* Vyp. 1, 2, 3 (St. Petersburg, 1911).

Turgueneff (Turgenev), N. *La Russie et les Russes.* 3 vols. Brux-elles, 1847.

———. "Dekabrist N. I. Turgenev," *Pis'ma k bratu S. I. Turgenevu (1811-1812).* St. Petersburg, 1936.

Historiography

Bestuzhev-Ryumin, K. "V. N. Tatishchev," *Biografii i Kharak-teristiki.* St. Petersburg, 1822.

Boltin, I. N. *Kriticheskiye primechaniya gen-mayora Boltina na pervyi vtoroi tom istorii knyazya Shcherbatova.* 2 vols. St. Petersburg, 1793-94.

Ikonnikov, V. S. *Opyt russkoi istoriografii.* 2 vols. in 4 pts. Mos-cow, 1889.

Karamzin, N. M. *Zapiska predstavlennaya Gosudaryu 18 Oktya-brya 1819 goda.* St. Petersburg, 1913.

———. *Zapiska o drevnei i novoi Rossii.* St. Petersburg, 1914.

———. *Pis'ma russkogo puteshestvennika (Letters of a Russian Trav-eller).* St. Petersburg, 1792.

Lambin, B. P. and P. P. *Russian Historical Bibliography, 1855-1864* (R). 10 vols. St. Petersburg, 1861-64.

Lappo-Danilevskii, A. S. "Ocherk razvitiya russkoi istoriografii. Vvedenie," *Russkii Istoricheskii Zhurnal,* Kn. 6 (1920), 5-29.

LeClerc, Nicolas-Gabriel. *Histoire physique, morale, civile et po-litique de la Russie ancienne.* 3 vols. Paris, 1783-84.

———. *Histoire physique, morale, civile et politique de la Russie moderne,* 2 vols. Paris, 1783-85.

Mazour, A. G. *An Outline of Modern Russian Historiography.* Berkeley, 1939.

Mezhov, V. I. *Bibliographical catalogue of Literature*, published on the Occasion of the Jubilee of Peter the Great (R). St. Petersburg, 1881.

———. *Russkaya Istoricheskaya Bibliografiya*. 8 vols. St. Petersburg, 1882–90.

Milyukov, P. N. *Istochniki russkoy istorii i russkaya istoriografiya*. N.p., n.d.

———. *Glavnye Techeniya russkoi istoricheskoi mysli*. Moscow. 1898.

———. "The Chief Currents of Russian Historical Thought," American Historical Association *Annual Report* for 1904. (Washington, 1905), 109–14.

Nikitin, S. A. *Istochnikovedenie Istorii SSSR XIX v.*, T. II. Moscow, 1940.

Otvyet gen-mayora Boltina na pis'mo Kn. Shcherbatova. St. Petersburg, 1793.

Pekarskii, P. P. *Noviye Izvestiya o V. N. Tatishchevye*. St. Petersburg, 1864.

Picheta, V. I. *Vvedenie v russkuyu Istoriyu (Istochniki i Istoriografiya)*, St. Petersburg, 1923.

Popov, N. A. "Ucheniye i literatur'niye Trudy V. N. Tatishcheva," *Zhurnal Ministerstva Narodnago Prosvyeshcheniya* (June, 1886).

Primechaniya na istoriyu Rossii g Leklerka. 2 vols. St. Petersburg, 1788.

Rubinstein, N. L. *Russkaya Istoriografiya*. Moscow and Leningrad, 1941.

Schelting, Alexander von. *Russland und Europa*. Bern, 1948.

Schlözer, A. L. von. *Histoire universelle*. Tübingen, 1781.

———. *Vorstellung seiner universal-historie*. Goettingen, 1772.

———. *Neuverändertes Russland, oder Leben Catharina der Zweyten*. Riga, 1771–72.

———. *Allgemeine geschichte der Nordischen* . . . Halle, 1771.

———. *Probe Russischer Annalen*. Bremen and Göttingen, 1768.

Sinopsis . . . St. Petersburg, 1762.

Starchevskii, A. *Ocherk Literatury russkoi istorii do Karamzina*. St. Petersburg, 1845.

Stryikowskiego, Maciera. *Kronika Polska*. Königsberg, 1583.

Tatishchev, V. N. *Istoriya rossiyskaya s samykh drevnykh vremen.* 5 vols. Moscow, 1768–1848.

Tikhomirov, M. N. *Istochnikovedenie Istorii SSSR: s drevneiskikh vremen do Kontsa XVIII v.* Ogiz, 1940.

Znamenskii, P. "Istoricheskie Trudy Shcherbatova i Boltina v Otnoshenii k russkoi istorii," *Trudy Kievskoi Dukhovnoi Akademii,* T. II, Sec. 65 (1862).

Varangians

For a recent discussion of the Varangian question from the anti-Normanist viewpoint, see V. Riasanovsky *Obzor russkoi kul'tury,* I. The titles listed below are only a few of the more important or readily accessible.

Bayer, Gottlieb Seigfried. "De Variagis," *Commentarii Academiae Scientiarum Imperialis Petropolitanae,* Vol. V (St. Petersburg, 1735), 273–311.

———. "Origines Russicae," *Commentarii Academiae Scientiarum Imperialis Petropolitanae,* T. III (St. Petersburg, 1741), 388–436.

Byelyaev, N. T. "Rorik Yutlandskii i Ryurik Nachal'noi Lyetopisi," *Sbornik Statei po Arkheologii.* Prague, 1929.

Chadwick, N. K. *The Beginnings of Russian History: an enquiry into sources.* Cambridge, 1946.

Gedeonov, S. *Varyagi i Rus'; (istoricheskoe izslyedovanie).* St. Petersburg, 1876.

Grekov, B. D. *Kievskaya Rus'.* Moscow, 1949.

Grushevskii, Mikhail. *Kievskaya Rus'.* St. Petersburg, 1911.

Harkavy, A. E. *Skazaniya mousoulmanskikh pisatelei o Slavyanakh i Russkikh.* St. Petersburg, 1870.

———. "Skazaniya evreyskikh pisatelei o Khazarakh," *Trudy Vostochnago Otdyeleniya Imp. Arkh. Obshch* (St. Petersburg, 1874), 259–421.

Krug, Philipp. *Forschungen in der älteren Geschichte Russlands.* 2 vols. St. Petersburg, 1848.

Kunik, A., and Baron Rosen. "Izvyestiya Al-Bekri o Slavyanakh i

ikh Sosyedyakh," Chast' I-*Prilozhenie* k XXXII Tomu *Zapisok Akademii Nauk*, No. 2. St. Petersburg, 1878.
———. *Die Berufung der Schwedischen Rodsen durch Finnen und Slawen*. St. Petersburg, 1842–45.
Lieder, Frederick W. C. "The Don Carlos Theme," S. H. Cross, "The Russian Primary Chronicle," *Harvard Studies and Notes in Philology and Literature, Vol. XII* (Cambridge, Mass., 1930), 77–320.
Marquart (Markvart) Joseph. *Osteuropäische und Ostasiatische Streitzüge*. Leipzig. 1903.
Pogodin, M. G. *Gedeonov i ego sistema o proiskhozhdenii Varyagov i Rusi*. St. Petersburg, 1864.
Riasanovsky, Nicholas. "The Norman Theory of the Origin of the Russian State," *The Russian Review*, Vol. VII, No. 1 (New York, 1947), 96–110.
Rostovtsev, M. I. "The Origin of the Russian State on the Dnieper," American Historical Association *Annual Report* (1920).
Schlözer, A. L. von. *Allgemeine Geschichte der Nordischen . . .* Halle, 1771.
Shakhmatov, Aleksei Aleksandrovich. *Skazanie o proizvanii Varyagov*. St. Petersburg, 1904.
———. *Razyskaniya o drevneishikh Russkikh Iyetopisnykh svodakh*. St. Petersburg, 1908.
———. "Drevneishnye sud'by russkago Plemeni," *Izd. Russ. Istor. Zhurnal* (Petrograd, 1919).
Shtritter, Ivan. *Izvyestiya Vizantiiskikh istorikov obyasnyayushchiya rossiiskuyu istoriyu drevnikh vremen i pereseleniya narodov*. St. Petersburg, 1774.
Sinopsis ili kratkoe opisanie ot razlichnikh lyetopistsev o nachale Slavenskago naroda. St. Petersburg, 1762.
Stender-Peterson, Al. "Die varägersage als Quelle der Altrussischen Chronik," *Acta Jutlandica*, Vol. VI, No. 1 (Copenhagen, 1934), 1–256.
Sturlason, Snorre. *Heimskringla* (or *The Life of the Norse Kings*). Cambridge, 1932.
Thomsen, Wilhelm. *The Relations between Ancient Russia and Scandinavia and the Origin of the Russian State*. Oxford, 1877.
———. *Nachalo Russkago Gosudarstva*. Moscow, 1891.

——. *Die Ursprung des russischen Staates*. Halle, 1870.

Tompkins, Stuart R. "The Varangians in Russian History," *Medieval and Historiographical Essays in Honor of James Westfall Thompson* (Chicago, 1937), 465–90.

Vasil'evskii, V. G. *Trudy*. 4 vols. in 3. St. Petersburg, 1908–30.

——. "Varyago-russkaya i Varyago-Angliiskaya drushina v Konstantinopolie XI i XII vyekov," reprinted in *Zhurnal Ministerstva Narodnago Prosvyeshcheniya* (St. Petersburg).

——. "O Varyago-russakh (otvet D. I. Ilovaiskomu)," *Trudy*, T. I, (St. Petersburg, 1908), 378–401.

——. *Russko-vizantiyskaya izsledovaniya*. St. Petersburg, 1893.

Venelin, D. Chl. Yurii. *Skandinovomaniya i ego Poklonniki*. Moscow, 1842.

Peasants

The literature on the peasant question even up to 1861 is vast. The list of titles as below is intended merely to be a guide to the study of opinion on the subject of the peasant.

Druzhinin, N. M. *Gosudarstvennye Krest'yane i reforma P. D. Kiseleva*. Vol. I. Moscow and Leningrad, 1946.

Grekov, B. A. *Krest'yane na Rusi: S drevneishikh Vremen do XVII veka*. Moscow and Leningrad, 1946.

Jacob, L. H. von. *Über die Arbeit leibeigener und freien Bauern in Beziehung auf die Nutzen der Landeigentümer vorzüglich in Russland*. St. Petersburg, 1814.

Kornilov, A. *Ocherki po istorii obshchestvennago dvizheniya i krestyanskago dyela v Rossii*. St. Petersburg, 1905.

Maslov, Petr Pavlovich. *Agrarnyi vopros v Rossii (Usloviya Razvitiya Krest'yanskago v Rossii)*. 3rd Ed. St. Petersburg, 1906.

——. *Krestyanskoe dvizhenie: obshchestvennoe dvizhenie Rossii*. St. Petersburg, 1909–12.

"Materialy po istorii krest'yanskoi promyshlennosti XVIII i pervoi poloviny XIX v. v.," *Trudy istoriko-arkheograficheskago Instituta Akademii Nauk*. T. XIV. Moscow and Leningrad, 1935.

Pokrovskii, A. A. *Krestyanstvo i natsionaly v revolyutsionnom Dvizhenii*. Leningrad, 1931.

Bibliography

Semevskii, V. I. *Krest'yanskii Vopros v Rossii v XVIII i pervoi polovinye XIX vyeka*. 2 vols. St. Petersburg, 1888.

———. "Krestyanskii Vopros v tsarstvovanie Imperatora Nikolaya," *Russkaya Mysl'*, Gl. 18 (Moscow, 1886), 133–74.

———. *Krest'yane v Tsarstvovanie Ekateriny II*. 2 vols. St. Petersburg, 1903.

Struve, Petr. *Serf Economy*. St. Petersburg, 1913.

Tomsinskii, S. G. (Ed.). *Krest'yanstvo i Natsionaly v revolyutsionnoi Dvizhenii-Razinshchina*. Moscow and Leningrad, 1931.

Vorontsov, Vasilii Pavlovich. *K istorii obshchiny v Rossii (Materialy po istorii obshchinnago Zemlevladyeniya)*. Moscow, 1902.

Glossary of Russian Terms

Adelspensionat: a boarding school for sons of the nobility.

Artel': a co-operative formed by craftsmen.

Collegium (plural, *collegia*): a department of the central government in the eighteenth century.

Donos: secret denunciation.

Dukhovnyi Reglament: "Ecclesiastical Regulation" of 1721 imposing upon the church certain obligations in the field of education.

Duma: a deliberative body.

Druzhina: warrior band who formed the personal armed following of the early grand princes; regarded as equivalent to the German *comitatus*.

Dvoryanin (plural, *dvoryane*): "courtier," a term applied to the noble of modern times.

Dvoryane gorodovye: "city nobles," who were actually provincial nobles.

Dvorovye: household serfs.

Dyak: scribe.

Glavnoe uchilishche: chief training school (for teachers).

Gymnasium: secondary school, roughly equivalent to the German *gymnasium*.

Immenoi ukaz: An *ukaz* or directive issued from the emperor's own chancery instead of through one of the usual agencies.

Intelligentsiya (English form, *intelligentsia*): the intellectual class in Russia.

Junker: a cadet in training for the army.

Knut: whip.

Krugovaya poruka: joint responsibility of the members of the village commune for payment of taxes, debts, crimes, etc.

Glossary

Kuptsy: merchants.

Mir: "world," the term sometimes applied to the village commune.

Myeshchanin (plural, *myeshchane*): craftsman or small tradesman.

Myestnichestvo: system of family precedence in vogue among the nobility until the end of the seventeenth century.

Nakaz: instruction.

Narodnik (plural, *narodniki*): one of a group of agitators who took their cue from Herzen and in the seventies and eighties preached the gospel "[back] to the people."

Nedorosl': a minor; a term applied to sons of the nobility who were too young for service and who were undergoing instruction at home.

Obrok: quit rent.

Obshchina: village commune.

Odnodvortsy: "one household men," a peasantry settled in frontier regions for purposes of defense; corresponds to English "yeoman."

Okol'nichi: a special rank among the boyars.

Okrug: "circle"; usually applied in the eighteenth and early nineteenth centuries to educational districts.

pension: French term applied in its Russian form, *pansion,* to a boarding school.

Pod'yachie: assistant scribes.

Pomyest'e: land held on conditional tenure, for service.

Puteshestvie iz Peterburga v Moskvu: Journey from St. Petersburg to Moscow, the name of Radishchev's famous book.

Raskol': "schism," applied to the great schism of the eighteenth century.

Raskol'niki: schismatics.

Raznochintsy: a group of persons drawn from all social classes.

Russkaya Pravda: "Russian Truth," the name applied to the constitutional treatise of Pestel' the Decembrist.

Shlyakhetstvo: from the Polish *Schlachta.* Peter applied this term to the serving nobility in his time, but it was later replaced by the ordinary Russian term, *dvoryanstvo,* of which it is the equivalent.

Slovo i dyelo: "word and deed," a formula used when making a denunciation which required the official to follow up the denunciation with an investigation.

Sluzhilye lyudi: "serving people," a general term for those in the service of the state, principally the nobility.

Stol'niki: a rank among the boyars.

Stryapchi: also a rank among the boyars.

Stryeltsi: "musketeers," the name applied to a group of professional soldiers who formed a hereditary caste in the sixteenth and seventeenth centuries.

Tyaglo: a tax in early times; sometimes a measure of land.

Tyaglie lyudi posadskie: townsmen subject to the payment of *tyaglo*.

Uchitel': teacher *(ouchitel)*.

Udyel': a "portion," in modern times applied to estates of members of the imperial family; at one time applied to the small "fiefs" held by the petty princes of north Russia.

Udelnyi period: the appanage period, a term at one time used by Russian historians for the period from 1169 to 1462. Sometimes called the "feudal period" or the "medieval period."

Ulozhenie: "code," usually although not always applied to the code of 1649.

Ukaz: a decree or directive of the monarch to the Governing Senate.

Uprava blagochiniya: office of security.

Uyezd: county.

Volost': township.

Votchina: land owned outright by a landowner; roughly equivalent to medieval *allod*.

Voyevode: local agent of central government; replaced in the eighteenth century by governors.

Vyeche: popular assembly.

Vyedomstvo: general term applied to any government department.

Index

Absolutism: 6, 7
Absolute monarch: 7
Absolute power: 7
Academies of Kiev and Moscow: 34
Academy of Sciences: 45, 46, 120, 196, 197; decree establishing, 1724, 43, 44; reorganized by Catherine, 44; university established in connection with, 51; Gymnasium of, 82, 83, 84; *Commentarii* of, 193
Adelspensionats: 81
Admiralty College: 45
Androsov, assistant editor of *Moskovskii Nablyuditel'*, 176
"Aesopian" language: 141, 142
Akademicheskie Peterburgskie Vyedomosti: 99
Aksakov, I. S.: 140
Aksakov, Konstantin S.: 140, 182; made contribution to Slavophil thought, 208; led to reverse himself, 210
Albigensian *Kathari*: 68
Alexander I: 65, 66, 69, 70, 73, 82, 87, 88, 109, 110, 112, 113, 118, 122, 124, 136, 143, 144, 150, 155, 159, 166, 195, 223; famous speech at opening of Polish *Syem*, 114; died at Taganrog, 156; attracted to Shishkov, 206; accession of, 217; and Kisel'ev, 221; "free husbandmen" created by, 224; puts Catherine's system of education into effect, 232
Alexander II: 160
Alexander Nevskii Monastery: 35
Anne (1730–41): 35, 44
Arakcheyev: 113, 156

Aristocracy, emancipation from service of: 28
Arkheograficheskaya Kommissiya came into existence through Stroyev: 195
Arkhiv Istoriko-Yuridicheskikh Svyedenii, Otnosyashchikhsya do Rossii of Kalachov: 185
Army Cadet Corps: 40, 46, 47, 50
Arndt, Johann: 59
Arnold, Matthew, and the term "philistine": 243
Artillery, school of (1721): 37, 42, 47
Assassination of the Tsar proposed: 150
Assembly of Urban Society: 18
Athenian democracy, teaching of: 94

Bacon: 12
Bakharevich proposes to start an official gazette: 115
Bakunin: 177
Ban on persons going abroad: 94
Baratynskii: 176
Bayer, a German scholar: 193, 194
Beaupré, Monsieur: 48, 49
Benckendorf, A. K.: 150
Benckendorf, Count: 128, 131
Bestuzhev, Alexander: 72
Bestuzhev-Ryumin, K.: 24, 150, 157, 159
Bestuzhev-Ryumin, Michael: 160, 219
Betskii: 194
Biblioteka dlya Chteniya (founded by Senkovskii): 136, 176, 178
Bielgorskii, Count Mikhail Yurievich: 173

281

Index

Jung-Stilling: 67, 69, 111
Junker College: 46, 47

Kachenovskii: continues *Vyestnik Evropy*, 174; a historian of the skeptical school, 209
Kachovskii: 160
Kankrin, minister of finance: 129
Kantemir: 25
Karamzin, N. M.: 9, 13, 194, 195, 205; *Vyestnik Evropy* begun in 1802 by, 174; influenced by the Masons at University of Moscow, 203; named historiographer and wrote his *History of the Russian State*, 203; on the Varangians, 204; *On the Old and New Russia*, 206; in Paris, 230
Karamzin, Madame, the salon of: 173
Kareyev: 210
Karneyev: 59, 68, 88
Katkov: 178; takes over *Moskovskii Vyedomosti*, 1863, 179
Keith, James: 55
Khan of the Golden Horde: 188
Khomyakov, Aleksei: 176, 207
Kiev Academy: 30; enlightenment imported from, 36; and left bank of Dnieper passed to Russian hands, 30
Kireyevskii, I. V.: 138, 140; edits *Evropeyets*, 175, 176
Kireyevskii brothers, Ivan and Peter: 207
Kisel'ev, P. D.: 225, 227, 228, 246; administrator of Danubian principalities, 221; return of, 224; named to secret committee, 226
Klingstedt: 78
Klyuchevsky: 6, 13; Russia's greatest historian, 212; on the lower classes, in his *History of the Classes in Russia* and his *History of Russia*, 247
Klyushnikov: 182
Knights Templars: 55, 69
Kolokol, Herzen's underground organ: 180
Korf, Baron: 133, 134, 135
Krayevich: 59

Krayevskii, A. A., edits *Russkii Vyestnik*: 174
Krizanich: 11
Krüdener, Madame de: 67, 68, 111
Kruitskii Monastery: 36
Krylov, Andrei: 101, 173
Küchelbecker, William and Michael: 72
Kulczycki: 162
Kuptsy: 17, 172
Kurakin, Prince Alexander: 56, 57
Kutuzov: 144

Labzin, A. F.: 67, 112
Labzin's *Messenger of Zion*: 73
Laharpe, tutor to Alexander I: 118, 217
Landlords' peasants: 20, 21
Lanin, pseudonym of Dr. Dillon in *Fortnightly Review*: 236
LeClerc, a French physician, visits Russia: 203
Ledru-Rollins: 139
Lefort, François: 41
Leibniz, German philosopher: 41, 43, 139
Lenin, V. I., calls liberals compromisers: 237
Lermontov: 130
Levashov: 160
Leverriers: 139
"Liberal" had become discredited: 237
Lieven, Prince: 89, 91, 128
Ligerides, Paisos, Metropolitan of Gaza: 30
Likhudis, Iohannikii and Sophronii: 31
Lisovskii: 135
Literature, modern Russian: 100
Little Russian Society, the: 146
Locke, English philosopher: 169
Lomonosov, Michael V.: 44, 45, 199; persisted in opposition to Müller, 201; reported to Senate that Schlözer intended writing a history, 202
Lopukhin, I. V.: 59, 60, 63, 103
Louis XIV founded *Académie des Sciences*: 43

285

Index

nym Nadoumka) articles in *Vyestnik Evropy*, 174, 205
Nakaz: 17; of 1767, 76
Naval Academy, the: 40, 47
Naval Shlachta Corps: 40
Navigation, School of at St. Petersburg: 37, 42
Nekrasov and Panayev take over *Sovremennik*: 176, 182, 184
Nesselrode: 129
Nestor, a German translation in 1802 by Schlözer: 195
Nevzorov, M. I.: 68
New General Charter for the universities: 90
New Learning: 30
Nicholas I, Emperor: 26, 88, 89, 92, 94, 124, 130, 131, 136, 137, 140, 143, 156, 159, 160, 161, 162, 171, 172, 232; at head of Finland Regiment, 158; suppresses Bible Society, 206; age of, 222; on the peasants, 223; names secret committee, 224; takes counsel with members of State Council, 228
Niebuhr stimulates Polevoi: 205
Nikon, Patriarch: 10, 11, 19
Nobility, formed from different ranks: 25, 168; squabbles between middle class and, 215
Nobles, emancipation of: 25, 28
Normanists and anti-Normanists: 202
Northern *okrug*: 151, 152, 154, 155
Novgorod seminary: 40
Novikov, Nikolai Ivanovich: 57, 58, 67, 80, 100, 102, 103, 104, 106, 108, 111, 122, 166, 203; publications of, 59; in Moscow, 63; revives *Moskovskii Vyedomosti*, 179; works of, 212
Novodyevichy Institute: 77
Number of students in attendance at universities: 95

Obmanshchik, a play by Catherine: 62, 80
Obolenskoi: 151
"*Obshchestvo istorii i drevnostei Rossiiskikh*," organized by Schlözer: 195
October Revolution: 202
Odnodvortsy: 39

Odoyevskii, Knyaz V. F.: 173; popularizes Schelling, 183
Okol-nichi: 15
Olearius: 9, 11
Ordyn-Nashchokin: 11
Origines Russicae of the Academy of Sciences: 193
Orthodox church: 18, 19, 30, 37, 65, 91, 112, 129, 187; Orthodox Russians, 30; exaltation of by Slavophils, 208
Orthodox faith: 53, 140
Orthodoxy: 10; "Orthodoxy, autocracy and nationalism," 89
Otechestvennye Zapiski: 174, 176; mouthpiece of the Westerners, 184

Pages Corps at St. Petersburg: 51
Panayev, I. I., and Nekrasov take over *Sovremennik*: 176, 184
Parish schools: 83, 84
Patriotic Society: 149
Paul, Grand Duke, betrothed to Sophia Dorothea: 56, 65
Paul, Tsar: 81, 109, 110, 122, 144; issues edict limiting landlords' demands on peasants, 216; death of, 217
Pavlov, M. G., popularizes Schelling: 183
Pavlov-Silvanskii: 210
Peasants: 20, 212; have good will of Alexander, 221; not relieved by Peter, 244
Pedagogical Institute: 82, 88; and universities, 93; seminaries, 103
Pekarskii, P. P.: 39
Pensions for the gentry: 93
Pereyaslavl' Zalesskii Monastery: 36
Perovskii, Minister of the Interior: 226
Persia, war with: 130
Pestel', Pavel: 72, 147, 148, 150, 151, 152, 153, 154, 159, 160, 166; evidence of, 155; evidence of, 169; outstanding figure in the Decembrists, 218
Peter the Great: 3, 8, 190, 191, 192, 195, 198, 213, 249; reforms of, 14; Table of Ranks, 15; and merchants and craftsmen, 17, 19; decrees of, 22,

Index

Roman church: 8, 205
Rome, the third: 8, 189
Rosicrucians: 54, 58, 69, 111
Rostopchin: 65
Rosy Cross: 54
Rousseau: 144
Royal Society, founded by Charles II: 43
Royal York de l'Amitié: 56
Rumyantsev, Count N. P.: 195
Runich: 89
Rurik, princely line of: 8
Russian Academy of Arts: 73, 109
Russian Bible Society: 67, 68, 72, 74, 87, 88, 111, 112; closed down, 124; suppressed by Nicholas in 1826, 206
Russian church: 189
Russian Free Masonry: 55, 66, 73
Russian Knights, the: 146
Russian press: 105
Russian revolutionaries: 170
Russians, scores of, dispatched abroad: 33
Russkii Invalid: 179
Russkie Vyedomosti: 99
Russkii Vyestnik, founded by N. Glinka, 1808: 174
Ryleev, Kondratii (poet): 26, 72, 146, 151, 155, 157, 160, 161, 163, 168
Rytsarstvo-Knighthood (Order of Strict Observance): 56

St. John of Jerusalem, Order of Knights of: 65, 69
St. Martin: 63
St. Petersburg Bible Society: 67

Saint Simon: 130
Samarin, Yu: 137, 207
Sammlung Russischer Geschichte of G. F. Müller: 193, 201
Sankovskii's *Good Intentions*: 99
Sankt Peterburgskie Kommercheskie Vyedomosti: 179
Schelling: 130, 183, 184, 234
Schlözer: 202, 205; left Russia in 1769, 194; published his *Probe Russischer Annalen*, 195
Schnor given permission to print Russian books: 101

Schröder, Friedrich Ludwig: 72
Schumacher: 44
Schwartz, Johann Georg: 57, 58, 102, 103, 104, 111, 203
Secondary schools: 78
Second Section of the Imperial Chancellery: 226
Secret Chancellery: 5
Secret denunciation: 130
Secularization of church lands: 79
Semenov: 151
Semenovskii Guards, meeting of: 73
Semevskii, V. I.: 221, 228
Seminaries after 1737: 39
Senate Square: 157, 158, 162
Senkovskii edits articles for *Syn Otechestva*: 175; founded *Biblioteka dlya Chteniya* in 1834, 176
Sergiev-Troitskii Monastery: 36
Serving class: 7
Sevastopol, fall of: 142, 186
Severnoe Obozryenie, a private publication: 185
Shchepin-Rostovskii: 157
Shcherbatov: 165; his *Corruption of Morals in Russia*, 203
Sherwood, an Englishman: 155, 156
Sheshkovskii, Stepan Ivanovich: 108
Shevyrev conducted *Moskovskii Nablyuditel'*: 176, 206
Shirinskii-Shikhmatov, Prince: 137
Shirley, English ambassador: 216
Shishkov, Admiral: 88, 89, 114, 124, 125; code of, 126, 128; strongly anti-foreign, 206
Shylakhetstvo: 16, 25
Shlyakhta: 16
Shuiskii: 135
Shumizorskii: 65
Shuvalov, A. I.: 55
Sionskii Vyestnik: 112
Skabichevskii: 201
Slavophil doctrine: 234
Slavophils: 140, 209, 223; patriarchal argument a great blow to, 210
Slavophilism: 205
Slovo i dyelo: 6
Sluzhilie i tyaglie lyudie: 25
Smith, Adam: 164
Smolnyi Institute: 77

289

Index

Tyaglo-paying persons: 13, 16, 17, 50
Tyaglye lyudi posadskie: 17

Uchenoe Druzheskoe Obshchestvo (Society of Friends of Learning): 102, 104
Ukaz: of 1732, 39; of 1833, 90; of January 15, 1783, 103; of March 31, 1801, 123; of 1797, 224; issued in 1842, 225; based on committee's report, 1844, 226
Ukraine: 10, 11; Cossacks of, 30; annexation of, 34; schools of *Odnodvortsy*, 39; peasants in, 212; peasants in, returned to serfdom, 216
Ulozhenie: 24, 77
Union of Florence in 1439: 189
Union of Salvation: 147, 148
Union of Welfare: 148, 149, 150
United Slavs, the: 146
Universities lost autonomy: 94
University of Kazan, 1758: 51, 87, 88
University of Kharkov: 87
University of Kiev: 89
University of Moscow, 1755: 51, 57, 99, 102, 114, 122, 141, 209
University of St. Petersburg: 87
Unofficial press established in 1771: 121
Uprava Blagochiniya to review publications: 121
Ursinus: 77
Uvarov, Sergei Semenovich: 85, 89, 128, 131, 136, 137, 141

Varangians: 190, 191; the question of, 204
Vasil'chikov, Adjutant General: 150
Vasilii III (Grand Prince Vasilii Ivanovich): 192
Velikii Novgorod Academy: 34
Venediktov, Yakov: 5
Venetian merchants: 10
Venevitinov promoted *Moskovskii Vyestnik* (1827–30): 175
Vladimirskii-Budanov: 40
Vladimirskii Monastery: 36
Voltaire: 76, 144, 164, 169
Vorontsov, Roman Ilarionovich: 55
Votchina: 15

Vremya, published in 1772: 99
Vyazemskii, Knyaz: 173, 176
Vyedomostvo (department of court peasants): 22
Vyestnik Evropy, begun in 1802 by Karamzin: 113, 174

Walch, Johann Georg, whose *Philosophisches Lexicon* was used by Tatishchev: 198
Watts: 139
Wax candles, sale of: 86
Weibrecht given permission to print Russian books: 101–102
Weishaupt, an unfrocked Jesuit: 55
White clergy: 34
Wilhelmsbad: conference of German Masons, 58; independent Russian province set up at, 64, 71
Witte, Count: 156
Wolff, German philosopher: 41
Wöllner: 55
World Mission of Russia: 97

Yakob, professor of University of Moscow gets prize for Free Economic Society competition: 218
Yakubovich: 152, 155, 157
Yakushkin: 147; offered to assassinate the emperor, 148
Yaroslavl' Academy: 34
Yatsenko, Grigorii Maksimovich: 114, 115
Yazykov: 176
Yelagin, leader in Russian Masonry: 56, 57
Yezhemesyachnyye Sochineniya, formerly *Primyecheniya* of Müller: 99, 201

Zapadniki advocates utopian socialism: 176, 184
Zavalashin, Decembrist: 166, holds extreme views on serfdom, 219
Zhukovskii: 173, 174, 176
Zhurnal dlya Dyevits: 185
Zhurnal Ministerstva Gosudarstvennykh imushchestv: 180
Zinnendorf, Dr. von: 56
Zolotnitskii: 77

291

UNIVERSITY OF OKLAHOMA PRESS

NORMAN